Sex Expression

AND AMERICAN WOMEN WRITERS, 1860–1940

The University of North Carolina Press
Chapel Hill

Sex Expression

AND AMERICAN WOMEN WRITERS, 1860–1940

Dale M. Bauer

Illustrations from James Thurber and E. B. White, *Is Sex Necessary?* (1929), © 2008 Rosemary A. Thurber, have been reproduced by permission.

The paper in this book meets the guidelines for permanence and durability of the Committee on Production Guidelines for Book Longevity of the Council on Library Resources.

The University of North Carolina Press has been a member of the Green Press Initiative since 2003.

LIBRARY OF CONGRESS CATALOGING-IN-PUBLICATION DATA
Bauer, Dale M., 1956–
Sex expression and American women writers, 1860–1940 / Dale M. Bauer.
p. cm.
Includes bibliographical references and index.
ISBN 978-0-8078-3230-1 (cloth : alk. paper) —
ISBN 978-0-8078-5906-3 (pbk. : alk. paper)
1. American fiction—Women authors—History and criticism. 2. American fiction—19th century—History and criticism. 3. American fiction—20th century—History and criticism. 4. Sex in literature. 5. Language and sex. 6. Expression in literature. I. Title.
PS151.B38 2009
810.9'9287—dc22   2008045181

cloth   13 12 11 10 09   5 4 3 2 1
paper   13 12 11 10 09   5 4 3 2 1

TO Gordon, THE LOVE OF MY LIFE

CONTENTS

ACKNOWLEDGMENTS

This book has been a long time coming, since I taught my first graduate seminar on sex expression in 1999 at the University of Wisconsin-Madison, a seminar I have now taught three times at the University of Illinois, Urbana-Champaign. I owe a huge debt to the students in those courses, particularly Christine DeVine at Madison and Ted Faust, Stephanie Henvaux, Andy Gustin, Katie Maulbetsch, Susan Rodgers, Ryan Haas, and Kyle Garton at Illinois. Past and present colleagues at Madison and the University of Kentucky have been crucial in shaping this project: Bruce Burgett, who invented the term "American Sex"; Susan Friedman and Susan Bernstein, two of the best feminist critics around; and Amy Mohr and Kirstin Wilcox, excellent colleagues at UIUC. One of the finest academic communities I've known was at the University of Kentucky, where Jeff Clymer, Andy Doolen, Janet Eldred, Ellen Rosenman, and Steve Weisenburger were all generous readers and terrific friends.

Many invited talks allowed me to test my ideas in public, and I'm grateful to the *Arizona Quarterly* Symposium, the University of Florida, the University of Kansas, Wesleyan University, the University of Louisiana-Lafayette, the Twentieth-Century Literature and Culture Conference at the University of Louisville, and North Central College. I thank my hosts at these talks for their warmth and engagement: Ed Dryden, Phil Wegner, David Leverenz, Tom Byers, Frank Farmer, Joel Pfister, Lisa Long, and Christine DeVine. Parts of this book were originally published in various journals. I thank Heldref Publications for permission to reprint "Refusing Middle Age," *ANQ* 15.1 (Winter 2002): 46–60. I especially thank Phil Gould and Len Tennenhouse for including my article, " 'In the Blood': Sentiment, Sex, and the Ugly Girl," in *America the Feminine*, special issue of *differences* 11.3 (Fall 1999–2000): 57–75, © 1999–2000 Brown University and *differences*, used by permission of the publisher, Duke University Press.

Chris Green, Mary Unger, and Mandy Wescott are amazing researchers, filled with all sorts of courage and intellect. Lisa Long and Jean Lutes have helped me immeasurably with their careful comments and support. Tina Karageorgos read my work with striking enthusiasm and intelligence. Kim O'Neill is a wonderful editor, someone whose skill and talent are matched by her wit and kindness.

Joel Pfister, Eva Illouz, Eric Haralson, Priscilla Wald, Susan Ryan, and Ann Ardis—friends from various universities all over the world— offered keen insights and astute recommendations. Both Priscilla and Joel were instrumental in leading me at the beginning of my work on the book.

Nina Baym is always there as a counselor, resource, and source of encouragement. And she's a remarkable reader. Bruce Michelson gave me several new ways of looking at the topic of this book, teaching me how to growl in the process. Besides giving on-target advice, Peter Mortensen exemplified dedication; his writing continues to inspire me. Bob Markley—friend and colleague—was there for me while I finished the manuscript, especially while I was recovering from brain surgery. He knew exactly the right amount of goodwill to get me through those hard times.

Susan Griffin brought her incredible wit and energy to the project when I first began work on this book and again when I most needed it, during my recovery.

Virginia Blum, at Kentucky, was one of the most amazing comrades throughout this process; nothing stopped her from giving help and offering love. Over the last eight years, a constant exchange of work with Dana Nelson has made a huge difference in my life. Dana's advice is the gold standard for toughness and engagement.

Lynda Zwinger kept me writing, and rewriting, always giving me words of enthusiasm and encouragement. Her friendship sustained me through this last year, keeping me both living and working. There's no colleague wiser than she is.

My love to Elana Crane, who has been there during every change, every transformation, of the book. I couldn't have done it without her. Many thanks and much love, too, to Mary Pinard, whose strong presence can be found on every page.

Sian Hunter, my editor at the University of North Carolina Press, was patient and smart, especially during the last year of the project. Sian has made this book worth doing. The Press is also lucky to have Ellen Bush and Dino Battista. I am also grateful for the wisdom of copyeditor Paula Wald. Nancy Bentley read the manuscript twice: she is the perfect interlocutor, giving me the best of her acumen in the process. It's been a pleasure to earn her meticulous remarks. Both readers for the press were invaluable, and I'm grateful for Sian's wisdom in locating them.

My gratitude to Samira Didos and Michael Chicoine—for saving my life this year.

As always, I thank my parents, Dorothy and Daniel Bauer, and my brother David for their love and support. Through the course of writing this book, my brother became one of my closest friends, and I'm grateful for his presence in my life.

The Hutners—Gordon, Dan, and Jake—have been there through every page of this manuscript. Dan and Jake grew up asking questions about sex expression—the topic and the book—and kept me inventing new ways to answer them. Gordon is a terrific editor and an even better friend, father, and—above all—partner. He's incomparable, and I'm lucky to share my life with him.

Sex Expression

AND AMERICAN WOMEN WRITERS, 1860–1940

INTRODUCTION

Sex behaviors, sex experience, sex rationalism, sex propensity, sex excess, sex values, sex suppression, sex starvation, sex freedom, sex inclination, sex impulses, sex distinction, sexual efficiency, sex morality, sex potentiality—Mary Austin deploys all of these terms in *Love and the Soul Maker* (1914), her treatise on how women might understand "the great adventure of sex life" in the twentieth century (137). In explaining the modernization of sexuality, including the moral values associated with love and the emergence of women's sex expression, Austin uses these and other similar phrases to devise a new rhetoric of sexuality. Nor was she alone in using these phrases, of which only "sex appeal" seems to have survived. The term "sex expression" was thus introduced into the cultural lexicon as a means of describing this radical upheaval in sex imagination, a new discourse that corresponded to the visual signs of women's signifying on the body and putting on style, a discourse that belonged to expressive culture rather than to nature or the marketplace. In this way, the new sexualization of American culture at the end of the nineteenth century and the beginning of the twentieth was indeed both material and rhetorical.

Much of the fiction concerning sex expression is inevitably middle class since these are stories written by women fitting narrative styles (like dresses in Anzia Yezierska's fiction) to passions that have no settings or forms. These women would even seem at odds with themselves since they were, according to Freudian theories of their sexual constitution, conflicted by the opposing desires of self- and sex expression, the former through work and power and the latter through heterosexual pleasure. And that conflict is deflected onto age and aging, beauty and ugliness, race and ethnicity, and psychology: women must "do" sex first while young, then—as middle-aged agents in the world—move on to power. Working-class women's stories, on the other hand, are mediated through middle-class desires to discover sexual ownership. But there is no prevailing narrative of young, sexually active women with power or of middle-aged women with sex lives. My work here concerns how various women writers—some better known than others—tried to create these new stories.

Seventy years prior to Austin's declaration about the sexualization of U.S. culture and its resonance for women's social and political meanings, Margaret Fuller advocated the primacy of woman's self-culture in "The Great Lawsuit" (1843): "We would have every arbitrary barrier thrown down. We would have every path laid open to woman as freely as to man . . . to bring forth ravishing harmony" (1629). Self-expression for American women took shape in Fuller's demand to have all arbitrary barriers flung open so that women could use any of the available venues for self-culture. The new narratives of sex expression that emerged in women's writing after Fuller's call heralded a new sphere of combined public and private life. Fuller famously protested that without freedom to engage in contract relations, women's marital state was no less a confinement than chattel slavery. This increasingly open private life allowed women writers over the century to create a new mode of self-expression, to the extent that they pushed the boundaries of sexual norms beyond conventional rituals of romance.

By 1890, for example, U.S. anarchist and sex radical Voltairine de Cleyre would denounce men's "sexual authority" in marriage (Delamotte 224) and the violence of the sex act: "A young mother . . . had been stabbed, remorselessly, cruelly, brutally stabbed, not with a knife, but with the procreative organ of her husband, stabbed to the doors of death, and yet there was no redress" (226). De Cleyre would contend that marriage was worse than chattel slavery because of the romantic illusions that undergirded the institution: "Young girls! If any one of you is contemplating marriage remember that is what the contract means. The sale of the control of your person in return for 'protection and support.' The sad part of it is, the majority of women think it is all right" (238). Fuller's and de Cleyre's positions frame the debate over female desires for self-expression by claiming that these desires culminate either in a "ravishing harmony" of the sexes or in the violent punishment of "enslaved sex" (Delamotte 229).

While Karen Sánchez-Eppler's "Bodily Bonds" teaches us to read the hyperbole of equating marriage with slavery (the former based on contract), Fuller's gesture speaks to the investment in sexuality that women used to express how self-culture might liberate them. As Fuller discovered, there was no way to invent a rhetoric of female self-culture without recourse to the language of sexuality. Despite her ambivalence about sex expression, the forces of the culture and female self-understanding pushed in that direction. Bound up with "ravishing harmony," women's desire for sexual expression, according to Fuller, *is* part of self-culture. She thereby anticipates issues that writers a half-century later tackled more explicitly. By the time de Cleyre passionately denounced sex authority, women writers had already begun to express their continued hope for and troubling ambivalences about sexual equality. Writers such as de Cleyre and Austin speculated courageously about the consequences of discarding sentimentality, even as they moved into psychological and social realms new to women writers. My book moves from sentimental sexuality to an analysis of modern sexual exhaustion, the refusal to accept sex expression as potentially liberating.

To that end, I consider how sex expression is embedded in the move from sentimentality to sexuality and, thus, from self-expression to sex expression. The nineteenth-century classical liberal emphasis on self-culture or, more specifically, self-expression—with the self understood as an autonomous and private being—gives way in modern American writing to a focus on intimacy and sexuality as the primary modes of personal expression. Women authors helped fashion a dominant idiom of sexual expression (with intimacy as the necessary condition for interrelational equality) to replace self-expression as the primary goal of the modern self. The heterosexual couple thus appeared as the rightful social arrangement in the United States. Self-expression paled next to the possibilities of sex expression, grounded as these new sexual, liberal possibilities were in the political transformations of contract relations. I also examine what the rhetoric of sex expression has meant in the literary history of U.S. women writers.

By studying the tradition of women writing on this transition from self-expression to sex expression, I follow the lead of scholars such as

Nina Baym who study women's writing as a coherent literary tradition. Following Baym's pioneering work, Susan Williams contends in her thoughtful study of nineteenth-century women's writing, *Reclaiming Authorship*, that we need to develop a nonoppositional approach to men's and women's writings. I, too, will argue for women's development of their own sexual lexicon, not in contrast or contradiction to men's[1] but from inside their own diverse psychological and social positionings. In analyzing their treatments of female sexuality, I prove Williams's contention that women's writing was a distinct nineteenth-century classification, insofar as women writers wrote in conversation with and sometimes against each other.

I examine how women turned from the general, possibly desexualized desire for self-culture (at its zenith in the 1840s to the 1870s) to an investment in sex power and sex expression. "Sex expression," a term circulating in the 1880s, was not really popularized until 1926, when V. F. Calverton published *Sex Expression in Literature*, which argued that sex expression constituted all the ways of representing a culture's measure of sexual life, a phrase bridging bodily practice and literary production.[2] Beginning with Elizabeth Stuart Phelps and Harriet Beecher Stowe and through the opening decades of the twentieth century, women writers celebrated sex expression as a linguistic and physical "style."[3] These writers constructed a psychological and social transition from sentimentality to intimacy, moved the culture from a praxis of self-expression to a praxis of *sexual* expression, and won a Pyrrhic victory. Although these new modes of sex expression might ultimately be co-opted or normalized over time, they had historically specific and culturally relevant moments of illumination for women, moments when women *appeared* or *felt* able to change the way they could imagine themselves as sexual beings. I explore those symbolic episodes in a history in which changes come fitfully, partially, and often uncertainly. The sum of these changes, however, affirms a sexual dimension to identity, whereby women writers found themselves confined within sex expression; it created a new circumscription, another social and imaginative strategy for being reduced to an "It" that, ironically and perhaps inadvertently, women had helped to construct themselves.

This transition from self-expression to the ideal of sexual intimacy was profoundly reflexive—a complex discourse about the transition itself—and a self-conscious inquiry into the strengths and treacheries of language and social custom as forces for stasis or change. "Sex expression" is a simple term for these combined rhetorical and material practices that takes into account not only physical and conjugal affirmation and adventurousness but also expression in social interaction, clothes, the body, politics, and the forms, perspectives, and rhetoric of American fiction.

I began this study with two major questions in mind: Who was presumed to have sexuality in the nineteenth century, and when did sexuality emerge as a modern identity for women in ways that qualified it as a subject for American women writers? In pursuing these questions, I encountered a tradition, previously either inchoate or openly determined, of women writing about sex and teaching readers how to understand the new languages of sexuality, including how to interpret American literary realism, postsentimentality, modernity, and their codes. Some of these new sexual norms were in ascendancy, while others were just emerging; still others (like sex power) were evolving and perhaps would not become demonstrable for another decade or two. This has been a long process of unearthing women's writing on matters of sexuality and distinguishing the newness of their claims. Instead of reading for these claims against the grain or for resistance, my method is to read for signs of an emerging style, whether in terms of characterization, tropes, setting, rendering of consciousness, or new language and sexual styles. I have found that this history of sex expression is not linear but richly recursive and startlingly dynamic.

At the same time, not everyone envisioned sexuality in the same liberatory ways. Some writers I study, like Fannie Hurst, were more conservative than others. Some were apologists for the status quo; others eschewed transgression or resistance as a means of dealing with sexuality. Few discussed lesbianism, bisexuality, or other sexual arrangements, although I explore some of these hopes for freedom in chapter 6 and the conclusion; fewer still featured interracial sexuality. Despite these conventional limits, the writers I examine tested sex expression as the means to argue for women's social ascension and equality. Even the most mainstream writers did not accept heterosexual norms without glossing them or trying to change them for their own purposes. I focus on those writers who invested hope in the emancipatory dimensions of sexuality for a mainstream audience, some of whom are quite familiar, like Edith Wharton, others almost forgotten but once admired, like Fannie Hurst. In many ways, I follow through on the hope that sexuality could be imagined as an equalizing, democratic force, taking my lead from such activists as Jane Addams, Mary Austin, and even Charlotte Perkins Gilman, who dourly predicated that sex was just a bribe to keep women from transforming the status quo.

More recently, my work has been informed by theories of intimacy and analyses of new forms of social suffering, along with recent critical studies of sexuality in U.S. culture like Ann duCille's *The Coupling Convention*, Pamela Haag's *Consent*, and Eva Illouz's *Cold Intimacies*. Uniting these books, and others, is their interest in the increasing complexity of sexuality in modern American culture. According to Mary Odem, in the late nineteenth and early twentieth centuries, Americans exhibited deep anxieties "about the increased potential for sexual expression outside of marriage—a situation that threatened middle-class Victorian ideals of sexual restraint and marital, reproductive sex" (2). Odem's *Delinquent Daughters* focuses on efforts to control "young single women"; Siobhan Somerville's concerns in *Queering the Color Line* are lesbian and gay desire and the color line; Sharon Ullman's *Sex Seen* features the intersecting language of court documents juxtaposed with film and vaudeville (3); Nina Miller's *Making Love Modern* studies the bohemian literati of the 1920s; David Shumway's *Modern Love* details the creation of intimacy as the dominant form of romance in the twentieth century; and Susan Koshy's *Sexual Naturalization* analyzes interracial sex. All of these important arguments suggest the cultural complications around sexuality itself and its significations, which result in changes to the meaning of "It" with each expression.

WHY "SEX EXPRESSION"?

In 1926, V. F. Calverton's *Sex Expression in Literature* helped to codify for modern Americans what sexual freedom in literature might be. Like other modernists, Calverton trusted that the greater liberation of sex discourse would lead to an even greater freedom in American culture. Calverton also thought of sex expression as "sex-imagination" or "sex-magnetism," terms signifying the new ideas about sexuality as a fantasy of personal empowerment. A host of similar studies followed, including Calverton and Samuel Schmalhausen's *Sex in Civilization* (1929) and Floyd Dell's much-debated *Love in the Machine Age* (1930), to which I turn in chapter 6. Following a sociological line, Calverton claimed that a greater sex expression would democratize the language of sexuality, opening it up to the repressed middle class and liberating sexual gratification from its reproductive ends. Once language was freed from its bourgeois restrictions, Calverton ascertained, sexual activity would follow: "The greatest cultural degradation and decline have been accompanied by increased sex repression and purity" (*Sex Expression* xxii). For him, sex *expression* countered the sex *repression* that the bourgeoisie had wrought. Class rivalry, he contended, produced an equally intense literary rivalry between "free flowing sex expression" and more restrictive bourgeois art (55, 58). Calverton reaches these conclusions by way of an overview of the literary history of sexuality—both English and American—and a history of bourgeois culture. In Calverton's view, a regenerated art and literature should instruct the masses in how to behave sexually and how to rebel against bourgeois constraints. Insofar as literature reflects either the bourgeois restrictions on sex or the liberation of sex from repression (58), he argues that sex expression registers the cultural freedom of both writers and readers (92, 126). Ultimately, for Calverton there was something even more emancipating in sex expression than sex itself: a liberation of the masses.

From the tropes of sex expression in 1860 through the novels by popular women writers of the first four decades of the twentieth century, I analyze the rhetorical figures enabling such writers to explore the representation of sexuality. In doing so, I trace how they move from self-expression as a cultural idea to sex expression as a personal ideal. Such values for sexual consent also validate the individual. Yet when we come to questions of consent, as Pamela Haag argues, sex is no longer simply a private issue. In reform work of the 1870s to the 1930s, Haag writes,

7

America celebrated the image of the sexually autonomous and desirous female. If a woman needed money, however, she could not truly consent, for sexual consent, Haag posits, is a *"class-specific luxury"* afforded only to those women who were beyond need or wages (*Consent* 45; Haag's emphasis).

Could women ever get beyond need or wages to a sexual equality of expression? Once women writers invoked sexuality as a pleasure, they also questioned when women consented to pleasure and when sexuality was coerced. In short, what would it mean to be considered a "consenting adult"? Did consent depend on context—like identity categories? How, for example, could marginalized racial or ethnic groups, like Jews, be considered consenting adults when they were often not yet recognized as citizens? Indeed, for some cultural observers such as sociologist E. A. Ross, Jews inherited sexuality as a racial characteristic and could never truly be liberal American individuals, free to create sexual selves— perhaps the central challenge of Anzia Yezierska's oeuvre. Could African American women consent to sex? Did lesbianism count as consent? In African American literature, women writers attempted to create an authentic language of sexual experience transcending race and class, ethnicity and age. According to Ann duCille, Hazel Carby, and Nancy Bentley, slavery's legacy made writing about sexuality an anxious topic since questions of consent were problematic or remote. Much of this sex expression was coded and deflected, and by the time references to lesbianism did appear in mainstream fiction—for example, in Gale Wilhelm's 1935 *We Too Are Drifting*, Fannie Hurst's 1942 *Lonely Parade*, or Mary McCarthy's 1963 *The Group*—the ideal of authenticity in sex expression was exhausted and replaced with a new quantification of sexuality. The new sexual expression was normalized through the therapeutic management of intimacy. With this new therapeutic goal, how were American women writers to define—and possibly defend—sexual autonomy? How much could American society regulate the norms of sexuality for its female sexual citizens? Who even counted as a sexual citizen?

In creating a new lexicon for sex expression, women writers confronted economic and market discourses that kept the language of contract distinct from sexual consent and the transcendence of "real love" (see Haag, " 'Real Thing' " 554). Love—as transcendence, as "It," as the "real thing," or as sexual magnetism—replaced earlier assumptions about intimacy as doing harm or leaving scars, the physical as well as psychological marks of passionate expression. What was once on the body or "in the blood" became instead an interior state characterized by a refusal of material or somatic conditions. "Real love" was imagined as a condition of transcendence of blood inheritance, not a situation emerging from bodily circumstances or social conditions like desire or need.

Whether performed on the streets or configured in marriage, prostitution symbolized women's failure to achieve this sexual equality. As Amy Dru Stanley argues in *From Bondage to Contract*, "Sex represented the human essence whose sale as a market commodity transformed its owners from free persons into slaves" (263). Neither marriage nor wage work guaranteed women's freedom from this transformation since men in power lowered women's wages to maintain their control. Selling sex on the market did not guarantee women much greater freedom since men (and women) of the middle and upper classes denounced and legislated against such sexual market exchanges. Selling sex seemed to be as much about slavery as it was about power, given that prostitution was a symbol of both slavery and a free market society. How could one sell oneself and still be free? Sex, in this formulation, was the "essence" of one's self-ownership. Prostitution—the literal exchange of intercourse for money—did not afford women much power, but the symbolic value of sexuality did have its own rhetorical weight. If the only option most women had on the marriage market was to wait for the most eligible bachelor, how could women extend that market power into marriage itself? Only when women could use sex as a symbolic power—rather than as a commodity to be sold or as an identity to be cultivated for emotional capital or influence—could women writers imagine sex power as a liberating social possibility.

The following chapters trace the shifting articulations about female sexuality and their spiraling effects. Rather than taking a linear path, this history tends to double back on itself or blend together tropes, thereby yielding nuances of development; period norms are often fused together, competing for dominance, instead of straightforwardly leading from one to the next. I begin with the mid-nineteenth-century transition from the ideal of sexual purity to the goal of sexual pleasure, which is not to say that at any point in time an ideal of sexual purity was out of place or the goal of finding sexual pleasure had not yet been conceived. These tentative explorations of pleasure proliferated in the literature of sex power, even as other stories about changes in sexual norms appeared: while some women argued for the class expansion of sex expression, other women focused on age as sexuality's most crucial liberation. As much as I have wished to adhere to a literary historical progression, these fictions about sex expression moved in sometimes conflicting, sometimes circular directions; stories about sex expression often occurred at the same time, in layers and palimpsests. Even in the career of one American writer, Fannie Hurst, overlapping concerns complicated the range of possible sex expressions and the fears that emerged as part of her fictions about therapeutic sexuality.

Chapter 1 explores the origins of sex expression in women's writing, although male writers, too, alternately profited and suffered from sex expression. Much of the fiction by writers such as Gertrude Atherton, Mary Austin, and Willa Cather was generated to help women assess new sexual norms. Because of their relation to the emotional labor of sentiment and sympathy, such writers had a head start on creating the fictions of sexuality, especially those exploring who was allowed to have sex or what sort of sex it was. Their major questions led me to generate three categorical questions: *Who* spoke about sexuality in these decades? *How* did women writers create a new sexual rhetoric? And *why* did sex expression become the focus of women writers' literary expertise?

First, *who* spoke about sexuality in these decades? We know that, by the 1920s, new sexual discourses were debated everywhere, by eugenicists, social scientists, and psychologists, as well as by cultural critics and philosophers. As Christine Stansell writes in *American Moderns*, "sex talk" went public (275). New terms and studies defined sex power and its various manifestations. More important, as Hurst dramatizes in *Back Street* (1931), sex style was a new power: "When [Ray Schmidt] so much as walked past the Stag Hotel, skirts held up off the sidewalk with that ineffable turn of wrist which again denoted 'style,' there was that in her demeanor which caused each male head and eye to turn" (7). For Hurst and a host of American women writers before her, style expressed both physical and material desires. American women developed and performed sexual style—in contrast to character and personality—as a series of gestures, codes, even clothing. American women novelists created a corresponding literary style to convey these new sexual gestures and purposes, a commensurate way to get readers' heads to turn—such as the idea of "pleasuring" that appears in Julia Peterkin's *Scarlet Sister Mary* (1928)—to their unspoken desires. The changes in sexual style required adjustments in the class status of sexuality, from the realm of the working class to the domain of middle-class women, so these writers also had to distinguish sexual rhetoric from talk of prostitution, fallen women, and "bad" or "fly" girls.

Second, *how* did American women writers go beyond thematizing issues of sexuality and invent a literary tradition—and a style—of their own? How did they develop a literary style equal to the new sexual styles of their heroines and their readers? Would there be a new genre of sexual melodrama and female complaint (Berlant), a gendered naturalism (Fleissner), or a sexual modernism (Boone)? As I demonstrate, many women writers contributed to the making of a comprehensive code of sexual legibility and rhetoric. That code was necessary because sexuality underwent a status change in these decades from an ostensibly "unconscious" reaction of the body, to a consciously motivated set of acts and speech, and finally to a style devoted to personal pleasure.

My premise is that we have not yet learned to read how the new languages of sex expression shaped both ambiguous reactions to and qualified acceptances of modern sexuality. This lexicon of shifting codes enables us to grasp how American women writers created a normative vocabulary to express the "unconscious" desires they presumed women to possess and embody. Although modern liberalism helped to make sexuality the predominant sign of individuality, giving it the terms of depth, interiority, and subtextuality to draw on, the writers I study give sex expression its own *literary* style. In the examples that follow, we can see these writers' challenges to once conventional notions of sexuality in

11

terms of new heroines (middle-aged women), new themes for fiction (the kept woman or mistress), and new literary styles (such as Anita Loos's *Gentlemen Prefer Blondes* in 1925 and Mary McCarthy's *The Company She Keeps* in 1942). In examining these challenges, I have embarked on a double project of demonstrating the sexual conventionality many of these women assumed even as they sought to change it. These new styles converge most often in the rendering of new kinds of heroines, those whose burgeoning self-consciousness about sexuality is the focus of these fictions.

Finally, *why* did women writers create new sexual dramas for their readers? Other critics have looked at sexology and the increasing visibility of sexuality in modern culture or, as historian Helen Horowitz has done, observed the rise of "American vernacular sexual culture" that was "passed down through the generations and sideways among peers" (4–5). In tandem with this vernacular sexual culture arose a new set of codes for what was not yet nameable and for which no literary tradition I know of has been previously assigned. The fallen woman, the New Woman, racialized and exoticized sexual identities, and gay and lesbian cultures have been cultural preoccupations (see Somerville 36), yet many women writers created narratives that refused immediate intelligibility and identification. Reading these novels offers a glimpse into the alternative discourses of sexual fulfillment to which American women writers had access when they reacted to the social control and scientific discipline that channeled women's search for sexual equality. Even though reading vernacular culture is an important way to decode these desires, it is equally necessary to study, as I do here, the sexual style inherent in conventions, codes, and choices that both mainstream and marginal American women writers designed for their fictions. Within these conventions, we can find the emergent notion of a sexual interiority, the first step toward the sexualization of U.S. culture.

The remaining chapters represent test cases—challenges to the limits of proscribed or normative sexuality—over the course of the decades I study. At each stage of a newly emergent sexual discourse, another discourse was about to be forgotten or silenced concerning issues like the sexualities of the ugly, the middle-aged, the ambivalent and powerless, the inarticulate, the ethnic, the conservative, the poor, and the broke. Whose sexuality is most easily codified and expressed? The beautiful, glamorous, or young; the rich, liberated, or liberal—all of these categories inform the general rubrics of normative sexuality. As previously marginalized sexualities emerge, other types remain suppressed.[4] Women writers' sex expression, as readers will see, did not reject heterosexual plots—the mainstay of their popularity—but drew on the predominant ideas of sexual norms that the new social sciences, mass culture, and capitalist consumption fueled. In their efforts at social regulation, sociologists and social engineers policed those who could practice sexuality and those excluded from standardized American Sex. So even as various sexual practices were marginalized or exoticized, pathologized or criminalized, certain categories of sexuality were considered beyond the borders of inquiry. The writers in my purview contended with these consequences for women's sexuality.

Chapter 2 begins by examining the cultural terms through which sexual behavior was alternately recommended and condemned during America's rise as an industrial power. My focus on the "ugly girl" reveals that sexuality was not always associated exclusively with youth and beauty, as it had been in the twentieth century (*pace* Fanny Brice). Rather, as various nineteenth-century novels demonstrate, "ugly girls" had sex; at the very least, the "ugly girl" struggled to repress desires that the innocent, attractive woman was loath to admit to consciousness. Beautiful girls strived to be considered morally and sexually pure. As Margaret Fuller explains, actresses, singers, female authors, "even learned women, if not insufferably ugly and slovenly" (1632), could expect to profit from their "beauty and grace." But "ugliness" was a category sui generis. In this context, I examine the eugenic discourse of the body and inheritance, which sought to explain ugliness as a cultural trait, in order to reveal how sexuality was "in the blood." Sexual otherness—caused by degeneracy, decline, or disability—and desire were often coupled in fictions by Rebecca Harding Davis ("Anne" [1889]), Elizabeth Stoddard (*The Morgesons* [1862]), and Elizabeth Stuart Phelps (*The Silent Partner* [1871]), whose works I explore subsequently.

With the advance of the eugenics movement, in order for women to be sexual, it became irrelevant whether they were ugly or beautiful. Rather, as it was for Gertrude Atherton in *Hermia Suydam* (1889) (see chapter 1), social class and status—more than aesthetics, health, or inheritance—determined a woman's sexual rights. Women's greater access to commodities and, indeed, ubiquitous shopping made sex expression all the more a desire (because sexual style could be bought and performed simultaneously), especially for middle-class women. Following this consumer explosion was a heated cultural debate about whether women could or should have sex once their reproductive and consumer capacities were exhausted. Chapter 3, "Refusing Middle Age," studies the changing ages at which midlife was assumed to set in: once thirty to thirty-five (early to mid-nineteenth century), then forty to forty-five (turn of the century), then fifty (by the 1920s). More important, this chapter shows how middle-aged women from 1871 to 1923—in works by Harriet Beecher Stowe, Rebecca Harding Davis, Gertrude Atherton, and Willa Cather—displayed sexual needs. As Laura Daintrey writes in her novel *Actaeon* (1892), "At forty, a woman finds it sweet to begin life, or rather love anew" (130). Once past reproductive capacity, middle-aged women had to invent new reasons to desire, including sex madness—a postreproductive desire for sex pleasure and self-assertion, even sex as an outlet for aggression and rage, as Atherton figures it in *Black Oxen* (1923) when her forty-two-year-old virgin character goes mad for mating. As Mary Austin writes, "In the states of adolescence, however, and at the climacteric, sexual energy is naturally convertible into other forms, passes easily, and without volition into creative processes such as have to do with the higher manifestations of consciousness" (*Soul Maker* 276). Yet some women wanted to hold onto their sex energy for sex, not for "higher consciousness." This new extrareproductive sex consciousness correlates with the self-consciousness animating an earlier generation of women, and it finds its analogue in the political and economic consciousness of such social activists as Charlotte Perkins Gilman and Jane Addams, the great settlement house philanthropist who disdained liberation as undesirable for working women.

More often than not, these middle-aged women writers who focused on sex desire also doubted its power. In novels about women's sex power, from Stowe's *Pink and White Tyranny* (1871) to Cather's *A Lost Lady* (1923), the heroines reject a new sense of libidinal force as liberating and are represented as being alienated from it. Chapter 4 moves to the concept of "sex power," focusing on how Stowe, Austin, Wharton, Louisa May Alcott, and Dorothy Parker associate sex with addiction, disability, racial antagonism, and death. By the time Wharton, for example, reached middle age and began her life-defining affair with Morton Fullerton in 1908, her fictions more and more expressed profound ambivalence about sex expression. Casting doubts about the hope that sex would liberate women from patriarchal control, Wharton's heroines despair over women's sexual rivalry over men, as in *Custom of the Country* (1913). Wharton pursued a more spiritual connection than modern liberalism promised to women in the version of American Sex commodified and packaged for the young. Other writers followed suit, describing sex power as a failed bid for equality.

By the 1920s, the prevailing discourse of *personal* self-fulfillment eclipses this earlier notion of sex as social power. Figures of sexual desire need not take indirect, often twisted forms (quite literally, given how Wharton's heroines end up deformed or disfigured by desire). Instead, a new generation of women writers—including Anzia Yezierska, Jessie Fauset, Viña Delmar, and Julia Peterkin—found more increasingly direct ways to express the ideal of women's pleasure, mostly borrowed from minority and working-class women's sexual experiences (or fantasies of what these were). White writers grafted white women's desires onto working-class intimacy and ethnicity in popular writings of the late 1910s and 1920s. In chapter 5, "Inarticulate Sex," I juxtapose white women writers' fictions with Yezierska's treatment of an immigrant in her 1923 novel, *Salome of the Tenements*. Yezierska's narrative of Jewish passion contrasts vividly with these writers' reflections on "other" women, for her heroines are not modern-day Nanas, or Maggies of the street, or even middle class and white. How far did sexual choice and pleasure extend beyond white, middle-class spheres? Working-class women characters enjoy sex and emerge with neither pox nor stigma upon them. These heroines enjoy "pleasuring" themselves and survive to profit by their sexual adventures. Sex power loses its compromising connection with ugliness, prostitution, middle age, addiction, and disability; yet women with sex power, "It," or sexual magnetism still are incoherent about pleasure, unreflective about desire. In Viña Delmar's *Bad Girl* (1928), for example, female sexuality loses almost all of its association with illicit-ness, even while the heroine remains almost entirely inarticulate about sex.[5] So what? As long as women could express sexual desires, what need did they have for sexual explicitness, as the prevailing logic held.

Sex expression as a creed reached its zenith in the 1920s when sexual freedoms are supposed to have proliferated, despite the limits of language in keeping up with these stories of female sexual success. Chapter 6 identifies and examines a counterdiscourse that emerges in the 1920s, 1930s, and 1940s, dedicated to a rationalized, even bureaucratic idea of "sexual magnetism." By the Depression years, American women writers typically represented sexuality as more conservative than ever before. There still may have been plenty of "It" girls, but in novels like Hurst's *Back Street* or *Family!* (1960) (in which Virgie refuses her lover's presents) or stories by leftist radical Meridel Le Sueur, sex expression gives way to examining conservative arguments about how women could survive the aftereffects of the Crash when a more prohibitive economic climate and more vigorous reproductive control took hold. Taking great pains to show that women do not profit by their sexuality, these novels save sexuality from its previous associations with prostitution and with contract relations of any sort. In fact, just the opposite occurs in Hurst's parade of eighteen novels, where women do not profit but pay psychologically for their unself-conscious sex expressions and grow unwilling to trade in sexuality for intimacy or equality.

By the end of the 1930s, women seem to have paid enough. Sex expression gives way to a figurative sexual exhaustion. Perhaps the most sensational example of this profound, encompassing fatigue is presaged in *Back Street* when the heroine, Ray Schmidt, dies, shriveled and starved, clutching the money that her now deceased lover's son has unknowingly thrown her way at the gambling tables where women of her milieu sought alms. It is a fitting ironic conclusion to women's belief in the viability of sexual contracts as kept women. By the end of this novel, and so many others during the 1930s, women just want to stay home, forget about sex, and tell stories, as Janie does in Zora Neale Hurston's *Their Eyes Were Watching God* (1937). This is a development— the exhaustion of sexuality and liberatory hope—worth explaining, as I do in chapter 6.

In what follows, I analyze how American women writers explore a complex set of responses to sexual liberation, including such considerations as age, appearance (beauty and ugliness), health (disability and addiction), and sexual literacy. An array of women writers confronted the liberatory claims of sex expression—from Alice B. Stockham and Angela Heywood to Mary Austin and Fannie Hurst—and deliberated about the utopic possibilities of sexuality. In doing so, they created a hopeful discourse of sexual fulfillment and described a new sexual interiority. Their works teach us to read cultural codes that were not recognized as sexual until these writers articulated them. With this lesson in mind, I explore how American women writers created tropes representing sexual experience: tropes of blood, age, disability, disaster, inarticulateness and alienation, contagion and absorption. Eventually, women writers saw even sexual conservatism as volitional passivity, whether in sexual submission or in "frigidity," a term that emerged in sexological discourse of the 1920s as the obverse of the pathologized hypersexuality of the late nineteenth century.[6] The critical debate about sexuality until now has focused on sexual rights and contract, as well as what constitutes "normal" or standardized intimacy. What we haven't yet done— and what I contend that these writers were trying to do—is to make the varieties of sex expression the locus of that debate.

My focus is the transformation from self-expression as the greatest goal of the liberal individual to sex expression as the locus of possibility in which women sought the emancipatory power of passion and sexual relationships. U.S. women novelists from the 1860s through the 1940s invested heavily in the possibilities of sexual self-definition and freedom.[7] This transition from the sentimental to the postsentimental, from the feminization of American culture to its sexualization, could not have occurred without the women writers who gave it currency in a literary style, one that was co-extensive with a general shift in sexology, psychology, and sociology.

These writers, as I will show, took up sex expression for ever-widening purposes. Their efforts to give nuance to women's sexual being are important because of the way such new values qualified the meaning of sexuality in America. So rather than focusing on a literary history of women's emotional or sexual labor or a history of women doing the work of intimacy for the culture at large, I study how U.S. women writers imagined their heroines as sexual beings, not for biographical interest but for a cumulative record of the cultural imagination and its inflections. That concern leads me to ask, What terms did women invent to express the rise of women's sexual labor at home and on the market? Women writers felt they had special access to defining what intimacy between equals might become because they drew on the emotional work of sentimentality. Such fantasies of equality stimulated these women's writing, revealing the hope that community is possible between genders— that intimacy would be the new power of sympathy and sexuality might emerge as the new sentiment. Thus, this project is dedicated to explaining the sexualization of liberal individualism (once grounded in self-expression) that occurred in the nineteenth century and extended into the twentieth. I explain throughout this book how the core of liberal individualism still inhered in the move from self-expression to sex expression, until the dynamics of modern women's sexual expression turned from liberation to therapeutic agency by the 1940s. As pop psychologist David Seabury explained in 1927, sex was not a "unified urge" but an "expression through which other impulses, non-sexual, may play a part" (532). In this way, I am describing the development of a sexual rhetoric that emerged from the language of liberal self-expression.

By focusing here on sex expression over sexual performance, I stress the precedence of rhetoric over practice as the measure of sexual norms. To that end, my study takes up a set of significant women's novels not always in the critical purview of late nineteenth-century and early modern American scholarship. I examine the legitimate call-and-response among these women writers, especially regarding sexological advice and stylistic innovations targeted at women. Women writers of this era harnessed "sex power" in their pursuit of equality, which signified for them the intentional use of the visible style and linguistic codes created for expressing desire. As sexuality became more public, the rhetorics of both the body and language could express sexual desire, however contingent on social context. Women writers began to treat sex, once considered an urge or impulse, as a conscious act and a choice, deliberately enacted and embodied. Newly construed in this way, sex power could be seen as an act, an identity, or even an exchange value. Yet sex power failed in its promise to equalize heterosexual relations, and the rise of sex expression (as I show in chapter 6) also contained the seeds of its own depletion.

I hope that this book provides a new episode in what Jonathan Ned Katz calls "the invention of heterosexuality" and its alternatives. This first sexual revolution did not occur in the 1960s and 1970s but percolated after the Civil War and into the first decades of the twentieth century. I aim, then, to revive the memory of how important U.S. women writers used their influence to register their call for sexual expression and freedom. We need to recover this discourse of sexual expressions based on constant renegotiation of women's psychosexual selves, along with a more just appreciation of several women writers—like Gertrude Atherton and Mary Austin, Jessie Fauset and Fannie Hurst, Anzia Yezierska and Viña Delmar—who deployed sex expression to give voice and meaning to the sexualization of U.S. culture.

CHAPTER ONE

THE
Sexualization
OF AMERICAN CULTURE

FROM SELF-EXPRESSION TO SEX EXPRESSION

The story of three generations of U.S. women writers who wrote about sexuality from 1860 through 1940 concerns women's investment in sexuality, intimacy, and "sex power" as alternatives to what much of the nineteenth century saw as individual self-expression. Refusing to sentimentalize sexuality any longer and instead claiming sexual desire as a new form of women's power, many writers adopted the rhetoric of free choice to establish their own authority in sexual matters. In doing so, these women writers first had to distinguish sexuality from its previous configuration as a racial or class inheritance or even a Lamarckian characteristic, passed down over generations through acquired traits. For these writers, sex was not in the blood, a racial quality, or even part of social class and character. Sex expression as a discourse had to be liberated from its association with the degeneracy of the working classes, racial and ethnic others, and physical and moral weakness. "Sex power" was once women's hope for democratizing heterosexual relations; despite some (or even great) ambivalence about sexuality, the writers I discuss forged a new language of sexual expressions, even going so far as to suggest how sex expression and sex power could erase the divisions among women based on racial and ethnic experience or on class and privilege. In an American culture increasingly devoted to choice, these writers crafted a discourse that addressed the imagined emancipatory pleasure of sexuality coupled with the actual limits of women's sexual self-reliance. Once women imagined sex and power as no longer antithetical but coterminous, the hope was that democratized heterosexual relations would end the economic inequality and instability of traditional gender roles. Once women writers rejected sexuality as a vehicle for equality or even liberation (by my reckoning, shortly after the first waves of the Depression), as many inevitably did, they embraced a desire to forsake sex power as too ambivalent and as a potentially self-destructive strategy. Animating this dramatic process was a willed rejection of earlier versions of sex power, a refusal of sexuality as a viable form of liberation.

Nevertheless, focusing on sexuality itself—or creating it as a category of identity—limited the self-expression that Margaret Fuller and others advanced. Promoting the sexual self relied on its promise of liberation, since the sexual self transcended the boundary between private and public, between self and the social network through which women had to negotiate their power. As narrow as sexual expression might seem in a range of other possible expressions available to women (family, community, politics, work, vocation), it figured—however briefly—as one of the most expansive, most hopeful possibilities for women's development. My challenge here may be understood as how to write a history of this hope. This study addresses how to see these narratives as discourses of possibility rather than thwarted attempts at expressive culture. Women writers infused sexuality with hope of liberation, hope of power and authority, even as they sometimes doubted sexuality's possibilities or its compensations for limited economic equality. Even so, the proliferation of contract relations in the late nineteenth century led women writers to believe that sexual relations could be secularized, codified, and democratized (based on conscious choice between equals in terms of affective and libidinal investments in each other) once sexuality was released from reproductivity and no longer associated with sin or immorality. By creating their own sexual rhetoric, writers as different as Rebecca Harding Davis and Mary McCarthy elaborated on the possibilities of liberation. This feat in itself marked these authors as important historical precursors of the sexual liberationists of the 1960s and 1970s. The period of women's sex expression, in Pamela Haag's terms, the "'first' sexual revolution" (*Consent* 78), occurred in the early years of the twentieth century when sexual privacy and sexual desire were considered the hallmarks of the modern self. I argue that this first sexual revolution started in post–Civil War America.

This hope for sexuality was never naive or unalloyed, however. There were always limits to the possibilities of sex expression. Some who were driven by ambition, others by opposition (bohemians, radicals, free-lovers, feminists, or socialists), were seemingly beyond the sexual pale and thus excluded from the practices of sex power. At the end of the nineteenth century, many minority women and working-class authors rejected sex expression as too bourgeois, apolitical, or quietistic. For these writers, sex power always had to be transformed into some other sort of more literal or material power—economic or social—but was never primarily physical or symbolic, as Charlotte Perkins Gilman and Jane Addams advocated. Women writers' very conceptions of what counted as sex power provoked as much ambivalence as that power did celebration or satisfaction. As Edith Wharton suggested, the danger of sex expression lies in its standardization, in the real possibility that sexuality would become normalized and hence lose whatever individuating and psychologically liberating power it might otherwise have.

One famous sexual controversy is especially telling in this context of transforming sex power. In his infamous tract against coeducation, *Sex in Education* (1873), Edward Clarke suggested that women risk becoming "agenes"—thoroughly sterile creatures—if forced to keep up intellectually, let alone compete, with men. Clarke described the closed system of brain and sex power: women "graduated from school or college excellent scholars, but with undeveloped ovaries. Later they married, and were sterile" (39). Devoid of reproductive power (or what Clarke terms "arrested development of the female reproductive system"), the "agenes" represented what would happen to women whose brain power eradicated their sexual power (93), sex power then referring exclusively to reproduction.

In *Sex and Education* (1874), Julia Ward Howe's edited collection responding to Clarke's attack, contributors were careful to defend educated women against the dual, contradictory charges of being "fast" and of being sexless (93). Clarke imputed that "excessive culture" would result in female "degeneracy"; author and reformer Caroline Dall's rejoinder to Clarke was that such degeneracy was actually "inherited from a vicious father" (104). Dall suggests just how much Lamarckianism influenced notions of cultural decline; neither culture nor coeducation but inheritance altered women's lives. While Clarke feared that college-educated women might become hermaphroditic as a result of the spinsterhood that, for him, inevitably accompanied a bachelor's degree (123, 145), his detractors worried more about what would happen to women out in society who were made ill by the grosser contacts of social life and its dissipations: "Sadder even than the bloodless skin and intellectual face of the normal-school girl is the not uncommon spectacle of the bloodless skin and unintellectual face of the girl in our fashionable private schools, whose mind has become so enervated by parental indulgence, so demoralized by social excitement, that, to use her own words, 'the sight of a book makes her head ache'" (121). As nineteenth-century ethnologists explained, blood will tell: the "bloodless skin" is the mark of an endangered girl, threatened by either intellectual or fashionable pursuits. Women writers like Elizabeth Stuart Phelps, who contributed to Howe's volume on Clarke's folly, had to protect girls—and sex—from such reactionary responses to women's self-expression. They did so by creating a sexual expression that invested women with a particular kind of sex power. As some writers worried, if girls were endangered, so were middle-aged women, whose sex power would soon "expire" or who would find themselves needing other compensations than a presumably "free" sexual subjectivity.

This period saw the move from "free" love to sex trade work: that the sexualization of American culture accompanied the rise of commodity capitalism is clear, but whether it increased female power was a question women writers argued even as they sought to reconcile the paradoxes of heterosexual relations in commodity culture. Sex expression promised a transgressive or emancipatory force that could lead to women's greater health, psychological depth, and subjectivity, but the question was, how could sexual choice and consumerism be analyzed, whether to link these processes or to disentangle them?[1] At the same time, these writers understood sex expression as an illusion of choice or consent in market relations. For David Shumway in *Modern Love*, this greater standardization of culture, especially in the middle classes, created the need to imagine sexuality and intimacy as a refuge from the alienation of consumerism (23–24). Rejecting mass-marketing's new images of sexual relations, a number of women novelists responded to the standardization of culture in ever more inventive ways, claiming sexuality as a move away from standardization. Advertising helped to cement this standardization even as it made sex more palatable as a subject of cultural debate. And as Jackson Lears argues, the end of the nineteenth century saw an "exuberant outpouring" in the visual imagery associated with the "primitivist, exotic, and erotic" (*Fables* 144). That imagery seldom translated into a language that women writers accepted and promulgated, but it did spark them to pour out exuberantly their own language of sex expression.

SEXUAL PERSONS AND SEXUAL NEEDS

Among the most important pronouncements about sexual health in the late nineteenth century was that sex expression typically begins with the call for women's physical health before it becomes a demand for psychological help and, eventually, a plea for pleasure and therapeutic relations. According to the doctrine of *Karezza* (1896), an exhortation for male sexual withdrawal during intercourse, "the natural woman knows that virtue is not sexual repression but rather expression" (48). Dr. Alice B. Stockham wrote *Karezza* to protect women enslaved by outdated ideas about passion and husbands who insisted on unlimited (and unprotected) sexual access to their wives. Stockham proclaimed that "sex life and sex expression are a natural heritage" to both men and women (49)—if only both knew how to reach "equal pleasure" (83). Intercourse without the "flood," as Stockham describes it, is the perfect act of intimacy, occurring "completely under the control of the will" and at the consent of both husband and wife (23).

Stockham advocates will over sexual impulse in order that the young " 'old lady' should become the regenerated 'new woman' " (43), once she is saved from her husband's sexual urges. She quotes John Humphrey Noyes's *Male Continence* (1872) to highlight his terms of water imagery and fluidity: "In normal condition, men are entirely competent to choose in sexual intercourse whether they will stop at any point in the voluntary stages of it, and so make it simply an act of communion, or go through to the involuntary stage, and make it an act of propagation. . . . The situation may be compared to a stream in three conditions, viz., 1. a fall; 2. a course of rapids above the fall; and 3. still water above the rapids. The skillful boatman may choose whether he will remain in the still water, or venture more or less down the rapids, or run his boat over the fall" (121). While men could control their sexual fluids by firmly grasping their oar, whether women could control their sexual desires as easily as men was an open question. Kate Chopin's "The Storm" (1898), for instance, depicts women's sexual desire as nothing less than a down-pour. For Chopin, women's—not men's—sexual urgency is so torrential that it constantly threatens to overwhelm social relations.

Stockham's tract was part of the cultural debate over who exerted sexual power. Scholars of U.S. liberal culture have demonstrated the modernization of these new sexual norms, especially through the de-velopment of the ideas of consent and choice, and examined the varieties of rhetorical and ideological transformations about intimacy, self-owner-ship, and free love.[2] In describing the sexualization of American culture, critics have especially documented how sexuality emerged as a defining quality of modern selfhood with a new language of intimacy to codify sexual freedom. Sociologist Eva Illouz argues that the contemporary era is one of disembodied love, characterized by disappointment and psychic suffering. Julian Carter also contends that modern intimacy is a disciplinary ideal characterized by impossible principles rather than "an actually existing state" (154). Nevertheless, this fantasy of egalitarian connection galvanized so many novels that it fueled a new kind of sexual hope.

It might seem self-evident to proclaim that American women writers took sexuality as their subject by the turn of the twentieth century, given how ubiquitous the topic became. Yet this assumed openness about sexuality in modern American culture has kept critics from marking the evolution of this new sexualization, especially among nineteenth-century sex-expression precursors like Elizabeth Stuart Phelps and Harriet Beecher Stowe.[3] The sentimental tradition once allowed women writers to register their interests in various social concerns like slavery, temperance, abuse, and deprivation—like Harriet Beecher Stowe in *Uncle Tom's Cabin* (1852)—even as it codified the authors' physical and psychic pain in emotional terms. While the sentimentalizing of experience never disappeared, many women writers invented a new style of sex expression that found its metaphors and tropes in sexual intimacy so that they might replace sincerity with sexuality as the dominant means of cultural expression for men and women alike. This mixture of sentimentality and sexuality was powerful and remains so today, giving rise to what Lauren Berlant calls "the female complaint" or the genre of women's writing devoted to "disappointment management" (*Female Complaint* 1–2, 230).

Starting in the 1860s and 1870s, U.S. women's writing recorded a major shift in thinking about sentiments and sexual relations. Once part of the realm of sentiments, sexuality became a discourse about rights; private thoughts and acts, once distinct from economic metaphors, now replicated social relations (Haag, *Consent* 79). According to this logic, it is impossible to separate new ways of talking about sexuality from the historical and cultural contexts that first witnessed these expressions. Whether one imagines that sexuality was the trade-off for the "corrosion" or failure of the liberal "fictions of autonomous selfhood" (ibid. 174) or that sexuality was the ultimate prize—promising unconstrained choice and equality—of modern liberal culture, these alternatives tell

27

only part of the story. Whether compensatory or liberating, therapeutic or repressive, sexuality suddenly betokened women's agency in works of fiction that were reflexive insofar as authors expressed their doubts even as they proselytized for women's sexual freedom.

Many women writers imagined the self as best expressed through the dyad that sex and intimacy promised as its reward; they advised women to be themselves within the intimate coupling that they chose, however narrow the possibilities of object choice or sexual style. Just as personality replaced character as the dominant language of the self, intimacy replaced courtship and companionship as the predominant language of sexuality. Intimacy later signified the heightened sex consciousness of the 1920s and 1930s, even as once-public courtship rituals became ever-more privatized. That is, women writers affirmed their places in modern American culture—from 1860 to 1940—not just by purveying sentiment but also by exploring intimacy and explicitness. In displacing sentimentality, they did not embrace sexology so much as contemplate how to use their sexuality as a social power.[4] Sex expression in general looked attainable since it seemed to offer a sex equality that could compensate for the social equality not widely or readily available. After all, everyone could "have" sex or be "sexual," while the means of self-culture was mostly class-specific; self-expression was a luxury of self-ownership, denied to some races and classes.

For Anthony Giddens, the idea that sexuality is something one "cultivates" or "has"—a quality that can be "reflexively grasped, interrogated and developed"—is a modern creation (14–15), the effect of what he theorizes as "the transformation of intimacy." This shift makes intimacy less a "natural condition" (although it is uncertain that intimacy was ever truly conceived as natural) and more a cultivated, socialized, and historicized attribute of the self. Giddens describes the transformation of intimacy as a process of the democratization of sex. As he quite optimistically contends, expressing sexuality once seemed to have substantial potential for a democratic expansion of human relations. While work, race, and class relations became increasingly codified and even calcified, sexual relations opened up as the new space of freedom. This sexuality is more "plastic" and mutable than Foucault argues is true of the discourses that bolster it: "Sexual diversity, although still regarded by many hostile groups as perversion, has moved out of Freud's case-history notebooks into the everyday social world. Seen in these terms, the decline of perversion can be understood as a partly successful battle over rights of self-expression in the context of the liberal democratic state" (33). Celebrating the potential for change embedded in this "partly successful battle," Giddens offers the important caution that "sexual permissiveness is not at all the same as liberation" (168), just as writers like Wharton presaged how "sex power" failed her characters (see chapter 4). This expertise in intimacy, Giddens suggests, leads women to develop ever greater variations on sexual narratives or new styles that allow them to escape from domestic subservience and move toward a more equal, democratic envisioning of passion. Even so, as we shall see, self-expression gets channeled into the sometimes strait-jacketed constraints of sexual identity.[5]

My focus on the transformation of intimacy is historical: how did self-expression become fixated on sexuality as the prevailing, even defining quality of the self, the trait with the most potential for cultural change from the 1860s through the 1940s? How did the field of expression from the "self" become solely focused on "sex"? Although the self has always seemed greater than its sexual possibilities, sex expression seemed the strongest place to launch new freedoms. Yet this new emphasis is focused less on the qualities of persons (whether in terms of race or class, sexual object choice, or sexual geography) than on the character of relationships, what Giddens calls "confluent love": "Women's capacity and need for sexual expression were kept carefully under wraps until well into the twentieth century" (118). According to Giddens, people saw modern sexuality as both "promise and threat" (78); such a relationship presupposes female autonomy, the freedom and resources to choose (see Giddens 195). Such egalitarianism depends on the notion of contract: the ability of women to contract freely and independently with sexual partners. Women had to come to terms with "a culture organized by sex difference" but without succumbing to opposition and resistance (Haag, *Consent* 44). Women writers' new configurations of intimacy in these terms are the key to the following chapters.

That is, I wish to bring literary history to bear on Giddens's theory by analyzing how U.S. women's novels explain what the "sexual contract" might mean and how women might use it to their own ends—for equality or pleasure. I begin by explaining how "sexual persons" or American sexual character emerged as a new way of self-styling. While American liberalism touted its support of individual rights, those rights were exercised in ever more regulated and sanctioned ways, albeit through the promise of presumptive freedom and personal consent. Haag charts this move from nineteenth-century classic liberalism to modern liberalism in the twentieth century, a shift marked by "deeper privacy and personal autonomy" that was figured through the image of the single woman or *femme sole*, who became the true test case of new liberal freedoms (*Consent* xix).[6] These test cases are also to be found in women's fiction (for example, Wharton uses the language of Undine Spragg's "case" in *The Custom of the Country* [1913]), whose nuances allow us to imagine women's concerns about sexual consent. What powers did women imagine to inhere in their sexuality? How could women exert this sex power to achieve some measure of equality in what they projected democratic sexual relations to be? Why did heterosexual "free" choice come to signify the height of liberal freedom in modern America?

In so many ways, women writers found this transition ineluctable at the crucial moment of this literary history: while self-culture was inherently a public demonstration of education, acculturation, and self-representation based primarily on social class, sex expression could appeal to women across classes and races since it spoke to private needs and psychological unfoldings of modern culture. As I see it, the category of "sexual persons" evolved at the same time—neither strictly "private" nor merely "statistical"—along with the rise of mass culture, which presupposed the performance of sexuality as an essential component of the self. American women's fiction provided the link between "sexual persons" and new sexualities, a way to describe and, arguably, to adjudicate sexual behaviors.

Although public purity campaigns enforced and encouraged a normalized sexuality, fiction enabled readers to negotiate freedom in ostensibly private domains of leisure. Many women writers envisioned sexual persons as fundamentally different from the sexual victims or naïfs that had previously been characterized in terms of seduction, prostitution, purity, and marriage. In doing so, women writers created tropes symbolizing power and pleasure that they hoped would transcend market logic and patriarchal relations.

As individual choice gained support as a value in U.S. culture, the women writers I study increasingly explored the possibility of personal sex power. Sexual rights and contract relations did not spell out what women wanted, just what they could legally expect or be granted. If freedom was predicated on choice, expression was predicated on need.[7] And while classic liberalism categorized women's new rights to choose and to make contracts, it could not articulate or predict how women would respond. Women writers invested in sexual over market relations, albeit within the modern liberal culture they had inherited.

Thus, in response to the discourse of "rights," women writers created a rhetoric of sexual needs. This new needs discourse made them targets for exploitation as emotional workers, but it did not always seem so when they articulated—quite openly and exuberantly—women's psychological and sexual needs. Consider Dorothy Parker's notorious cynicism in this context, and one can imagine what hopes underlined her satiric disappointments. The absence of a linguistic register—a vocabulary of sexual desires that women could use to articulate their new freedoms—compounded the difficulty of discerning women's sexual needs. Women writers thus confronted the psychology of change, creating narratives of how sexuality could alter personal expression, such as mood and style. Whatever the motive, their achievement was to speak truth to conventional or contractual models of sexual power and to create their own intimate exchanges.

Seeking a retreat from standardized culture, many women writers imagined sexuality as the one place where they weren't categorized as consumers or "statistics." In a culture that addressed women primarily as customers or advertising commodities, a woman's self-expressions were supposed to distinguish her from other women. Yet the new consumer goods became associated with "romance" in the expansion of leisure, cultural events, and goods that could be marketed as part of courtship (see Illouz, *Consuming* 77). Self-expression grew more difficult when those choices open to the self were ever more homogeneous, mass-produced, or ready-made. In opposition to this mass commodification, women writers dramatized how women invested in sexuality as a salvation from the increase in choices and the decrease in their "personality" or uniqueness. Greater choices in material and personal things amounted to much less than met the eye, so people exercised their choices in realms where they thought the so-called standardizing forces of culture ostensibly could not encroach (though they certainly would in time)—sexuality and style. Sexuality seemed new and different enough —indeed, an individuated quality—to unleash a liberatory discourse. Until sexual debates in the 1920s began to homogenize representations of women's desires, women writers created newer tropes and narratives to explain themselves as sexual persons. Women never gave up entirely on self-expression, but they began to focus instead on sex power as a means to stylize the self, as we might see clearly in a novel like Gertrude Atherton's *Black Oxen* (1923) (see chapter 3). Both intricate and intimate, sex-power narratives became increasingly reflexive discussions of romance and sexual empowerment.

Even so, that sexual intimacy could be written from a woman's perspective made it an irresistible topic for many American women writers. By describing sexual needs within regulated, rationalized, even bureaucratic liberal contract relations, women writers advanced the cause of sex expression, even as their deployment of sex expression always needed to stay one step ahead of the social regulation that followed its appearance. When women attained the rights to bargain as individual sexual persons (as corollaries to their private and statistical selves), they imagined first creating female sex expression as *different* from the male sex expression that coincided with modern liberal contract relations, such as in Mary Austin's *A Woman of Genius* (1912). That is, attaining even a restricted equality meant that women could assert their sexual needs as different from men's, most typically in novels by Edith Wharton and Willa Cather. To demonstrate that difference, I chart the process by which intimacy and sex expression came to *seem* synonymous.

One last caveat from Giddens about the mistake of reading sexual activity as sexual liberation: "No viewpoint which pits the energy of sexuality against the disciplinary characteristics of the modern social order is likely to be of much value. Nor is one that looks to the more eccentric or non-conventional forms of sexuality as avant-garde. . . . Finally, if sexual pluralism is to be embraced, it has to offer more than just a sort of casual cosmopolitanism, particularly if other issues intrinsic to sexuality, including gender difference and the ethics of the pure relationship, are not addressed" (180). Echoing this warning in *Sex, Literature, and Censorship*, Jonathan Dollimore argues that sexual subversiveness alone—"pleasure, sex and shock" themselves—"are neither necessary nor sufficient conditions for radical political effect" (10). Desire itself is so unruly and unpredictable that demystifying human sexuality does not immediately yield sexual liberation or sexual democracy (17). Dollimore shows just how little truth there is to the notion that "sex is both the inner dynamic of the individual and the means of his or her liberation" (19).[8] While women's sexual ownership might be seen as resistance against male sex power, it is not true that sex power effectively challenges modern sexual liberalism and its insistence on free-market contractual relations. As I will show, for many women writers, these sexual exchanges inevitably result in alienation and exhaustion. Their disagreements about what sexuality and intimacy could actually do for women reveal a literary history whose contours we have not seen clearly enough.

FROM SEX POWER TO SEXUAL STYLE

The emerging discussion about modern women's sex power finds an important impetus in Harriet Beecher Stowe's *Pink and White Tyranny* (1871) and in Angela Fiducia Tilton Heywood's columns for *The Word* in the late 1880s and early 1890s. Stowe was as much against sex power as Heywood was for it: granted, Stowe was the wife of a Presbyterian professor of religion and sacred literature, and Tilton was the wife of Ezra Heywood, who was jailed for obscenity as the editor of the free love paper, *The Word*, which was published from 1872 to 1893. While the 1870s and 1880s saw the contest over the language of sexuality made public, it is also clear that Stowe imagined how women internalized the discussion of sex power, putting into practice the very ideas of sexual power emerging from those public debates (see chapter 4). Angela and Ezra Heywood staked their lives on externalizing the discussion of sex power; they theorized that publicizing words such as "penis," "fuck," and "cock" could balance the sexual equation between men and women. Stowe, by contrast, maintained that women's best hope lay in domestic influence and Christian millennialism.

Perhaps the most important consequence of this conversation about sexuality, Helen Horowitz suggests, was that "a new sensibility that placed sex at the center of life came into being" (5). Thus, sex expression gestured toward a social dimension, within which the call for free and liberal expression became paramount. In fact, the general calls for self-expression took root in the debates about sexual appetite. Contending that sexual contact was healthy for both men and women, some doctors urged women to eschew abstinence and to explore their sexual natures, an exhortation that was not so much an argument for the right to pleasure as an argument for the right to sexual health. Satisfying one's "sexual appetite" was likened to feeding the body and necessary for homeopathic balance.[9] Along with the growth of what Horowitz calls "sexual culture" came a vigorous outpouring of American women's writing that pursued women's own views of sexuality (9). In short, vernacular sexuality—including the sources that historians have amply documented—had its print-culture corollary in women's emerging postsentimental writings, stories, and novels that helped to expand the range of women's expertise from the domestic to the sexual and thus led to making modern sexuality a female topic.

By the 1880s, "sex power" was not so much an impulse or affect as a democratic symbol of women's right to seek sexual freedom and to express social aspirations for equality. Often women's claim to sex power was a symbolic freedom measured not in actions but in the words women could claim to express in a previously unavailable register. Writing for *The Word*, Angela Heywood argued that sex was an offshoot of free self-expression, a proposition that violated the idea of specifically female social and sexual self-control. Her columns promoted female

sexual pleasure but only after women achieved the freedom to use explicit sexual language: she may well have spoken for all women when
she declaimed that "little girls wish to know, young and middle aged
women wish to know, old and experienced wish to know" what she
knew about humans' "Sexed Being" ("Grace and Use of Sex Life" 3). The
1873 Comstock Law tried to suppress such publications as the Heywoods', but a new generation of women writers was already developing
tropes and figures of sexuality that dodged the charge of sexual obscenity
and explicitness. As Heywood contends, "What mother can look in the
face of her welcome child and not religiously respect the rigid, erect,
ready-for-service, persistent male-organ . . . ? Penis is a smooth, magical,
almost feminine word" ("Sex Nomenclature" 2).

Stories of sexual rejuvenation abound in the years following the Heywoods' once-scandalous pronouncements. Consider the vision of change
portrayed in one of Gertrude Atherton's earliest novels, *Hermia Suydam*
(1889), the story of an ugly, drab, ambitious young woman who inherits
her grandfather's money. Before his death, Hermia lives "a double life"
with her sister, abhorring the life of competency that her brother-in-law
offers her sister. Daydreaming of a romantic setting with "all the instincts
of a beautiful woman" and forgetting her "unseductive frame" (24–25),
she begins to write impassioned, unpublishable poetry, which she hawks
from editor to editor, until one eventually commits it to print. Once she
inherits a million dollars, however, she is better able to realize her
passionate fantasies. Soon, Hermia engages a fashionable physician and a
"trained and athletic nurse" to rejuvenate her (48). With diet and exercise and a good colorist, she attains an eccentric beauty (52). Atherton's
novel is obsessed with surfaces—with the appearance of youth and vigor
but also with clothing as self-expression—and treats ugliness as a condition that can be transcended through hard work. Atherton calls it "style,"
thereby anticipating the next generation of women novelists who defined
sex style for American readers.

Rather than continue writing, Hermia makes herself, not her poetry,
into a seductive work of art by conducting a salon and conversing with
the most famous dialect-author of her day. Smitten with this author's
cosmopolitanism, Hermia sleeps with him, an act represented in the

novel by seven asterisks across the page since sex itself was unrepresent-
able for Atherton. After her first night with the novelist, Hermia knows
she has made "a horrible mistake" (110) but goes on with the affair,
violating conventional respectability. Their scandalous liaison causes
Hermia pain after she falls in love with another intellectual who wants
to marry her and take her to Europe. When she confesses her sexual
experience to her new fiancé, he abruptly leaves her, but only for an
hour: just as she is about to drink poison to punish herself for her
indiscretion, he returns and evokes a promise that she will not commit
suicide. At this point, he dies of a heart condition and the novel ends.

This is a bad novel, certainly not up to the level of Atherton's best-selling fictions (see chapter 3) that are waiting to be recovered.[10] Linked at
the time with the "erotic" or "sensational" school of women writers—including Laura Jean Libbey and Laura Daintrey—Atherton was skewered
for her treatment of female passion.[11] Nevertheless, even in this early
work, Atherton contributes a key perspective in the conversation among
American women novelists about sexual freedom. That Hermia's fiancé
—Grettan Quintard—dies at the end does not negate Hermia's newfound
sexual expression, fostered in part by her New Woman friend, Helen
Simms—a "New York girl" who "had no beauty, but . . . had the clean,
clear, smooth, red-and-ivory complexion" and perfect teeth (55). What
distinguishes Helen from Hermia is the latter's intellectual commitment.
Helen advocates these sexual adventures and helps Hermia procure her
first lover, to whom she pretends a deeper attachment than she feels. One
mistake is forgivable; two (or more), sensationalistic.

Instead of killing off the heroine, Atherton kills off her fiancé, who
has a heart attack on the last page. Quintard's acceptance of her sexual
experience leads to his immediate death as soon as he knocks the poison
cup from her lips. His history is more dangerous than Hermia's, for he
has been involved with a married woman who committed suicide after
her husband discovered their affair. "Everybody cut Mrs. Maitland, and
she felt so horrible that she killed herself. Quintard was fearfully upset.
He went abroad at once and staid five years" (125). In courting Hermia,
he admits to wanting a woman "indifferent to public opinion" (132),
someone "companionable" rather than fashionable. Atherton kills him

off for professing his unconventionality; the heroine lives for acting on hers. In enjoining her "to let [her] past go" (204), Quintard means to erase centuries of traditional sexual morality, and for that acceptance he must be killed off. Here *Hermia Suydam* introduces the equation of sexuality with youth and beauty (and wealth) and distances sexuality from ugliness. Sexuality begins the move toward standardization: bodies must be exercised and styled, hair bleached so that sexual passion can move from fantasy to reality. Atherton again and again calls this facing "the actualities" of life (132), but the "face" that meets these actualities must be standardly pretty. Otherwise, sex is out of the picture.

Beyond its challenge to sexual morality, Atherton's novel is significant because it inaugurates the equating of sexuality with a new somatic standard of beauty. Atherton is less concerned with the fate of expressive individualism or with the idea of sexuality as democratization than with rejuvenation and sexual power, as we see in her phenomenal best seller of 1923, *Black Oxen*. While Stockham's *Karezza* might have been the salvation of women overwhelmed by sequential childbirths, Atherton celebrates a power of rejuvenation that makes clear her conviction that sexuality was not or should not be available only to young, rich, and beautiful women. Such stories of rejuvenation insist on the potential for a greater democratization of sex, in which women would be free, sexual citizens.

To make this claim stick, women writers had to show that sexual desire was a self-conscious act of will not to be dismissed or diminished as impulsive or unconscious. But women who acted on sexual desire often were accused of being sexual adventurers or opportunists. Creating hero ines who were neither gold diggers nor free lovers but true lovers, women writers invented a middle ground between the unconscious and the conscious, a discourse of choice that gave their imagination of sexual desire cultural legitimacy (see Haag, *Consent* 137). Negotiating the idea of sexual choice and freedom, the authors I study developed a language of sexual expression that was not completely dependent either on the will or on impulse. Women writers often defined sex by style (what women wore, how they talked, whom they met) and sexual subjectivity (including the emotional work they did to reconcile sexuality with character and personality). In response to the various discourses, these sexual metaphors were condensed—made compact, economic, even evocative—distant as they were from explicitness or literalness. (Not even in Mary McCarthy's raw *The Company She Keeps* [1942] is there a direct rendering of sex, only the marks upon the body that signify intercourse.)

Repeatedly, these tropes signaled abrupt shifts in how women envisioned sexuality. Some American women writers still maintained that sexuality was repressive; others saw sexuality as liberating; many wrote about sexuality's threat to women's economic and psychological security. The early twentieth-century claims of sexual liberation, like those of female sentimentality and sympathy in the nineteenth century, enabled American women writers to explore the complications and ramifications of their new circumstances, launching their own scenarios about what women actually did or didn't *do* or count as sexual and *how* they came to rationalize or justify their desires. Thus, I examine their means of persuading readers that sexuality might be positive or freeing, destructive or degenerate, or oppositional and corrupt.

THE RHETORIC OF SEX EXPRESSION

Although American culture was open to greater frankness in the 1890s about sex than ever before and the 1920s have been read as the era of proliferating sexual freedoms,[12] many women writers were suspicious about what this freedom really meant: was sexuality a liberating force or psychologically debilitating and even—as Charlotte Perkins Gilman had it—economically disempowering? In *Women and Economics* (1898), Gilman rejected outright sex power—the newly emancipated sexual norms of modern America. On the contrary, Wharton compared France's "sex-conventions" to those in America, which is "supposedly the country of the greatest sex-freedom" (*French Ways* 114). Wharton specifically challenged the rhetorical question many Americans proposed about social equality (not sexual congress): "But where is there so much freedom of intercourse between men and women as in America?"[13] She condemned the culture that celebrated women's newly emancipated sexuality without specifying what sex power could do for them.

What might seem a literal frankness about sex still had to be configured rhetorically, most often in metaphorical terms. As Nina Miller argues, "Popular sexology was peppered with calls for 'frankness' and scientific candor yet so often proceeded from the contrary discursive register of metaphor and even euphemism" (49). These metaphors and euphemisms (or even the dysphemisms that the Heywoods favored) were critical in American women writers' development of sexual literary style. In the end, these sexualities were part of the endlessly developing rhetoric about "sexual personae" and sexual possibilities, the "official and unofficial sexualities" of the American sexual citizen (Lindemann 11). These women writers challenged scientific theories of sexuality through literary forms and, in doing so, invented new ways of seeing intimacy and sex expression that rejected so-called scientific accuracy in favor of their sexual fantasies and tropes. American women writers gave a rhetorical spin to what social scientists described as women's unconscious response to sexual stimuli. Instead of seeing women's desire as coerced or involuntary, they invented a way of representing women's new interiority as thoroughly sexualized, invested as it was in their libidinal desires.

The sexualization of American culture—from its hope for gender democracy to the exhaustion of its potential for liberation—leads me to a conclusion about the sexual frankness of the subsequent generation of writers. The search for a new counterintimacy might have started in the 1930s, when metaphors for erotic experience seemed to disappear from American women's writing and researchers and reformers turned to the more problematic notions of sexual visibility and performance (Berlant and Warner 561).[14] Once sex expression was identified as women's work in a relationship, once it replaced self-expression as women's exclusive equitable form of public being, then sex became women's obligation rather than their right. Predicated on excluding homosexuality, interracial sex, and anything but sex between the young and the beautiful, sex expression was hardly a liberation, as it once had seemed.

CHAPTER TWO

Blood, Sex,

AND THE UGLY GIRL

Recovering the history of sex expression means exploring the evolving relation between sentiment and sexology, a once dynamic connection between conscious sympathy and overt sexuality inherited from sentimental culture. As early as the 1880s, sexology—the professional regulation of what was to be considered "normal" or healthy sex instincts—ostensibly reversed the stifling effects of sentimental culture, a sentimentality still so much with us, especially in our most romantic notions of the practices of physical intimacy. Even the modern obsessive linking of sex with youth and beauty—largely a vestige of early twentieth-century eugenic thinking—grows out of a cultural transition from sentiment to sex. By the end of the century, American literature would revivify sexuality by cleaning it up and replacing sentimental language with the more explicit lexicon of intimate contacts.

Here, this project of revivification—the revitalizing of sexuality out of the rigors of sentimentalism—leads me to explore how some important American women writers reconceived their relations to sex expression, along with how sex expression and its popularity changed the course of American women as writers and as sex experts. Such questions prompted the fiction of female Christian reformers in the 1860s and 1870s. Elizabeth Stoddard, Elizabeth Stuart Phelps, and Rebecca Harding Davis challenged the ugliness or sordidness associated with sexuality in order to distance it especially from its previous association with inheritance through blood. This inheritance denied volition, consigning sexuality to being a force outside oneself rather than a choice.

Sexuality had to become a choice, not a disposition or inheritance. Pleasure was, thus, made viable for middle-class women. Rescuing intimacy from its associations with vulgarity, Nina Miller argues, was the task of modern women writers belonging to the literary avant-garde. These writers, such as Dorothy Parker and Genevieve Taggard, sought to replace the notion of Bohemia as immigrant immoderation with the notion of bohemian as a personal style. But unlike Miller, I see this process occurring much earlier. The cultural work of the women writers I discuss here, which began with the charge to sublimate or reform sexuality, evolved into the injunction to make sexuality safe for the masses and for the home by arguing for liberation through sexuality.

This chapter describes such cultural nuances of what later came to be called sex expression and provides a way of understanding literary change in general. Sex expression was the means through which women writers rejected the literary forms of realism and naturalism and developed instead a gendered "popular modernism" and the middlebrow novel.[1] This shift from sentimentality to unmediated pleasure expressed a symbolic change in the cultural imaginary. These sex-expression narratives staged an increasingly public debate in a culture ever more insistent on standardization and codification, especially of women's social conduct.

Writers deployed the discourse of sex expression for political leverage in a culture stubbornly ambivalent about women's right to speak about sexuality. Under this aegis, many writers treated the crucial issues of birth control, race preservation (one of Charlotte Perkins Gilman's favorite topics), and eugenics. Yet women writers disagreed on the benefits and disadvantages of the newly proliferating discourses about sexuality. Even before William Dean Howells challenged the oversentimentalization of romance and sexuality, these women writers had begun the transformation of sentimental culture.

Consider the Howellsian formula of the "economy of pain," made famous in his 1885 novel, *The Rise of Silas Lapham*; this thesis provided a means through which other writers could consider an economy of pleasure *and* an erotics of pain. Howells's rejection of sentimentalism in that novel leads, in realists and naturalists, to the sexualizing of the pain he vetoes. For instance, Walter Michaels teaches that Frank Norris's *McTeague* (1899) represents sexual desire as a masochistic contract between lovers. Erotic pleasure is explicitly related to tyranny and to pain (51), so much so that Trina's hoarding of money and her submission to McTeague excite her. "The simultaneous desires to own and be owned," Michaels writes, "constitute the emotional paradox Norris sets himself to elaborate in *McTeague*" (54). This erotic economy—"between owning and being owned"—makes sense to Michaels given "the erotic potential of the self in a market economy" (55), an economy dependent upon the individual subject's ability to bargain for the fulfillment of his or her pleasure (even when that pleasure is masochistic).[2]

Also focused on pain, Theodore Dreiser mocks the idea of such an erotic economy between men and women in *Sister Carrie* (1900). No self-consciousness about masochism exists for Dreiser's characters, as it may for Norris's. According to Dreiser, men like Drouet, Carrie's first lover, "have no conception of the necessity of a well-organized society wherein all shall accept a certain quota of responsibility and all realize a reasonable amount of happiness. . . . When, after error, pain falls as a lash, they do not comprehend that their suffering is due to misbehavior" (132). Dreiser's erotic economy is based on the fulfillment of desire, where even shoes have expression and speak to potential buyers (98). His characters don't understand the erotic exchanges into which they enter. Their failure results from a refusal to see pain as caused by error; the "lash" is not part of any sexual or masochistic contract but merely another bewildering sentiment. No economy of pain here; rather, the

43

"lash" comes as a surprise to the sufferer, who is generally mystified about sexuality.

This mystification is no less true in Dreiser's sympathetic portrayal of the eponymous heroine of *Jennie Gerhardt* (1911), in which Jennie and her lover, Lester Kane, "drift" into the "sex relationship" and just as mysteriously drift out of it (187). As Dreiser puts it, "The sex relationship, which we study so passionately in the hope of finding heaven knows what key to the mystery of existence, holds no more difficult or trying situation than this—of mutual compatibility broken or disrupted by untoward conditions which, in themselves, have so little to do with the real force and beauty of the relationship itself" (364). Dreiser thus rejects the romance of companionate sexuality and domesticity for the pressures of social classifications. Jennie is just not of Lester's class, and thus, they cannot sustain their sex relationship. Dreiser everywhere insists on a kind of sexual balance in his own economy of pain and pleasure.

While Howells, Norris, and Dreiser were arguing in terms of economy and exchange or contract and consent, Stoddard and Phelps took a different tack and reimagined human relations in antieconomic, antisentimental terms. They bridged the gap between sentimentality and sexuality by creating new tropes—and a new lexicon in general—in order to move from an emotional "economy of pain" to a physical erotics of pain and pleasure. The rejection of sentimentality left a gap that sex expression could fill. With greater and greater candor, a language of sexuality replaced the once vibrant emotional economy that dominated American culture, in terms as varied as the public outcry against slavery and the private heartbreak of post–Civil War mourning. Whereas women writers had previously expressed economic realities and social relations of power in sentimental terms as influence and benevolence, they recast these as intimate feelings of individual fantasies of pleasure and intimacy—decidedly postsentimental.

Many American women writers certainly expressed the outcomes of sexuality before 1860; we need only remember the myriad seduction plots of the early nineteenth century. The crucial difference I find is that postbellum novels by women combined seduction plots and sentimental romances with stories of sexual intimacy, unlike those of John W. De-Forest or even Henry James. Benevolence gives way to sexualization; emotionalism, to physicality and passion. In these books, the middle classes could embrace sex expression as the defining impulse of human personality. Women writers no longer depended solely on sentimental language—of experience or of possessions—but began to express themselves in terms related to passion and physical pleasure.

With the rise of consumer culture, more and more Americans were assumed to be filled with passions, for things as well as for others. But sexuality as object relations took a long while to take hold in the popular imagination; while it did so, the compulsory pairing-off of couples held sway. As Eric Haralson writes about Henry James's major phase, James was reacting against the "compulsory sexuality as such, whether hetero-, homo-, or otherwise," demanded at the turn of the century ("Excellent Adventure" 178). The growing sexualization of the culture meant that sexual self-definition, along with sexual style, became more prominent in American literature. Whereas once the sentimental codes of tears, blushes, and emotional displays proliferated in the nineteenth century, the early twentieth century was saturated with a new sexual style of "fly" and fast girls rather than fallen women, like Gertrude Atherton's new heroines.

So powerful had the idea of sexual intimacy become by the turn of the century that it yielded a new form of power in relationships—sex power, by which women began to measure how much security they could count on in heterosexual relations. One perdurable modern trope—"the crash"—was a metaphor fraught with allusions from popular culture, from the new industrialization and the new technology of travel, even in images of the *Titanic* in Edith Wharton's *The Reef* (1912).[3] This "modernist poetics of disaster," as Nancy Bentley calls it, fuels many American women writers' postsentimental and protomodern plots, whether in postbellum novels or in early modern texts ("Wharton, Travel, and Modernity" 152). The "crash" was a way to create the power of a new relation between humans.

With amazing frequency, women writers imagined sexual desire as ending in crashes, accidents, or other disasters, which left scars on their faces and bodies or on their souls. For instance, Willa Cather's 1905 story "Paul's Case," which has been read as an exploration of homosexuality, concerns a gay aesthete who commits suicide by throwing himself in front of a speeding train at the end of the story. After a week of living out his fantasy in New York City (furnished with stolen funds from the office where he worked), the hero cannot go back to his father and school in Pittsburgh and chooses to end his life dramatically. "He stood watching the approaching locomotive, his teeth chattering, his lips drawn away from them in a frightened smile; once or twice he glanced nervously sidewise, as though he were being watched. When the right moment came, he jumped" (131). Cather describes his suicide as the "crushing" of his imagination while his "disturbing visions" fade into black. According to the story's enigmatic last line, Paul "drop[s] back into the immense design of things." By this design, does Cather refer to the market economy that creates desire (as Norris and Dreiser might do) or the "design" of sexuality that her work disrupts? Paul's "case" moves beyond the cultural possibilities of expression, and his suicide suggests how far his "disturbing visions" of life advanced beyond the sex expressions available to him.[4] Cather's Paul chooses to have both the erotics and the pain but experiences them separately.

These metaphors of the crash—before and after Cather's "Paul's Case" —ushered in a series of fictions about sexual accidents and disasters. In all of these metaphorical crashes, sexuality produces accidents—unexpected "babies," of course, but also ruined lives. "Paul's Case" compels us to look backward for the emerging languages of sexuality. In that past, Stoddard and Phelps, despite their ambivalence, challenge the idea that passion was an involuntary reaction, an inheritance of vice, or the inevitable showing of blood, predicting instead a future of voluntary sexuality.[5]

THE MORGESONS AND SEXUAL SCARS

I argue that Elizabeth Stoddard advances an idea of female sexuality as a conscious choice rather than an inherited condition or something "in the blood." Indeed, the inheritance of vice and of passion is one of Stoddard's central concerns, yet *The Morgesons* (1862) challenges the culture's belief in sexual inheritance, thereby distancing Stoddard from her culture's sexual Lamarckianism. Lamarckians believed that human traits are inherited and thus essentialized. By showing signs of passion as chosen, or at worst accidental, Stoddard opposes conventional logic about innate desire. Rather than inheriting passion, the heroine of Stoddard's *The Morgesons* discovers how deeply personal choice lies at the heart of female sexuality.

Stoddard's novel is one of the first to eschew sentimentalizing sexuality and to deal explicitly with the heroine's sex experience. Stoddard's own logic leads her to ask, What counts as sexual consciousness? Is it the desire itself, the drive that is first imagined and then enacted? Is sexuality a recognition of sexual pleasure and anticipation or the first contact between bodies? This is key for the developing idea of sex expression in the 1860s and 1870s, insofar as women writers were beginning to distinguish between unconscious and conscious sexual desires. Cassandra Morgeson, the delinquent daughter, is Stoddard's eccentric heroine, whose passion is figured metaphorically as a violent, physical encounter —a crash, a wreck—and is a trope that retains its symbolic power as a mode of sex expression for writers who follow in Stoddard's tradition, especially Wharton and Cather. Conventionally called a bildungsroman, the novel traces Cassandra's passions through two love affairs. The first is an unconsummated one with her married Cousin Charles and the second is with Desmond Somers, whom she eventually weds but only after Desmond, in self-exile, learns to control his own passions, including his drunkenness and temper. His brother, Ben Somers, once expelled from Harvard for fighting, marries Cassandra's sister, Veronica, but dies soon after the wedding from the long-term effects of his dissipation, so carried away by his passions that he has no self-control. Both men are seemingly cursed by the family inheritance of alcoholism.[6]

As the Somers sons must face their inheritance, so must the Morgeson daughters: Cassandra's legacy begins with gossip about her mother. In an odd sort of education in repression, she is sent to live with her grandfather so that she can gain an appreciation for her mother's upbringing. While there, she hears a rumor from one of her classmates about her mother. At school, Cassandra's peers torment her; says one accuser:

47

" 'Who are *you* that you should be angry? We have heard about your mother, when she was in love, poor thing' " (40). Cassandra responds by hitting her tormenter. In a novel that is predicated on blood inheritance (8), Stoddard ominously sets up the family secret of sexuality as an influence on Cassandra's future. Cassandra's eccentricity contrasts with her sister's "peculiar constitution" (238), which results in anorexia, neurosis, and depression. By the end of the novel, Veronica eats only milk and toast, taking to bed for weeks at a time. Her year-old baby testifies to the father's inheritance of vice: "It smiles continually, but never cries, never moves, except when it is moved" (252). The baby is "thin and melancholy. . . . A wall of darkness lies before her, which she will not penetrate" (252). Thus, the family legacy is visited upon the children as both a social and a sexual inheritance.

Although her sister Veronica is invested in an economy of pain and suffering as a way of knowing and identifying with the world, Cassandra chooses another route: desire. She recognizes, as Veronica does, that her grandfather had squelched the "wants" and "dreams" in her mother and aunt (64); Cassandra is opposed to anyone who would repress her passions. Instead, she opts for the destiny of her mother, who had ridden "the white colt bare-back round the big meadow, with her hair flying" (49). In this way, Mrs. Morgeson's suppressed sexuality gives rise to the daughter's rebellion against conventional sexual mores. (Wharton later uses horseback riding as a signal of women's sexuality in her 1907 *The Fruit of the Tree*.) This conventional image of sexuality—riding bareback—prefigures the accident in the carriage that Cassandra will experience with her first love.

After a year in her grandfather's house, Cassandra returns home more defiant than ever: "My acquaintances were always kind enough to let me know that I was generally thought proud, exacting, ill-natured, and apt to expect the best for myself. But one thing I know of myself then—that I concealed nothing; the desires and emotions which are usually kept as a private fund, I displayed and exhausted. My audacity shocked those who possessed this fund" (58–59). No conventional interiority or private self here: as the antithesis of the sentimental daughter, Cassandra is the perfect test case for Stoddard's version of sex expression. What her mother was forced to keep repressed, her daughter displays as bouts of passion, intent as Cassandra is on shocking her interlocutors with her confessions and audacity.

Such shocking displays are often literal in *The Morgesons*, such as the tattoo by which one character expresses her love. This mark on the body figures a voluntary expression of passion, a mark consciously chosen to represent an expression denied women in speech. While visiting her cousins Charles and Alice Morgeson, Cassandra begins her only friendship with a classmate, Helen. In a rare moment of confidentiality between them, Helen reveals a tattoo on her arm with the initials of her fiancé, "L.N." The tattoo startles Cassandra since it marks Helen's physical commitment to her fiancé. Cassandra is used to more sentimental codes of affection, such as the flowers Charles gives her from his greenhouse or the diamond ring he presents to her.[7] In contrast to these conventional signs of sentiment, the tattoo is a consciously chosen and indelible sign of sex expression, a quite deliberately unconventional mark.

Why must passion mark women physically? The tattoo literalizes the belief that sex or passion could be read on the body and made permanent. While cultural beliefs held that women's passion was always written on their bodies, Stoddard leaves this physical marking open to choice; it is not some internal impulse rising to the surface. Passion was once considered in the blood; perhaps, as Stoddard suggests, it can instead be found as marks on the body—less an inheritance than a remembrance, a scar based on experience. Earlier in the novel, Cassandra calls herself a creature of sensation, not sentiment. And Stoddard leaves us to wonder where sex expression emerges—whether in sensations or in affect. Not having had an education in sentimentality from her mother, Cassandra worries about the effects of a "vicious sentimentality" when she falls in love with her married cousin. She especially fears that sentimentality is vicious when she suffers from self-delusions about her love for her cousin. Does sexuality come from the impression of things upon the mind or from the affectual, even vicious, attachments one fantasizes?

Consider Cassandra Morgeson's dreams about her cousin: when he is away on business, she lapses into a dreamworld so real that she imagines he will leave tangible tokens of his affection in the morning when she awakes. Once he reappears in the household, her dreams cease, and instead, she imagines (correctly) that he has visited her bedside in the middle of the night.

> There was a change everywhere. The greatest change of all was in Charles. From the night of the sleigh-ride his manner toward me was totally altered. As far as I could discern, the change was a confirmed one. The days grew monotonous, but my mind avenged itself by night in dreams, which renewed our old relation in all its mysterious vitality. So strong were their impressions that each morning I expected to receive some token from him which would prove that they were not lies. As my expectation grew cold and faint, the sense of a double hallucination tormented me—the past and the present. (111)

While Charles is gone, Cassandra and Charles's "mysterious vitality" is carried on in Cassandra's dreams. When he returns, his face carries an "expression of unspeakable passion, pride, and anguish" (115). One night Cassandra imagines that someone is in her room, and the next morning she finds a dusty footprint on a handkerchief she had left on the floor. Which is her authentic sexuality—the dreams or his uninvited visits? (As I will show in chapter 3, Rebecca Harding Davis's "Anne" also suggests that erotic fantasies are more vivid than women's domestic reality.) In neither situation—the unconscious dreams or the strange visits of Charles at night—does she exercise sexual choice, but that's the point: middle-class women were not supposed to do so. Yet her confusion about the dreams and the actual world is telling since she reacts to her dreams and fantasies by expecting real and tangible tokens. Sexual dreams have real results. When Cassandra sees a tattoo on her friend's arm, she imagines that there might be sex expressions beyond sentimental materialism like flowers and rings. She lives through the unconscious impulses that surprise her and the dream-fantasies that fill her nights.

In her waking world, Cassandra's emotions change her appearance as well as her expressions. After Cassandra spends several months with her cousin Charles and his wife Alice, her father uncannily remarks on her appearance. "I examined my face as soon as he closed the door. There *was* a change. Not the change from health to disease, but an expression lurking there—a reflection of some unmoved, secret power" (101). The secret is her love for her cousin, and her mistake is to assume that it is a private, uninterpretable feeling rather than a public sign of passion, involuntarily disclosed. Cassandra's sex expression marks her intelligibly, just as Helen's tattoo does her.

Eventually she, too, wears what she calls her own "tattoo": scars from the accident that killed Charles when they were out riding together. "I had scarcely taken my arm inside the chaise when Aspen [the horse] stopped, turned his head, and looked at us with glazed eyes; flakes of foam flew from his mouth over his mane. The flesh on his back contracted and quivered. I thought he was frightened by the chaise-top, and looked at Charles in terror" (121). Charles dies saving Cassandra, but her wound attests to the danger of her own passions. Everyone knows how she got the scars and that her cousin's barely repressed love for her cost him his life in saving her. Passion cuts deep, leaves scars, and can kill.

After the accident, Cassandra confesses to Alice, the widow of her lover: "'You may, or you may not forgive me, but I was strangely bound to him. And I must tell you, that I hunger now for the kiss he never gave me'" (123). This confession of being "strangely bound" to the dead Charles suggests how complex female sexual desire is for Cassandra. Whatever sex expression Cassandra might have had with Charles is now channeled into her confession of desire to his wife. The greatest transgression in women's writing was once the sexual confession, as we see in *The Morgesons* or in fictions such as Nathaniel Hawthorne's *The Scarlet Letter* (1852), which had one of the greatest sexual confessions of all. For Cassandra, the transgression is *not* having consummated the affair, *not* having kissed; hers is a confession of thwarted desire.

Stoddard's rendering of sexuality as a physical mark directly contrasts with the idea of the secret sexual self, a condition Joseph Boone finds half a century later, when he describes the "early-twentieth-century belief, in the fields of both psychology and sexology, in 'interiority' as the site of the true self, in sexuality as the key to identity" (103). In other words, Stoddard leads her reader to see sexuality less as an interior or inherited state than as a series of experiences or events, ones that may indeed leave physical marks. The author rejects the notion that sexuality is an internal drive or impulse, let loose like a flood with unconscious motivations. Instead of being involuntary, sex expression is a choice—something one does rather than something one is or one inherits.

At the end of the novel, Desmond Somers chooses Cassandra as his bride precisely because her passion marks her. Her involuntary disclosures—first a facial expression, then scars—reveal her sexual passion, but only she can choose to act on it. The scars do not disfigure her but actually attract male attention because of their signification. When one of Cassandra's admirers asks how she got her facial scars, Cassandra replies, " 'In battle' " (173). The metaphor sticks. Later, Desmond comments on his interpretation of her face: " 'So, women like you, pure, with no vice of blood, sometimes struggle, suffer, and are tempted.' " Cassandra replies: " 'Even drawn battles bring their scars' " (183–84). These are marks of sexual temptation and resistance, an internal battle against sexual temptation. He announces in a letter: " 'I am yours, as I have been, since the night I asked you "How came those scars?" Did you guess that I read your story?' " (227). It doesn't matter that she hasn't actually done anything; she is marked—accidentally but no less remarkably—by the temptation.

I have been charting Stoddard's deviation from the cultural belief that women's sexual response was internal—an effect of heredity—and that women were more sentimental than sexual. Perhaps more important is Stoddard's insistence—through her heroine—that women were supremely aware of these sexual battles. The novel signals a shift from the idea of sexuality as an unconscious depth to the idea of sexuality as a voluntary and chosen act, that is, a will to exercise sexual choice. At one point, Ben Somers stares at her scars: "His eyes, darting sharp rays, pierced me through; they rested on the thread-like scars which marked my cheek, and which were more visible from the effect of cold." In response to his gaze, Cassandra remarks, " 'Tatooed still' "—a highly self-conscious invocation of her friend Helen's deliberate marking (156).

Thus, for Stoddard, sex expression is neither a blood inheritance nor a family curse but a deliberate act of desire and will. The novel's middle class assumes Cassandra Morgeson's sexuality to be private, focused on the interior rather than on the surface. Contemporaneous accounts posited sexuality as below the surface rather than on the body itself (see Boone 118). Stoddard inverts the surface-depth model at play in early accounts of sexuality. The author shows that sexuality is *on* the body, not *in* the body waiting to surface. People read the heroine's scars and expressions for signs of a public display of her individual will.

Crucial here is the distinction between self-expression and sex expression: women and men were encouraged to develop self-culture, based on individual talent and skill, but were not encouraged to develop sex expression, based on intersubjective modes. Desmond's mother, Bellevue Pickersgill Somers, claims her son has "broken" other women like "toys" (193). She sees it as part of her lineage. In confessing his past loves to Cassandra, Desmond claims that " 'if there was ruin, it was mutual' " (199). His brother Ben also confronts her about the terrible future with Desmond: " 'Have you so much passion, that you cannot discern the future you offer yourself?' " (200). Desmond's entire family so doubts his ability to love because of his heredity that they discount Cassandra's sex expression. The usually perspicacious Cassandra cannot "discern" her future with Desmond because "passion" stands in the way. Self-expression allows careful, deliberate self-disclosure, but sex expression promotes mutual revelation. Thus, Stoddard sets self-expression in opposition to sex expression, even as she works to reconcile the pleasures of both. But first, Desmond must go away for years in order to prove to both himself and Cassandra that he can overcome the Bellevue Pickersgill Somers curse of blood. As his brother describes him, " 'Desmond is a violent, tyrannical, sensual man; his perceptions are his pulses' " (226). Before he will marry, he leaves for two years to overcome his "pulses" and impulses—"to break [his] cursed habit of drunkenness" (250). Ben stays behind and does "*something worse*"—drinks himself to death (248; Stoddard's emphasis). What a culture imagines as "worse" is central to discussions of the early history of sex expression: Is sexual pleasure "worse" than alcoholism in its hierarchy of values? Or are there even worse expressions to imagine, not yet articulated? Alcoholism might be carried in the blood, but Stoddard shows that passion is not.

The novel ends strangely, just as it began. Now a widower, Cassandra's father marries Alice Morgeson, the widow of his cousin Charles Morgeson: "When father was married again, the Morgeson family denounced him for it" (248). After this marriage, Cassandra refuses to see her father anymore, given her love for Charles and her distrust of Alice. Yet it is also the strangeness of middle-aged women in this novel that troubles Stoddard. Middle-aged women reproduce at an unprecedented rate in postbellum American fiction. Ben and Desmond's mother gives birth to her last child—a boy—after she has turned forty (Julia Stern sees her as nearly fifty! [118]), since she is tying up the family inheritance until the last child turns twenty-one (169); Cassandra's mother gives birth to her brother Arthur at age thirty-nine or forty.[8] And Alice Morgeson, who had previously devoted herself to her children instead of her husband, hurriedly marries Cassandra's father, perhaps to reproduce with him as well. In the process, she manages her husband's business and reenters the social world. Middle age seems to bring out women's hidden powers. As Julia Stern has remarked about Mrs. Somers, "In her late forties, when the major health issue worrying most nineteenth-century women is impending death, not childbed fever, Bellevue Pickersgill Somers has produced a baby boy, whose unanticipated arrival impedes the distribution of Pickersgill capital held in trust until the youngest Somers male reaches twenty-one years of age. Is it fancifully Freudian to remark in this case that a mother's unnatural sexuality has paralyzed her sons?" (119). Perhaps, but it is also possible to remark in light of the whole novel that women's sexuality does not paralyze them but gives their desires free rein.

SEX AND SENTIMENT

Was working girls' sexuality different from middle-class daughters'? Elizabeth Stuart Phelps indicates that all sexuality was public and thereby subject to contractual, commercial relations. The working girl then either could be seduced or could sell her (sexual) labor. According to Pamela Haag, "Significantly for the future of women's sexual rights, the single woman's sexual and economic appetites were assumed to be inextricable, such that economic need or gain exteriorized and 'proved' women's *sexual* consent" (*Consent* 45; Haag's emphasis). In other words, when women needed or worked for money, the sheer physical fact of their existence in the world of business presupposed a sexual contract. Middle-class women might have private sexuality only insofar as they manifested no economic needs. Just as Stoddard suggests that the middle-class woman might have a sexual interiority, Phelps shows what the middle-class daughter has to learn from her working-class sexual sister—that sex is contractual, public, and dangerous, if also potentially liberating, however temporarily.[9]

The images of the sexually vulnerable heroine and the crash converge in Phelps's 1871 novel, *The Silent Partner*. Near the end of the novel, the sexually promiscuous Catty Garth falls to her death when a bridge collapses after lumber floating on the river crashes into it. A vulnerable wageworker, Catty indulges in sexual encounters that seem related to her disabilities, and her ultimate fall seems a metaphoric judgment upon her sexual delinquency. Catty's crash into the river is neither beautiful nor purposeful, but it is dramatic. While Catty's death may reinforce her status as the title's ironic "silent" partner, showing her centrality to Phelps's novel, it may also repudiate the Christian sympathy that the novel otherwise elicits (190). As her sister, Sip, asks, What sort of benevolent God would make something as ugly as Catty? Leaving her sister embarrassed by her own condescending pity and relief, Catty's death leads us to ask, What is it about Catty's ugliness and sexuality that seemingly prevent her sister's grief? And, concomitantly, how could a wayward, even repulsive understanding of sexuality be recuperated for mass culture?

In such a way, Phelps's career connects the sentimental with the antisentimental. Catty's illicit encounters capture a liminal moment in the last third of the nineteenth century when sexuality, not yet in the domain of mass culture, was on the brink of sentimentalization. Sentiment represented the culture's emphasis on affections and relations, what Joanne Dobson calls the "primacy of human connection" (273). In doing so, it also deliberately obscured physical intimacy since it could not yet contain or account for sexuality. A body such as Catty's, and the effects of sentimental culture on its instincts and desires, renders sentimentalization moot, its strategy of invoking readerly sympathy irrelevant (at least according to her sister's reaction). Yet even as sentimental language made the affections more transparent, it made sexual relations more opaque; sexuality was figured as a lack of sentiment, an unfortunate absence of right feeling.

Lacking sentiment, Catty's case seemingly invites transgression through the vicarious experience of her intimacies. Thus, she signals the other, often repressed half of the sentimental divide. That repression might best be made explicit by Jack London in *Martin Eden* (1908), when he describes English seaport prostitutes: "The women he had known . . . a grotesque and terrible nightmare brood" of "frowsy, shuffling creatures . . . , gin-bloated hags of the stews, and all the vast hell's following of harpies, vile-mouthed and filthy, that under the guise of monstrous female form prey upon sailors, the scrapings of the ports, the scum and slime of the human pit" (4–5). Coming at the moment when late nineteenth-century sexual reform movements had wavered and early twentieth-century social control had not yet reached its ascendancy, London's remarks about British women also crystallize American anxieties about female degeneracy.[10] His descriptions of "ugly women" reflect the shift over forty years that made beauty a prerequisite for sex, even as ugliness came to be seen as a vestige of a dysgenic atavism.

Phelps's novel shows how sex was displaced onto unsentimental— that is, ugly—bodies and how sexuality was later dissociated from ugliness, a change necessary in order to recuperate sexuality as a choice connected to consumer culture. I contend that this spiraling process of sentimentalization culminates in the sexualization of American culture, by which I mean that sexuality becomes an ideological and psychological basis of cultural authority. More important, sentimentalism rationalized this newly emerging sexual order in modern American culture, which determined who could have sex, with whom, at what age, and how.[11]

"IN THE BLOOD": THE UGLY GIRL

In *The Silent Partner*, Phelps gives a bourgeois account of an antibourgeois activity—sexual pleasure divorced from its procreative ends. While women's beauty culture has been analyzed as part of the rise of

MORE REPELLENT THAN INVITING.

"More Repellent than Inviting": *"Strongly sexed men do not seek the society of plain women like Miss Otta, whose likeness we subjoin." From Orson S. Fowler's* Creative and Sexual Science, or Manhood, Womanhood, and Their Mutual Inter-Relations *(ca. 1875).*

Love Small.

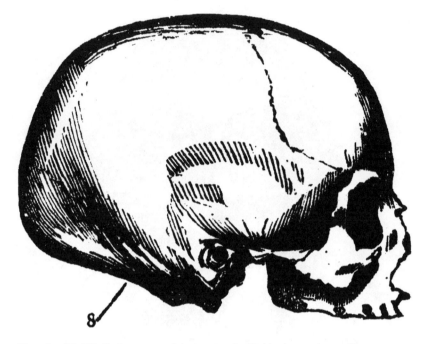

"Love Small": "Skull of a woman of sixty years who died in the poorhouse. Upon examination, her skull shows the organ of Love to be naturally very small. It is almost imperceptible." From Orson S. Fowler's Creative and Sexual Science, or Manhood, Womanhood, and Their Mutual Inter-Relations (ca. 1875).

capitalism, ugliness gets much less attention. The ugly girl came to embody sexual pleasure, and subsequent women writers liberated sex from this symbolic disfigurement and racial categorizing.[12] This sex expression was first recognized as a subject of fiction when Social Gospelers like Phelps and Davis addressed its presence in the working classes. From the 1860s through the 1880s, the Christian socialists preached the Social Gospel, promoting moral reform of the poor and the spread of Protestantism, especially among immigrants who practiced other religions or none at all. While the rising commercial culture was obsessed with advertising and selling beauty culture to middle-class women as an *alternative* to sex expression, the Social Gospelers imagined that they had discovered in working-class women perhaps the very source of cultural degeneration. Those who engaged in sex without procreation are depicted, curiously enough, as ugly girls. The cultural logic that links ugliness and sexuality goes like this: if sexuality originates in ugliness, then patriarchal control can flourish when it is exerted over beauty. The ugly, then, are seen as unmanageable sexual objects; indeed, mating among the ugly produces only deformed hybrids. The result is that by the end of the nineteenth century beauty is a necessity of pleasurable sex, thus negating what was once the ugly girl's sexual pleasure. Even by 1875, the phrenologist Orson S. Fowler would publish his theory of creative sexual science, explaining why "beautiful women enkindle, but homely allay, desire" (136). As American culture became sexualized, physical intimacy was first a fact of science and was imagined only later as an aesthetic experience.

Nineteenth-century Social Gospel fiction repeats this story: some men and women are born ugly and are born to belong to the mills or the working class. Karen Halttunen's *Confidence Men and Painted Women* explores how mid-century middle-class beauty was considered a sign of moral worth, whereas ugliness was thought to indicate inferiority. While women's beauty was a sign of their purity, ugliness indexes a cultural anxiety about sexuality. Although black women had traditionally been suspected of being oversexed, the ugly girl, too, was often cast as sexual prey. In Phelps's novel, as her sister tells it, Catty was an easy mark:

> "You see," said Sip, "I *told* you there's things you could n't understand. Now there ain't one of my own kind of folks, your age, would n't have understood half an hour ago, and saved me the trouble of telling. Catty's queer, don't you see? She runs away, don't you see? Sometimes she drinks, don't you understand? Drinks herself the dead kind. That ain't so often. Most times she just runs away about the streets. There's sometimes she does—worse." (84; Phelps's emphasis)

Sip wants to avoid speaking about Catty's sexual pursuits—her running about the streets and the "worse" behaviors to which she alludes. Like Ben Somers's "worse" behavior in *The Morgesons*, Phelps foregrounds what her culture considered worse than alcoholism. Sip's questions to Perley Kelso are rhetorical, merely indicating an equation of the dysgenic with promiscuity that many in Phelps's reading public would have accepted as fact.

Sexual acts are associated in these moral reform tracts with the deformed, the dirty workers in the mills, factories, and sweatshops. This construction links sex and work, but not sex *as* work, either as reproduction or as prostitution. Instead, sex provides relief from the drudgery of work, and sex expression itself is the corollary of working-class tedium, its only alleviation. While the Social Gospel writers could not change the situation in the mills, they could attack leisure sex, along with the mass entertainment invested in sex expression.

Christian reformers in the 1860s and 1870s drew on the new pseudoscience of ethnology—the categorizing of what was in the blood—and its relation to working-class women's sexuality. They provide the crucial prehistory of sex expression, which originally focused on the conflicts and alignments between the study of blood inheritance and Social Gospel writings as they inform nineteenth-century interpretations of sexuality. As Rosemarie Garland Thomson argues, "The Cripple, the Lame, the Blind, the Halt, the Mute, the Deaf—figures we today term physically disabled—appear with some frequency in the fiction of nineteenth-century American women writers" ("Crippled Girls" 128). Unlike the discourse of reform and disability that Thomson describes, ugliness was a separate category, one that initiated a language used to delimit the categories of sexuality. Ugly girls seemed to be everywhere in postbellum literature, from the pages of reform novels to mass-market magazines and even the newly created literature of the social sciences (whether in urban or rural sociology). The ugly girl was a product of her society in multiple forms—a wayward and untrained worker, a misguided consumer, a sexual sport.[13]

Early anthropologists who studied blood and heredity to determine racial characteristics and, eventually, racial superiority often spoke of blood as carrying distinguishing or inherited traits. Not surprisingly, this discourse was also transmitted through the popular literature of the 1860s and 1870s and gave credence to the ethnologists' decrees of racial and class traits inherited through the blood. Susan Gillman expertly documents Pauline Hopkins's subversion of these earlier doctrines in *Of One Blood* (1903), arguing that Hopkins revises the term "blood" as something that simultaneously signified "a mystical vision of (black) racial distinctiveness and interracial harmony, while remaining a biologism, rooted in racial and social inequities" ("Pauline Hopkins" 61). By having "blood" signify both visionary and essentialist thinking, Gillman contends, Hopkins promotes transculturation, an exchange between cultures achieved in large part by the mixing of bloods. A similar discourse can be traced to Davis and Phelps, who employed their fictions in the aid of the working classes. Yet complicating their social reformist vision is the notion of "blood" as the somatic cause for class divisions and stratifications.[14]

The mid-nineteenth-century discourse of beauty—and its subsequent commodification—produced another discourse of ugliness that was blood related, often manifested in dark skin, deformity, and immoral behavior. Middle-class beauty rituals were not only skin-deep but also habits of mind. By turning their attention so obsessively to surface appearance, middle-class women could keep themselves from focusing on sex expression as an urge, even as they stylized or cosmeticized it. While middle-class women were exercising their power as consumers, the working classes were continuing to reproduce with what social engineers deemed disastrous results, as the presence and proliferation of the ugly girl evinces.

BLOODLINES AND BORDERLINES

Phelps expresses her doubts about the ugly girl as the cultural carrier of sexuality. When one of her heroines in *The Silent Partner* exclaims, "It's in the blood" (200), her "it" alludes to degeneracy, waywardness, and illicit sexuality, among other failures. Such degeneracy was thus linked to cultural explanations for criminality. As Nicole Rafter reminds us, "In the criminological context [of eugenics], what eugenicists spoke of with greatest alarm was the degeneracy of poor whites" (50). It was their sexuality in the blood that associated them with the assumed promiscuity of racial and ethnic others. The "female defective delinquent" "fornicated for pleasure, with no thought of the consequences" (Rafter 159).

In *The Silent Partner*, Phelps documents a sentiment common among ethnologists and pervasive in the culture: what is in the blood includes the working-class heroine's own unsuitability for any other kind of labor as well as her sister's sexual degeneracy. Yet even Sip's self-assessment as being unfit for service-economy labor is bland compared to the narrator's description of Sip's dysgenic sister, Catty: "A girl possibly of fifteen years,—a girl with a low forehead, with wandering eyes, with a dull stoop to the head, with long, lithe, magnetic fingers, with a thick, dropping under lip,—a girl walled up and walled in from that labyrinth of sympathies, that difficult evolution of brain from beast, the gorgeous peril of that play at good and evil which we call life, except at the wandering eyes, and at the long, lithe, magnetic fingers. An ugly girl" (86). The only feeling that can break through her dysgenic state is the sympathy of the mill-owner's daughter, Perley, which she offers "for love's sake" (88). Instead of charity, acts of sympathy seem to confirm "blood" as the source of irreconcilable difference between the leisure and working classes. Sympathy, according to Social Gospel novelists like Phelps, is a negative or exclusionary identification; it separates the "good" blood from the "bad" even as it affirms the middle-class philanthropy that seeks to bridge the somatic and aesthetic gap between classes. An ugly girl is beyond any real help except the sympathetic gesture, usually eliciting more antipathy than sympathy.

Reform fiction's fixation on the ugly girl is the obverse of its creation of the middle-class cult of beauty.[15] (Given the choice of sex or makeup, the middle-class woman would choose the latter.) The ugly girl becomes the image of what reform cannot fix: the physical or inherited ugliness that results from miscegenation, maternal or paternal culpability for genetic sports, or sexual promiscuity. While reform fiction rarely took birth control as its central topic, the obsession with dysgenic progeny registers a worry about a problem much larger (perhaps unspeakable) than the concern about the working classes: the sexuality and unchecked proliferation of the working classes. Reform fiction offers its ostensible concern with labor conditions as a way to address the uncontrolled sexuality of the workers, which resulted not in wayward workers but in dysgenic laborers. What is in the blood is an urge to procreate, a far greater urge than the middle-class cult of beauty and its commodification could fulfill.

Twentieth-century birth-control novels, such as Edith Summers Kelley's 1923 *Weeds* and Charles Norris's 1930 *Seed*, would eventually follow in this tradition. *Seed* tells the story of an extended Catholic family torn apart by too many children. Refusing birth control, the wives banish their husbands from their bedrooms, and one of the husbands lives in "hell," developing "the worst case of neurasthenia." He ends up in the Diablo Sanitarium, fearing that his developing insanity resulted from the lack of any "sex indulgence" (401). For Norris and many others, abstinence and continence drive good men to temptation with dysgenic women, whose hereditary dispensation for sexual promiscuity makes them vulnerable.

Ugliness, poverty, class, and sex are all assumed to be in the blood, since the environment is heritable after it crosses bloodlines. Rebecca Harding Davis's 1862 novel *Margret Howth* also repeats, with greater frequency, the litany of "It's in the blood": " 'Blood will out,' " one character says of a half-breed Creek (85); character assessments such as "very pure blood" (103) or " 'crippled there by my Yorkshire blood' " (111) are also common. In Davis's novel, blood must be overcome through hard work, if it can be overcome at all: " 'Think of the centuries of serfdom and superstition through which their blood has crawled' " (151). By the conclusion, Davis's thinking seems to be in line with the dominant theories of ethnology, reiterating the thesis that " 'there's a good deal of an obstacle in blood' " (187) or that "a vice of blood" (250) overrules charity, sympathy, and social welfare work. Whether because of "blood or vice or poverty" (259), the novel of sexual reform depends on an inherent sense that change in the social situation is impossible because of essential differences between social classes.[16]

So why did such authors as Stoddard and Phelps take on an impossible task—to imagine the pleasures of the biologically, ethnologically, inherently irretrievable, such as Cassandra Morgeson and Catty Garth?

Why would they redeem sexual passion? My argument is not that the best efforts at social sympathy by writers such as Phelps or Davis ultimately capitulated to regressive thinking, although such an argument could be made. Rather, the pedagogy of sympathy—which Elizabeth Barnes and Glenn Hendler claim needed to be taught through the domestic or sentimental novel—depended for its rhetoric on sexual hierarchies. One could not have sympathy without having it rest on a discourse of sexual restraint. Blood inheritance *naturalizes* sexuality so that one need not discuss reforming sexuality in the working class; such sexuality was assumed. After all, how could one alter what was in the blood?

More important, the Social Gospel reformers led to the development of the pernicious doctrines of the eugenicists, such as those in the 1860s and 1870s who promoted "family studies" as a way to root out dysgenic blood in American communities. These family studies often generated conclusions that linked—in Rafter's phrase—"maternal culpability" to familial degeneracy (*White Trash* 66). While the father might be more blatant in his defiance of middle-class sexual codes, the mother's promiscuity was ultimately responsible for the failure of the family genes; the children, as in slavery, shared their mother's condition. Davis seems to subscribe to this notion in *Margret Howth* in her portrait of Lois Yare, the daughter of a white mother and a black father, who leaves jail less reformed than willing to conform. Lois Yare is configured as the standard ugly girl of so much reform fiction: "You would think, perhaps, pitifully, that not much pleasure or warmth would ever go down so low, within her reach. Now that she stood on the ground, she scarcely came up to the level of the wheel; some deformity of her legs made her walk with a curious rolling jerk, very comical to see. . . . The face would have startled you on so old and stunted a body. It was a child's face, quick, eager, with that pitiful beauty you always see in deformed people" (55). Her deformity is a matter of jest; her acceptance in the community depends on it. Moreover, as Jean Fagan Yellin claims, she is "asexual, victimized by industrial abuse" (210). Otherwise, she could end up alienated and vulnerable prey, as Catty does in Phelps's novel.

Davis is more ambivalent about Lois's deformity than Phelps is about

Catty's; it accords a "pitiful beauty" usually not reserved for a "skin [that] betrayed the fact that set Lois apart from even the poorest poor,—the taint in her veins of black blood" (56). Even more important, her ugliness just about precludes pleasure and desire, two discourses that reined in the newly emergent commodity culture. In imagining blood as justification for ugliness and sexual profligacy, among other social "crimes," many reform writers typically reinforced the equation of somatic appearance with moral health. As a hybrid of white and black races, Lois exemplifies the cultural fears of miscegenation. She also reminds readers that social reform has its limits and that the body reveals "the truth about its bearer" (Thomson, "Crippled Girls" 132). Reform cannot change blood; it can only ameliorate the conditions of the working class to which such dysmorphic "sports" must inevitably belong, while giving some pleasure to the reformer.

The Silent Partner is a protofiction of sexual exploration. While Catty is the only character in Phelps's novel to have sex, presumably for the physical pleasure, both Sip and Perley—the parallel heroines—are concerned about reproduction, as well as saving Nynee Mell from the sexual designs of "foreigners," such as the shift boss, Irish Jim. Too much personal, physical contact in the mills causes girls like Nynee to become accustomed to the pleasure of physicality. Sip explains to Perley:

> "A miserable Irishman, Jim is; has n't been in Five Falls a month, but long enough to show his colors, and a devilish black mustache, as you see. You see, they put him to work next to Nynee; he must go somewhere; they put him where the work was; they did n't bother their heads about the girl; they're never bothered with such things. And there ain't much room in the alley. So she spends the day with him, pushing in and out. So she gets used to him and all that. She's a good girl, Nynee Mell; wildish, and spends her money on her ribbons, but a good girl. She'll go to the devil, sure as death, at this rate. Who would n't? Leastways, being Nynee Mell." (123)

Nynee is saved when her attention turns to Dirk, Sip's former suitor, who despairs that his true love Sip will never allow her passion to become physical. The uncomfortably close conditions in the workplace, along with the indiscriminate "pushing in and out" that the girls must do in the aisles with the men, prefigure the other casual physical contact that the working girl "gets used to." "And all that," as Sip implies, is the code for intercourse, then as now expressed in the language of senti-mental indirection. In thus masking physical pleasure, the novel seem-ingly argues for a physical transcendence of the body, for a spiritual and, hence, future satisfaction.[17]

Or does it? Is Phelps ambivalent enough to leave the gates of passion ajar? When both Perley and Sip decide to forgo marriage, Perley does not complain, but Sip registers her hopelessness over being denied the com-fort of intimacy. After refusing Dirk's offer of marriage, she dejectedly returns to her room and ponders her sexual purity: "She felt as if her life had just been through a 'house-cleaning.' It was clean and washed, and proper and right, and as it should be, and drearily in order forever" (290). When she ponders her future, she vaguely refers to the sexuality she will be missing: "'I don't see why I could n't have had *that*, leastways,' she cried between her hands. 'I have n't ever had much else. I don't see why *that* should go too'" (287; Phelps's emphasis). She wants to have had *something* to offset the drudgery of working-class labor. She eventually turns to ministering and preaching, but her first choice—as it was for both Nynee and Catty—was sex. (The novel does not broach the question of birth control, but for Phelps it seems to be a nonissue, although social historians from Linda Gordon to Christine Stansell to Janet Brodie de-clare its availability in both the upper and the working classes.) That all the mothers—Perley's, Sip's, Nynee's—are dead or dying is also key to Phelps's rejection of reproduction. Yet Phelps does not reject pleasure: both Sip and Perley enjoy the performance of the opera and the musicale at the Blue Plum, two places that are parallel in the novel's sexual geography.

Phelps's 1871 novel illustrates the complex mystification of women's work of domesticating or obfuscating their sexuality in a culture that wanted to know about "It," but not too directly. Phelps is necessarily ambiguous about sexual desire because it threatens her model of cross-class sympathy and the power of sentiment. We might argue that sex expression replaced the cultural work of socialization upon which sentimentality depended. This new dynamic gave women an alternate route to self-expression (through a tentative sexuality), what has been since Margaret Fuller the ultimate goal in a culture of liberal individualism.

FEMINIZATION AND VICTIMOLOGY

If, as Rosemarie Garland Thomson posits, the nineteenth-century reform genre "requires a victim and a rescuer" ("Crippled Girls" 135), Phelps's novel challenges the victimology of such reform and, in doing so, contests the feminization of the culture. Phelps shows what happens when the victim does not submit to a disciplinary code, one she has not intuited or recognized; Catty Garth refuses to submit when she pursues sexual activity over sentimental commitment. That Catty presumably gets nothing but pleasure from sexuality—the pleasure of intimate contact—might be troubling for nineteenth-century reformers, who mostly fail to address sexuality except through sentimentality. Because it was predicated on the cultural doctrine of sympathy, reform became the barrier to sexual pleasure insofar as the reformers saw their objective as instructing readers in a kind of self- and sexual control.

Thus, Catty's anomalous appearance augurs a strange new idea in Victorian America about sexuality: physical pleasure. The next phase, however, was to make such impure sex "pure," not in the ways that the Victorians insisted on but in the newly modern sense of spectacle— whether such exhibitions were theatrical as in *Sister Carrie*, strictly commodified as in the emergence of the burlesque in the Floradora girls, or even the transcendent expression of passion untainted by exchange. In these new forms, American fiction aestheticizes sexuality, making it into a sort of tableau vivant (literally so in *The House of Mirth*) that, on the one hand, is visually stimulating yet, on the other, renders sexuality a sterile still life. "Transcendent sexuality" is the fantasy—like the developing one about sexual "magnetism"—that allowed middle-class women the possibility of imagining pleasure without the complications of declassing or unclassing themselves. The ugly girl is a postsentimental figure in which sexuality was once isolated, an image that social reformers used to deflect sex and a figure that the commodification of beauty and modern consum-

erism eradicated. (See chapter 6 for one story of the move from transcendent to therapeutic sexuality. Fannie Hurst's *Lummox* [1923] treats the
ugly girl as a figure who inspires sexuality.)

Some social reformers could see sexuality only as something to contain or prevent, even to breed out, just as they would try to do with
ugliness. In doing so, their arguments coincided with the rise of the "sex
expert" in the new social sciences. At the turn of the century, sociologist
E. A. Ross, with his doctrine of engineering social change, argued for a
birth control predicated on the failure of social reform to fix the nation:
"It is not too much to expect that in a few thousand years all hereditary
blemish, defect and ugliness will have been bred out of us, so that noble
and beautiful beings will be the usual thing. What could be more sense-
less than that birth control, the one facile means by which the ill-
constituted can have a satisfying sex life yet refrain from handing on
their defects to offspring, should be branded by religious authorities as
God-offending!" ("Positions" 7). Ross's sociology makes explicit that
reproduction rightly belongs to the eugenically fit, while mere "sex" is
for the dysgenic or ugly. Ross continues, "The grim reality of years of
gnawing, aching desire is sh'sh-sh-ed; religious leaders, faculty men and
athletic directors agree in insisting that hard work and hard play ex-
orcise the demon" (17). In acknowledging sexual desire, Ross takes us
closer to what Phelps could only describe as the "worse" that women
could attain or want: unmediated, unproductive pleasure rather than
work or play, spirituality or consumerism.

SEX EXPRESSION AND AMERICAN UGLINESS

One of the most interesting results of sex expression is that it allowed
bourgeois and antibourgeois representations of sexuality to exist simultaneously. As we see in *The Silent Partner*, Phelps cannot quite banish
sexuality or its appeal, however unintentionally she holds to pleasurable
sex. It also registers the new association of sex with youth. Catty is
fifteen, whereas the older middle-class heroine, Perley, is twenty-three
and, once she breaks off her engagement, already seems beyond the
sexual pale. Both the advent of consumerism and the failure of social

reform movements in the 1880s herald the sexualization of American culture, wherein ugliness ceases to be sexual, while beauty becomes the prerequisite for sex. By the end of the nineteenth century, sexual pleasure becomes another valuable commodity in culture rather than retaining the questionable status it held in Phelps's time. For the inheritors of sentimental culture, the goal is to reimagine and revise the notions of physical worth, to free sexuality from bloodlines and race, and to sever the eugenic link between beauty/youth and sexuality.

Thus, female sexuality in Stoddard's novel is more about voluntary response than is the working-class sexuality that Phelps portrays, which is purportedly involuntary, a blood-inherited response to the world. The middle-class woman is presumed to have an inviolable private self that the working-class woman does not also enjoy. On the contrary, working-class sexuality was never assumed to be private but was always a matter of public debate and potential reform. Although Sip's sister Catty has sex in public for pure pleasure and not for economic gain, Phelps's novel ends with two great acts of will—Perley Kelso's and Sip Garth's renunciations of sexual pleasure. Perley and Sip prefer to forgo sexual pleasure for the security of self-ownership and self-expression. Sex expression, as of the 1860s and 1870s, was too insecure and uncertain.

The next chapter is also concerned with the outer limits of youth and beauty—not ugliness but middle-age sexuality. By middle age, women no longer wanted to consume or reproduce; they wanted to feel. And their feelings moved them beyond sentimental attachment or community service to sex expression itself. While working women's sexuality remained a primary interest and concern, these writers also began elaborating an interest in women's passion and age.[18] No longer sentimentalized, sexuality became the stock-in-trade of young women. Nevertheless, a new generation of women writers developed a language of desire for middle-aged women, who seemed to fall through the cracks of class- and race-based arguments for what women's desires might mean.

CHAPTER THREE

Refusing

MIDDLE AGE

This chapter explores the changes in how several American women writers—from Rebecca Harding Davis to Willa Cather—imagined the oversexualization of working women and then the undersexualization, even "frigidity," of middle-aged females. If earlier writers identified sexuality with race (black women had it), then with social class (working women had it), and finally with age (young women were doing it), this shifting set of anxieties about who is having sex—and why—is key to the new "problem" of middle age. If ugly girls existed on one side of the sexual divide, on the other side were middle-aged women; ugly girls and middle-aged women were pitted against an emerging ideal of sexual productivity for young women.

Pauline Hopkins's *Of One Blood* (1903) exemplifies the limits of aging sex power. The novel charts the career of African American Reuel Briggs, a mesmerist-doctor in Cambridge, Massachusetts, who is passing as white in order to practice medicine among his peers at Harvard. To earn money to marry one of his African American patients, Dianthe Lusk, he accompanies an expedition to Africa as the company's doctor since he is unable to find work in the United States once his rival reveals Briggs's racial origins. While there, the doctor is discovered to be the lost king of Ethiopia. "Queen Candace" is to be his future wife, chosen from among a group of virgins awaiting the appearance of the lost King Ergamenes to revitalize the African city of Telessar and restore Africa to its rightful place of power. And a long wait it is, so long that Candace must be dethroned every fifteen years, during which she "chooses her successor" —a new virgin queen—while the city prepares for its king (561). Since Hopkins has no place for a middle-aged virgin in her novel, why, we might ask, does virginity expire in middle age (close to age thirty)? For Hopkins, the project of African renewal is tied to the revitalization of the Queen's sexuality so that nationhood depends on the trope of youthful virginity—a quality that ostensibly expires. Of course, reproductivity is an issue, but virginity in this kingdom is primarily a symbolic value indicating power.

While Hopkins's racial politics is linked to youthful sexuality, the association of sexuality with youth is only one of the ways that sex expression condenses the notion of individual self-culture. In this light, youthful sexuality is the primary source of women's power in lieu of a larger domain of possible self-expressions. Forgoing sex for fifteen years, as Hopkins's virgins do in preparation for the king, might have been a small price to pay to secure the kingdom. As for Hopkins, so the United States: sexuality became a way to imagine national politics and national culture, a way to secure the concept of heterosexual relations through women's consent to a new language and practice of sexuality. And part of that consent was tied to the idea of sex as a practice of youth, while older women would find in it as yet unspecified power—either from rejection of sex or from renunciation of desire. The question is not *whether* sexuality was capitalized or commodified, since it was both, but *what* effects these changes had and what the changing conceptions of sexual needs were.

As much as the culture might have sentimentalized the aging woman's role as socializing agent, the writers I study in this chapter suggest what middle-aged women might expect as an answer to their passions and impulses. The reform work that Phelps described in *The Silent Partner*, for example, did not always lead to altruistic desires or to a vow of celibacy, as Gertrude Atherton shows in *Black Oxen* (1923). Rather, some middle-aged women who observed younger women's displays of sexuality began to imagine such sex lives for themselves. As Jennifer Fleissner writes about naturalist fiction, "Turn-of-the-century women wanted something, but they had no idea what it was, and so they would never get it" (188). Fleissner's point is that women's desires may never have been "expressed" (247). That they had "no idea" what they wanted was not entirely true: many women saw their desires reflected in a working-class context against which they defined themselves and, thus, would not admit their sexual desires to consciousness. It's not so much that women had limitless desires, as psychologists feared, but that they had very specific desires that transcended the social order governing age and sex.

To that end, this chapter addresses the transition in the nineteenth century from the condemnation of pleasurable sexuality to the twentieth-century commodification of youthful sexuality. Between 1850 and 1900, a period circumscribed by Nathaniel Hawthorne's *The Scarlet Letter* and Theodore Dreiser's *Sister Carrie*, the foibles of youthful sexuality and its decline were a salient part of canonical literary history. The responses to Hester Prynne and Carrie Meeber frame the change in the meaning of sexuality during the second half of the nineteenth century. Hawthorne's contemporaries see his heroine's passion as romantic excess, and that passion is integrated only when the culture can see it as a symbol. For Dreiser's readers, Carrie's sexuality is a commodity offered onstage as spectacle and offstage as exchange value. That is, Hawthorne portrays Hester's sexuality as symbolic, while Dreiser sees Carrie's as salable, but Carrie is even less an anomaly than is George Hurstwood. Crucial is Hurstwood's age: Hurstwood, unlike Carrie, is a sad joke because, at thirty-nine, he is middle-aged, and his lust for Carrie looks ridiculous. As this frame exemplifies, mid-nineteenth-century sexuality was often a shameful vehicle for pleasure, while in the late nineteenth century sexuality was often an act of self-promotion.

Beyond the possibility of reproduction, midlife sexuality is demonized as opposed to the cultural uses to which that libidinal energy might be put. Various examples of middle-age consciousness in American literature show how middle age became a site of cultural aggression, as antisentimental, antipathetic an experience as Catty's sexuality in *The Silent Partner*. Middle age quickly became a category of life beyond sympathy, a loss so great that no amount of sentimentality could save it. From Harriet Wilson's *Our Nig* (1859) to Rebecca Harding Davis's stories and newspaper columns to popular fictions by Gertrude Atherton and Willa Cather, middle-age sexuality is represented as the stuff of jokes or, when taken seriously, linked to catastrophe. Even today, middle age represents a crisis to be resolved, a residual effect of the culture's sentimentalizing of youth.

Studies such as Mary Odem's *Delinquent Daughters* have made the debate over "age of consent"—when girls were considered of legal age to consent to sex—a focal point in American cultural studies, especially the surprising fact that state laws suggested that girls as young as seven could consent to sex.[1] Social-purity reformers campaigned vigorously to legislate the new age of consent at puberty (roughly twelve to sixteen years). Yet at the opposite end of the spectrum, we have no upper limit for the "age of irrelevance," when consent is assumed to be moot or unnecessary. Once youth and beauty were gone, as Lois Banner argues in *In Full Flower*, women's power was supposed to offer compensation for the failure of desire. Thus, sex expression among middle-aged women is an especially complex topic, given that competing analyses suggest two different ways of reading middle age in American culture: in terms of invisibility and erasure or in terms of unexamined power. Margaret Gullette posits another alternative: declining to decline, a resistance to cultural scripts of aging bodies and failing desire. So my question is, What is the upper age limit of sex expression in American literature?

Middle-aged women—especially mothers and mothers-in-law— prove to be among the most debated and dismissed figures of modern culture, representing as they do the cessation of sexual desire and, thus, its prohibition. The story of aging female reproductive organs in modern American writing is one that configures male projection and female invigoration or rejuvenation. The spinster in American literature elicits

74

the fears surrounding the figure of the unattached woman, even as the mother-in-law is deemed scariest of all. In *Bachelor Girl*, Betsy Israel describes the anxiety generated by the sexologist's description of the "intersexual": "a single woman who because of her odd experience somehow had fused with a male inner soul and who, though she appeared female, acted like a man" (142–43). How far did a single woman's "odd experiences" go? When a woman asserts "a male inner soul," does she also assert a masculine desire? The performance of gender roles preoccupied those interested in categorizing sexual identity and sexual acts—who was supposed to be sexual and with whom—no less than age.

The mother-in-law attracted a great deal of negative attention about an aging woman's sexuality. As novels like Edith Wharton's *The Mother's Recompense* (1925) and Atherton's *Black Oxen* demonstrate, middle-age sexuality was represented either as symbolic incest, as when an older woman took up with a younger man, or as child endangerment. Both of these novels, and a host of others (including Floyd Dell's 1931 *Love without Money*), portray a mother's sexuality as an either-or dilemma: either a mother is selfish and devotes time to herself, or she gives herself over to sexual denial and secondary narcissism by living through her children. Mothers are perceived as the general enemies of sexuality since they use both sentiment and sensation to stop their adult children from having intercourse.[2] Wharton's novel is a case in point: the power of middle-age womanhood remains untapped—either relegated to gambling and cards or distorted in the aggression displayed in mother-in-law jokes.

Freud describes this aggression in *Totem and Taboo* (1913) and traces it to the incest prohibitions that J. G. Frazer outlines in *Totemism and Exogamy* (1910). Based on Frazer's ethnographic evidence of mother-in-law ambivalence, Freud theorizes that this profound anxiety leads to the universality of the incest taboo, since he focuses on the son-in-law's attraction for his mother-in-law. This taboo is predicated on the ostensible dangers of mixing young and old bodies. Considering the taboo one of the "protective measures against incest," Freud nonetheless balks at the notion that these prohibitions result from the "great fear of the temptation presented to a man by an elderly woman, who might have been, but in fact was not, his mother." Freud takes pains to dismiss the possibility that the younger man could be attracted to an "elderly" woman, twice raising the interpretation only to dash it. Incest cannot be a viable interpretation because the elderly woman could not possibly attract a man. Freud deems such a "temptation" to be "incomprehensible" (13).

Instead, the mother-in-law is the totemic substitute for the attraction the male child once felt for his mother, "and perhaps his sister as well," Freud adds (16). As the boy grows up, he "liberates" himself from this earliest "incestuous attraction." Hence, Freud explains the rejection of the middle-aged woman as a necessary prerequisite for male liberation from infantile sexuality and attachment. After the man is liberated, the older female must be banished and replaced with a younger woman who does not remind him of his mother, sister, or even the younger woman's mother (hence, the repulsion toward the mother-in-law). For Freud, the mother-in-law taboo embodies the psychic fear of middle-aged women's continuing desires. She is, as Freud depicts her, "a woman whose psychosexual needs should find satisfaction in her marriage and her family life [but who] is often threatened with the danger of being left unsatisfied, because her marriage relation has come to a premature end and because of the uneventfulness of her emotional life" (15). Modern women are so potent a threat because marriage fails to satisfy them; whatever desires they may have had are unsatisfied in family life and, thus, are unattached and free-floating.

Yet this Freudian analysis does nothing to explain the middle-aged or elderly woman's temptation at all, especially in terms of her sexual attractions. As feminist critics have noted, Freud's theories are centered on the critical period of childhood, after which nothing means as much or feels as intense (see Gullette 65). After childhood, human beings enter into a "decline narrative," a scenario whose persuasiveness was compounded by the ever-growing cult of youth in the twentieth century. Age thirty triggers the decline narrative because that age suggests the end of women's sexual power and, often, male sexual reliability. In this light, Freud declared that psychoanalysis was useless for those over forty since middle age represented the rigidity associated with old age (see Brennan 134).[3]

At the same time that Freud explained away the sexual temptations of middle-aged women, the social engineers (many rabidly anti-Freudian) proclaimed these women devoid of sexual interest and desire. The University of Wisconsin sociologist E. A. Ross saw the great changes in modern culture as demanding new social arrangements, particularly concerning age. In asserting that sex absorbs "not more than twenty per cent" of our minds and lives, Ross claimed to differ with "Freudians, popular fictionists and scenario writers" ("Positions" 15). Our attractiveness to strangers, Ross argues, "declines rapidly in the thirties and in the forties touches zero" (18). "Age creep[s] on," and with it, one's magnetism and energy disappear. "Therefore, the part of wisdom is during your time of greatest bloom to attach some satisfying member of the opposite sex so firmly to you that he (she) will stand by you even if some day you become crippled or bedridden or crabbed or poor" (19). For Ross, only youth has inspirational power; age is nothing but a curse.

Much of Ross's logic is linked to the notion that the sex urge of young men and women must be tapped before it dissipates by the magical age of forty (481). He posits the sociological value of marrying early so that the "sex urge" can be channeled before its "inevitable loss." As he suggests, "The dalliance of shepherds and nymphs is charming but what will be the lot of the nymph after she is past forty?" He continues: " 'Tell me,' you who assert the right to flit responsibility from amour to amour, 'how will it be after you are forty-five'? Your former love partners have gone on to other affairs, in their hearts your image has been effaced. Time has deprived you of the power to inspire love in the young, and those of your own age do not appeal to you. Unless money gives you a dazzling setting, blooming youth is going to cut you out" ("Society of Western South America" 16). As we see here, the question of sex expression, as many sociologists and sexologists posed it, turned on the transience of youth. Ross does not forbid sex after forty or forty-five so much as he chastises youth for "flitting" responsibility. Sex after forty, like psychoanalysis itself, seems irresponsible and immaterial, useless as an effort to reinvigorate or cure something—either ego or desires—that would be better off laid to rest. In middle age, sexuality becomes a negotiable rather than a strictly utilitarian value—linked to keeping married heterosexual couples together through infirmity and crippling.

The utilitarian values with which the new American sociologists, especially Ross, invested sexuality conflicted openly with the emancipated ones that writers such as Atherton and Cather used to avoid reifying age. These women belong among those who advanced what Lauren Berlant has called "the female complaint"—"that space between feminism and conservative femininity" in American culture ("Poor Eliza" 652). That they were seen as "never satisfied" meant that they refused the image of middle-aged women's unattractiveness (while that incapacity to be satisfied with social issues indicated a kind of social unattractiveness). To be sure, some of these women writers reinforced sexual stereotypes, but others rejected the sentimentalizing of youthful sexuality for a more radical vision of sexual availability. This is exactly what Freud distrusted in women over forty: their ability to forget the traumas of sexuality and regain the pleasures of the sixteen-year-old girl. Age is scripted as lost youth, not gained experience, and the cultural script of aging reinforces the notion that women are better as blank pages before they have gained experience through the cultural process of sexuality and aging (see Mellencamp 300–301).

THE PROBLEM OF MIDDLE AGE

In his compelling argument about sentimentality in *Hard Facts*, Philip Fisher observes that "emotional life not based on sexual passion" (102) was sentimentalized in the nineteenth century, along with "the prisoner, the madman, the child, the very old, the animal, and the slave" (99). Unlike the experiences of the child and the very old, the desires of middle-aged people—of whatever race—could not be subsumed or sublimated for work, reproduction, or citizenship and, therefore, came under increasing suspicion. The culture expressed its growing discomfort with the indeterminacy of middle age through a discourse of irrelevancy, most problematically for women who were now expected to keep their mind on social rather than biological reproduction. Middle-aged women were especially vulnerable to these cultural projections. The literary culture I explore here shows middle-aged women as prone to what are considered sexually useless adventures.

In a society increasingly dependent on "sex for self-expression," Jackson Lears observes, the strictures against middle-age desire emerged out of the worries that romantic self-expression would devolve into merely modern sex expression, a narrowing of human possibility into one category of experience ("Sherwood Anderson" 28). In part, the rejection of middle-age sexuality responded to the greater sexualization of American culture. While the culture accommodated itself to sex expression for youth (almost as an inevitability), youth and its accompanying drive for sex expression were treated as a stage or a phase to be outgrown. Indeed, this is the historical argument that G. Stanley Hall invented in his category of *adolescence* in his 1902 book of that title. Once American psychology "discovered" postadolescent sexuality, it was labeled a "problem," to be solved by replacing it with more culturally meaningful activities in middle age. This channeling of middle-age desire into the nation's collective desires was an aggressive attempt to cordon off a decade or two of human life for a public purpose, even national projects. Middle-aged women, especially those who did not marry and have children, were supposed to channel their excess energies into social welfare, such as settlement houses or reform work.

Given the social investments in depicting the middle-aged woman as beyond desire, the age of forty is imagined as symbolic, free of sexual drives and impulses and, therefore, free of the pain and ambivalence of wanting and lust. At the beginning of the twentieth century, Mrs. Emma Angell Drake published her guidebook for forty-five-year-old women, *What a Woman of 45 Ought to Know* (1902), which ushered in a new era for middle age. Drake argues for the functionality of women at midlife, suggesting that these women "pass simply and easily, from the reproductive or child-bearing period, into one of sexual inactivity" (23). Rather than sexuality, women should promote "physical and spiritual redemption" (25). As Drake preaches:

Conserve your strength for a few years, and then you will be fitted to take up any line of work you wish, and carry it on for years. One such noble woman whom I have come to know recently, said to me when I remarked upon her young looks, though she had passed her fifty-second year, "I should not have been so well had I not followed my physician's directions. I came near a nervous breakdown, (she was a teacher) when upon consulting my physician he advised a year of perfect rest. I did not see how I could well take it but felt I must. At the end of the year I reported to him and he said, 'another year is necessary, and then I feel sure you will have many years of healthy usefulness before you.' I again followed his advice to the letter, and to-day at fifty-two, I feel as young as I did at forty, and am so well." She is still teaching in one of the Indian schools, an exacting position, with mind active and alert, and in splendid vigor. (109)

Drake's response to middle age is a promise of years of healthy usefulness. Women's dead reproductive organs—the end of women's germinal ability to reproduce—are the figures for men's liberation from their mothers and from their submissive attachment to older women. As Drake cautions, "Avoid passion and excitement. A moment's anger may be fatal" (114). Drake figures middle age as the emptying out or absence of desire rather than as a time of surplus pleasure or sexuality. In Drake's words, for a woman of forty-five, "all the physical passion has died, or is dying a natural death in her, in the right order of things, and it is more than sacrilege to demand from her, what she cannot and should not give. For your own sake as well as hers," she admonishes husbands, "be the protector to your wife in these things" (148).

Much earlier than Ross and Hall, however, Harriet Beecher Stowe contemplated a national life for middle-aged women. So careful was she to banish "shiftlessness" from her domestic arena that in her portrait of Ophelia in *Uncle Tom's Cabin* Stowe models middle-age usefulness. Stowe celebrates this middle-age power, but her vision is met with resistance. Stowe's Ophelia is seemingly without sexual interest, but as early as 1852, we can see this siphoning of individual middle-age desire into a heteronormative project in George L. Aiken and George C. Howard's stage version of *Uncle Tom's Cabin*, which adds a suitor for Miss Ophelia upon her return to Vermont with Topsy (act 5, scene 2). Given how closely the first four acts adhere to Stowe's novel, this adaptation strangely displaces Stowe's focus on Ophelia and Topsy's new familial arrangement. The following scene introduces a new character, the Reverend Deacon Perry, a widower who is searching for another bride to fill his dead wife's place. Ophelia is his choice. But why does she need a husband, especially after forming a new family with Topsy and moving back to the North after St. Clare's death in New Orleans? So uncomfortable is the idea of an unattached middle-aged woman that she is presumed marriageable despite her lack of interest in the normative heterosexual family. As an unmarried man, the Deacon may be shiftless, but as an unmarried woman, Ophelia has proven herself politically and socially powerful:

> OPH. Why, Deacon, by this time you ought to be setting your cap for another wife.
> DEA. Do you think so, Miss Ophelia?
> OPH. I don't see why you shouldn't—you are still a good-looking man, Deacon.
> DEA. Ah! well, I think I do wear well—in fact, I may say remarkably well. It has been observed to me before.
> OPH. And you are not much over fifty?
> DEA. Just turned of forty, I assure you.

An age joke is made at his expense but not at hers. Ophelia mistakes his age for ten years older than he is, making his claim about his age "wearing well" even more ridiculous and vain. Ophelia goes along with his courting, but it's not clear why. It's not Ophelia's age—Stowe gives it as forty-five (245)—but her relation to Topsy that almost scares the Deacon off. Because Ophelia introduces Topsy as her "daughter," the Deacon fears miscegenation, that she married "a colored man off South" and produced a "somewhat tanned" young lady (45–46). In this stage version, middle age and miscegenation are weirdly entwined, so troubling are they to mid-nineteenth-century culture. His proposal (and her presumed acceptance) effectively substitutes heterosexual marriage for her adoption of Topsy as Ophelia's central relationship. Thus, Aiken and Howard foreground the cultural anxiety surrounding the interracial family by substituting fears of unmarried middle-aged men and women. The latter worry is powerful enough to pose a threat to the sentimental order that the novel discloses in the evidence of interracial sex. The play adapts Ophelia's political agency—her ability to adopt the African American daughter and thereby change the national family—for the theatergoing audience by changing it into a heterosexual fantasy of family and middle-age social standing.

Which is to say that Ophelia's unattached status points to the unpredictability of women's desire as a sexual "problem" for the culture. The problem of midlife sexuality was that women were not fulfilling their cultural function; any expression of sexuality was then seen as selfish. The real problem was that women wanted to define their own roles— distinct from the family and from reproduction.

Or they wanted to define sex expression as a refusal of slavery. Harriet Wilson's 1859 *Our Nig* illustrates how the heroine's aging is tied to her need to write her story for profit. Wilson ties Frado's authorship to her need to make money now that she is graying. While Wilson describes Frado as beautiful, that beauty is fraught with the abuse that Mrs. Bellmont heaped upon her out of sexual jealousy. Once that beauty fades, Frado faces the crisis of growing older in a culture that privileges youth and sexuality when she succumbs to poverty and defeat as a result of years of abuse. Before Frado is "forced to some experiment" (Preface, n.p.) in publishing a novel, she sells a "recipe" for "restoring gray hair to its former color" (74), one which staves off poverty for a while. The change from marketing hair dye to selling a story is heralded as experimental. Nevertheless, Wilson dismisses it as a permanent strategy and turns to publishing as the means of her heroine's survival.

Wilson's comment about her recipe is one of the first to signal how showing age was an issue for African American women in antebellum culture, arguably more so than for white women insofar as free blacks needed to prove their worth—their youth—in the North's difficult labor market. Never very fit after her abuse by the Bellmonts, Frado is doubly endangered by showing signs of age. Her story represents the beginning of a trend in American literature: women may be able to control their hair color, but they cannot control their own histories. Selling one's story, the preface suggests, makes one vulnerable; selling one's middle-age story initiates the image of the older woman desperate and out of control.

Wilson's narrative prophesies the sea change in American women's writing about age. Because of the bias against middle age, especially in terms of employment and sexuality, women were compelled to invent new narratives for midlife desire. As it did for Wilson's heroine Frado, turning gray meant trying a new experiment—novel writing. For other female authors such as Atherton and Cather, turning gray meant turning to sex expression.

Focusing on the drama of desire rather than the deprivation of poverty, Mark Twain's sexual satire in *Letters from the Earth* suggests that the fundamental difference between male and female sexuality is the basis of culture itself:

> During twenty-three days in every month (in the absences of pregnancy) from the time a woman is seven years old till she dies of old age, she is ready for action, and *competent*. As competent as the candlestick is to receive the candle. Competent every day, competent every night. Also, she *wants* that candle—yearns for it, longs for it, hankers after it, as commanded by the law of God in her heart.
>
> But man is only briefly competent; and only then in the moderate measure applicable to the word in *his* sex's case. He is competent from the age of sixteen or seventeen thenceforward for thirty-five years. After fifty his performance is of poor quality, the intervals between are wide, and its satisfactions of no great value to either party; whereas his great-grandmother is as good as new. There is nothing the matter with her plant. Her candlestick is as firm as ever, whereas his candle is increasingly softened and weakened by the weather of age, as the years go by, until at last it can no longer stand, and is mournfully laid to rest in the hope of a blessed resurrection which is never to come. (40; Twain's emphasis)

Twain parodies male fears of sexual burnout by projecting illusions of sexual energy onto the ever-ready female, who presumably reaches the age of consent at seven and enjoys the guarantee of "competence" until old age. Typically deflating, his joke attacks the idea of male sexual prowess after fifty. In a reversal of the usual roles assigned to middle-aged women—"the overbearing mother-in-law, the wretched sexual has-been, the maternal nag" (see Gullette 78)—Twain imagines that women enjoy an active state of desire until they die, from the apparent sexual rapacity of seven-year-olds to death-bound desiring women. Men may entertain these illusions but to no avail since sexuality belongs exclusively to women and some youthful men. Women thus had to combat the problematic illusion that they were always ready for sex and, at the same time, that reaching middle age negated sexual desires. In doing so, they imagined a new kind of sex power that was not healthy, useful, or competent; instead, they yearned for pleasure.

THE REVOLT FROM MIDDLE AGE

The train wreck in Rebecca Harding Davis's 1889 short story "Anne" is one of the earliest examples of how fantasies of youth end with a literal catastrophe in order to bring the heroine back to her middle-age senses. The story concerns a successful middle-aged widow—Nancy Palmer—with grown children who dreams of herself as a beautiful sixteen-year-old; "Anne" is the name she gives the teenager within. In her dreams, "Anne" is still in love with a man from her youth; the memory of that love is so vivifying that Nancy Palmer grows "so alive and throbbing with youth and beauty" (329). Awakened from her reverie by the demands of her grown children and the house servants, the middle-aged widow returns to her quotidian tasks of bill paying, babysitting, and housekeeping: she is a woman, it is said, of dispassionate "masculine intellect" (331). Nancy wonders whether it is "quite decent in a middle-aged respectable woman to have such a dream" (331). Her dream of singing to and kissing her youthful lover means a regression to a time of oral pleasures, when the banal repressions of daily life did not constrict her.

In her real life, she fantasizes again, but this time about an escape that she literally enacts: on a train to Philadelphia to empty her bank vaults, she encounters the lover about whom she has been dreaming. But she realizes how shallow he has been in marrying an "ugly, stupid, and older" woman for her money (329). Moments after this realization, the train crashes and brings an end to her immediate dreams of sexual attraction and possible fulfillment. Her children rescue her and take her back home. Although returned to her family, she is still in the thrall of her sense of herself as youthful, alluring. Remembering her dream-fantasy of herself as a sixteen-year-old, she thinks: "*Is* she dead? she feebly wonders; and if she is dead here, will she ever live again?" (339; Davis's emphasis). Davis leaves the question open, as if to suggest that "a stout woman of fifty with grizzled hair and a big nose" with yellow cheeks and sallow jaws might still find passion again (330–31).

As Davis shows, representations of aging have more to do with generationalism—the demarcation of life cycles, such as adolescence, adulthood, and middle age—than with subjectivity or an inner life of desire. That the heroine acknowledges the "girl within" does not so much reject middle age as rejuvenate desires earlier surrendered to more immediate —domestic and familial—needs (see Apter 277). Davis renders midlife desire mostly through the perspective of the yearning child who sees only the mother's digression from the child's needs: "Susy glanced at her with indignation. Was mamma deranged?" (333). Even though "Anne" starts out as the story of the aging mother, it ends with the mother policing her own desires as though she were her own daughter. The moment of release comes when she leaves family behind to reinvent herself. That reinvention means capturing the sense of being sixteen again, before her advanced age places her in a personal and national drama of reproductive centrality and race preservation.

In this story, the mother is forced to live out her family's fantasy of her being beyond desire, forced to settle for the pleasures of secondary narcissism that parenthood presumably delivers. Moreover, the spectacle of a desirous middle-aged woman disrupts the cultural fantasy of moving beyond primary needs to secondary ones. Insofar as she still harbors sexual desire, the sexual middle-aged woman comes to be viewed as awkward, foolish, even ugly. Thus, sexuality becomes age- and beauty-defined at the moment that American women writers began exploiting the ambiguity about when sexuality begins (is it at sixteen?) and ends (at thirty or thirty-five, forty or forty-five, fifty or later?). These erotic fantasies include rejecting the strict distinction between reproductive adulthood and the next stage, productive middle age.

The ideological function of these narratives about aging is to establish middle age as its own temporal location, distancing the postreproductive years from productive sexuality. The identification of productivity with youth and beauty aims to sever a sense of aging-as-process. As a result of sharp divisions between stages—adolescence/adulthood, middle age/senescence—we see aging as moving through demarcated stages, not as a gradual process. As Gullette explains: "Age theory reminds us that the very concept of a 'beginning' depends on accepting the positivist claim of age ideology: that there's a real category of being there, separable from earlier stages or age classes and distinguishable from continuous processes as well. The midlife is now localizable" (159). The stages of middle age are rigidly demarcated by jokes, aggression, catastrophe, crisis, and death. This splitting off of adulthood from what follows redirects midlife energy to other cultural uses: politics, nurturing, charity. Such temporal segregation also renders sexuality a necessary distraction, so that women ostensibly beyond sexuality inhabit a de-eroticized social world where libidinal energies are channeled into cultural ideologies.

Throughout the nineteenth century, the United States entertained changing ideas about aging, as evinced by the continually shifting year of middle age's inception: from thirty to thirty-five, to forty, then to forty-five. In *Figuring Age*, Kathleen Woodward posits fifty as the "symbolic date" when aging occurs in contemporary society (xiii). Beyond the demographic and actuarial changes this movement implies, Atherton and Cather challenged the normative cultural conception of what midlife in general, and middle-age sexuality in particular, signifies. What is crucial is not that middle age seems to get further and further away, no longer at thirty but now at fifty; instead, the delaying of middle age is a sign of greater cultural distress about aging, signaling a panic and an attempt to distance the invisibility, indeed emptiness, of the middle-aged. Middle age was designated as a time when nothing happens, or can happen, to the self. Thus, "decline" or "invisibility" narratives about middle age give way to stories of midlife emptiness. The only presence that middle-aged Americans are allowed is that of benevolent service to the nation—as members of heterosexual white families or as teachers, social and settlement workers, or caretakers.

MIDDLE-AGE SEX

By the 1920s, the culture may have been accustomed to all sorts of expressions of lust, but such desires did not ostensibly emanate from middle-aged women. Wharton and Cather, for instance, increasingly found it in their own best interests to revamp the stereotypes about middle-aged women, and they began to explore how the promise of sexual fulfillment was a diversionary tactic that routed middle-aged women's unmoored power back into a secure space: whether middle-aged women were chasing young men or sublimating their desires, they were still self-regulating. Instead, Wharton and Cather imagined middle-age power as outside of modern categories of sexuality. Their response was not prudish, unlike certain authors, such as Kathleen Norris, whose 1911 novel *Mother* celebrates "something magnificent in a woman like your mother, who begins eight destinies instead of one!" (179–80). For Norris, the Catholic impulse to bear children is a "higher tribunal than the social tribunal of this world" (180).

For Atherton, however, middle-age power might be seen as a refusal to take a "liberatory" bribe, one that has everything to do with constructions of age and sex. One of her earliest novels, *A Question of Time* (1891), directly addresses a topic that would become her calling card in later fiction: middle-aged women's combined social and sexual power. Here Boradil Trevor, a forty-six-year-old widow, falls in love with and marries a twenty-two-year-old "genius," whose potential as a great poet she hopes to nurture. There is not much more to the plot, except for the horrified reactions of the young man's aunt and the town gossip. Just as Boradil is about to cancel the engagement, her lover, Mark Saltonstall, plans a surprise wedding, and the union takes place. While this ending sidesteps the issue of Boradil's agency, it does not let us forget that the novel is concerned with her unconventional sexual desires and her sexual viability.

The drama turns on the dissonance between Boradil's age and her youthful appearance. The novel opens with this description: "She was young, as many women of her age are, because trouble had scarcely brushed her in passing, nor the world scorched her with its hot breath;

because no illness had come to rift her perfect health, nor ill-placed passion to consume and wither. In a word, she had never lived, and a certain coquetry, too light for discontent, yet strong enough to guard and enhance her beauty, made her still look like a flower half bloomed, then passed by and forgotten of Time" (5). The rest of *A Question of Time* is similarly punctuated by frequent discussions of Boradil's age, appearance, demeanor, and passions. All of the conventional arguments against this December-May romance are trotted out and dismissed because of Atherton's disdain for the double standard that holds that what is fine for older men is not suitable for middle-aged women. By comparison to women half her age, Boradil "understands" men and knows how to appease their egos effortlessly. Mark explains that her "mysterious power" over men is that she "believes" in them (92). Her "coquetry," a "dainty feminine gift," proves as "dangerous as the fiercer charms of the equatorial sisterhood," whose passion (as conventional racists like Atherton assume) is a result of their darker skin color (20). What is acceptable for "equatorial" women should be equally acceptable for their northern, middle-aged "sisters."

Atherton is one of the first women novelists to explore this sex expression, a "mysterious power" not part of a woman's reproductive duties or ascribed to her because of her race or ethnicity. Boradil, like Mary Zattiany in Atherton's *Black Oxen*, is a white, middle-aged woman who wants sex with a younger man and social power, a power that she has not garnered because of her matronly status or her husband's property. On their midnight walk in the woods, the lovers discover "the great mystery of sex": "In her wide eyes was an expression of horror fighting with rapture; the knowledge of age and the knowledge of youth" (110). Atherton remarks, "What an awakening!": "You are forty-six! forty-six! forty-six! Boradil Trevor; the age of many a grandmother; yet here you are thrilling and quivering under the kiss of a boy, passionate as a girl in her first awakening. What have you to do with passion, O Boradil Trevor!" (111–12). It seems she has everything to do with passion, for despite declaring herself "an old woman—old woman—old woman" (115), the sex-awakening gets her past the "hideous irony" of this new relation (116).

The question, then, is what a forty-six-year-old woman is allowed—

conventionally—to do. At their first meeting, her future lover tells her,
" 'You do look so awfully young for forty-six,' " after which he asks her to
"adopt" him as a companion (21). In her presence, he writes until
midnight, and when he becomes exhausted, she lets him spend the rest of
the night on her sofa. Yet his presence leads her to feel "old," although the
catalog of her charms remains intact: she has no wrinkles, firm flesh, no
"loose look," perfect teeth, fresh—not faded—skin, no stringy or soft
throat, shapely and smooth hands, "rich abundant hair," curved bust (22).
This catalog echoes the compartmentalization of aging that emerges at
the turn of the century since appearance has everything to do with
sexuality. Mark and Boradil ultimately marry, not because of her age but
because of her appearance. She is still amenable to passion and is willing
to risk her future for a few years of intense sexuality, even as she imagines
that Mark will abandon her by the time she turns fifty. "At least she could
make him happy for some years. A younger woman might make him
miserable in less. When the time came wherein he looked at her with
aversion, she could go and leave him to his own full life. . . . And passion,
long unfelt, is a tremendous factor in deciding such questions as these"
(128). In calculating the exchange of a year of passion for rejection after
fifty, Boradil imagines that passion is better than convention since its
arousal in middle age undoes a lifetime of conventional respectability.
Her newfound sense of companionship with Mark invigorates her so
much that "twenty-five years slipped out of the century" (48)—a conve-
nient number, for that quarter century would make Boradil only twenty-
one to Mark's twenty-two years.

The "question" Atherton poses in the title also concerns how passion
works: does it age a woman or keep her young? Those characters who
have been touched by passion seem to have been marked physically by
it, as both Phelps and Stoddard mark their passionate characters. Boradil
had felt no passion for her first husband, a man twenty years older than
she. Although two years younger than Boradil, one of her friends assesses the difference in their appearance on the basis of their experience: "I . . . have had trouble, and ten children, and many duties. She has
had an eventless life" (12). Childbearing duties age a woman, while a
passionless marriage does not. Boradil loses her baby after seeing it only

once (60). Her friend Hetty wonders how she could love someone who might be her son (148), and she reminds Boradil that it is only by the accident of an actual stillborn baby that she does not have children his age. Arguably, this is part of Atherton's dismissal of Boradil's eugenic capacity to reproduce her race, but it is also a suggestion that women who don't mother have passion to spare. (But is it then only an accident that middle-aged women have not used up their passionate natures in childbirth? Is the compulsion to maternity a way to drain women of "unnatural" desires later in life?) More important, as eugenicists feared and Atherton's later fiction will bear out, Boradil's childlessness leaves her restless in middle age. Even though Boradil has read books about passion, her "ego" is untouched by it (27). "Intellectual women are mentally polygamous," Atherton's most forward-looking character argues (166). And so the smarter the woman is, the more sexually adventurous she might become.

Boradil has no relatives to accost her, but Mark's relatives accuse him of insanity of a specific kind: dysgenics. His cousin, Elnora Brewster, wants to marry him to advance his genius. She has spent the passion of her first great love and promises Mark "never to love again." Through him, she believes that she can "become famous." As she argues, "'Men of genius are apt to be low-born, but there is no better blood in America than the Saltonstall's, and you are one of the few men I could endure as a husband'" (142–43). Making the eugenic appeal, Elnora proposes a genetic dynasty as their "duty."

How Mark arranges the marriage to Boradil is key to understanding Atherton's take on middle-age passion. Sensing that Boradil will renege on her promise, he plans a secret wedding, which his father gladly attends. Only Mark's father supports his decision, for he believes that Boradil's passion will sustain them and that his son needs the mature woman's experience to guide his genius. Boradil knows nothing about his plans but follows his will unconsciously. So the novel ends. Her aroused passion initially gives way to her social sense, which is the conventional restraint imposed on middle-aged women. But when passion comes, Boradil declares that she does not have "the strength to resist it" (148). "Such is the imperious demand of my woman's nature for its rights" (150). Boradil's argument suggests that she cannot own her desire for respectability demands that she resist it. Her instinctual passion, once aroused, demands its "rights," but Atherton gives her no outlet except for a twenty-two-year-old companionate "son." So Freud was wrong: men can and do feel passion for older women, so much so that marrying younger women for the good of the race and to solidify male genius and female power must become national custom and a matter of civic duty. Even as Boradil tries to repress her sexual instincts, Mark Saltonstall is in control of them: he arranges a secret wedding at precisely the moment that he fears Boradil will surrender to conventional age relations. His conscious and unconscious desires are aligned, while hers seem out of sync, her sexual impulse at odds with her conscious revolt from her promise to marry Mark.

Jennifer Fleissner argues that the tendency in naturalist fiction is to chart both the impulsive and compulsive natures of women's responses to modernity. Such compulsions are part of Atherton's sex expression: her characters are self-divided between unconscious sexuality and sublimation of those impulses into poetic genius and motherhood. For example, the woman denied maternity through such accidents as stillbirth retreats into compulsive domesticity, but that domesticity fails, time after time, to fulfill women's desires. Domestic work, like material consumption, involves a series of activities that have to be done over and over again, repetitive actions that are never really done and, hence, never really satisfying. Alas, that domestic logic of routinization is the same language that women inherited for sexuality: fulfilling a lack, providing an exchange value on the market, but not having any real definition of its own. Sex as work and sex as power were the only frames established for sexuality with any social currency. So women saved or spent themselves in fairly traditional, even domesticated ways.

A Question of Time looks forward to Atherton's extended treatment of aging three decades later in *Black Oxen*. As the hero of the former novel predicts, " 'I have not the faintest doubt that a couple of centuries hence a woman will not be thought old enough to make her bow into society until she is fifty,' " though at present, in 1891, thirty marked the beginning of "old age," when "teeth begin to drop, the eyes to dim, the vigor to fail" (34). Atherton's 1923 best seller depicts a profound tension between "adult" and middle-age sexuality. Middle age seems to mark the division between productive adulthood and nonreproductive midlife. The heroine of *Black Oxen* gives up youthful sexuality, too, as insufficient for adult productivity, namely politics and nationalism. Written when Atherton was sixty-six, the novel makes the case for a mature woman's position in the culture, which turns on the fate of Mary Ogden Zattiany, a woman whose marriage at age twenty-four—"the beauty and the belle of her day"—to a Hungarian diplomat "withers" her youthful beauty (8). Yet when she returns to New York society after a thirty-year absence, she does so looking no older than twenty-eight and becomes a mystery to old and new New York (6). While some imagine her to be a Bolshevik retreating from Europe or even a "rich man's mistress" (20), eventually she reveals the secret of her rejuvenation: the Steinach treatment—a procedure involving X-ray stimulation of the ovaries, which left women sterilized, although seemingly revitalized, to which Zattiany submitted in order to advance her political cause.[4] While Atherton makes it clear that Mary Zattiany is everyone's idol, the mature *and* youthful woman, she also shows how sex distracts her heroine from arguably more important pursuits. And it is precisely this separation between the categories of adulthood and middle age that is demarcated and ossified from the 1890s through the 1920s.

In analyzing Atherton's novel, Susan Squier writes about the process of "scientific rejuvenation," a companion project to reproductive technology from 1909 through the 1930s. The cultural climate for Atherton's novel, Squier notes (contra Lois Banner), is revealed by the heroine's "motivation for undergoing rejuvenation—and thus, the motivation of all women—not as a desire for youth, sex, and love, but rather as an attempt to achieve agency" (97). In this way, Atherton distances her heroine from sex expression, which radicals and conservatives alike, according to Charlotte Perkins Gilman, saw as "a morbid excess . . . whether in marriage or out, which makes the health and happiness of humanity in this relation so precarious" (*Woman* 30). Atherton shares Gilman's and Wharton's enthusiasm for debunking flapper culture and advocating either maternal stability or the individual will of the feminist. From the first pages, she declares, "The world was marching to the tune of youth, damn it" (3), and the novel is all about overcoming the infatuation with youth for a more meaningful age.[5]

The difference between *A Question of Time* and *Black Oxen* can be found in Atherton's measuring sexual repression and liberation not through the young widow but through the flapper. Youth and personality were the reigning normative values of 1920s culture, which eroticized rather than sentimentalized young women. The culture of youth distanced middle-aged women even further from the feelings of competence we saw in Twain's description of women's lifelong readiness for sex. What is dangerous about the flapper era is not only its fetishizing of youth but also its ability to get women to identify with flappers against their own interests. *Black Oxen* focuses on the contradictions of a society that promotes the slogan "Youth reigns" and represses women's "sex-imagination" in exchange for power (as we will see in chapter 4). Although the flapper pursued self-gratification in sexuality, Atherton's heroine must choose political commitment to Austrian refugees rather than her own newfound sexuality.

The locus of Atherton's attack is America's obsession with youth, embodied in the flapper, and the "Ancient Idea" (42) that the young are essential in populating the earth. In eugenics, women's reproductive power is central, but Atherton wants a more enduring authority. After the Steinach treatment, Atherton's heroine "radiated power" (53), and she is not duped by romantic love when she acknowledges that "man was essentially polygamous and woman essentially the vehicle of the race" (56). In regard to a young girl who drinks, smokes, and cavorts, Mary Zattiany wonders why "her people" do not put the young flapper "in a sanitarium" (109). Professing an anti-Freudian dismissal of sex urges (what Atherton calls "young love. The urge of the race" [92]) in favor of mature power, Atherton's heroine promotes her own kind of sex expression. But first, Mary Zattiany has to harness science to "reenergize" her tired body and mind (137): this was "an interior drama . . . a drama of one's insides, and especially one that dealt with the raising from the dead of that section which refined women ceased to discuss after they had got rid of it—it was positively ghoulish" (139).

Atherton's approach to this "interior drama" is not about psychologi-cal or psychoanalytic force; rather, it literalizes the issue of women's sex power. Through the Steinach treatment, her heroine "raises from the dead" her sexual desire and, hence, her political power. The drama concerns how her culture responds to a reborn woman. The once mori-bund, now irradiated reproductive organs restore Mary Zattiany's youth-ful beauty, though she cannot reproduce. So Atherton separates youth from reproduction, thereby giving free rein to her ideas about middle-aged women's potential power in a legitimate political marriage.

Casting flapperism as the antithesis of power, Atherton's novel main-tains that women's true expression lies in their forgetting about sexuality and investing themselves in intellect and politics. Gora Dwight may be plain, but she is an important novelist; Mary Zattiany may be beautiful, but she must also be a politician. As Prince Hohenhauer tells her: " 'With your splendid mental gifts, your political genius, your acquired statecraft, your wealth, and your restored beauty, you could become the most powerful woman in Europe. But only as my wife. Even you are not strong enough to play the part alone. There is too much prejudice against women to permit you to pull more than hidden strings' " (322). For Atherton, sexuality cannot lead to power; only politics can.

The reverse of the flapper is the middle-aged settlement worker who tries to keep her charges from engaging in sexual congress. Mary Zat-tiany sickens at the confession of one "old maid" to her repressed urges. Agnes Trevor is "the admirable spinster," aged forty-two, who is devoted to settlement work (258). Yet she speaks passionately of her desire for sex: " 'Oh, I tell you that unless I can be young again and have some man—any man—I don't care whether he'll marry me or not—I'll go mad—mad!' " (264). Trevor's confession is filled with self-loathing.[6] She is ambivalent about her interlocutor, Mary Zattiany, and equally ambiva-lent about herself and her now unrepressed desires.

The spinster's sex repression results in a middle-age mania. At first, Agnes is oblivious of the sexual intimacies of her female charges in the settlements, then she is sure she can control them. Most settlement workers hoped to focus their charges' energies on proper self-expres-sion. Similarly, many middle-class reformers imagined that the influence in the settlements would go all one way, from the middle class down to the settlement girls. None of the settlement literature suggests that "problem girls" and wayward sexuality might influence the middle-aged and middle-class matrons and chaperons who labored there.[7] And in fact, one novelist, Hamilton Fyfe in *Peoples of All Nations* (1922), created a category called the "Third Sex" to cover women who did not want to marry and who were so invested in work as to foresee "no probability of marriage to provide them with interest and occupation, [who] either worked for a living or threw their energies into work of a social or charitable kind" (Fyfe qtd. in North 185). This "Third Sex" was to define the gap between those women who stayed home after marriage and those who found marriage too dull to sustain them. Charity, then, was supposed to drain women's libidinal energies.[8]

Atherton, however, reverses the direction of influence. Before long, the working-class girls entice their mentor to imagine the pleasures they experience:

> "[Sexuality] horrified me so that for several years I hardly could go on with it [settlement work], and I have always refused to mix the sexes in my house down there, but, of course, I could not help hearing things—seeing things—and after a while I did get hardened—and ceased to be revolted. I learned to look upon all that sort of thing as a matter of course. But it was too late then. I had lost what little looks I had ever possessed. I grew to look like an old maid before I was thirty. Why is nature so cruel, Mary?" (261)

Agnes's confession opens up the topic to the only cultural analysis the novel offers: hearing and seeing "things" compel the spinster to imagine them, to experience vicariously the desires long repressed. Settlement work and a stable domestic life cannot hold a candle (*pace* Twain) to sexual adventure and fantasy. Mary counsels her that "a good many American women develop very slowly sexually. You were merely one of them. I wonder you had the climacteric so early. But nature is very fond of taking her little revenges. You defied her and she smote you" (261). To get even with nature, the heroine urges the spinster to have the Steinach treatment and, once rejuvenated, to have sex.

Settlement work is an especially apt setting for Agnes's midlife sexual frustrations to the extent that the scene of Agnes's sexual awakening highlights the power of youthful sexuality to ameliorate the conditions of wage slavery. As *The Silent Partner* intimates, workers' promiscuous proximity to heterosexual partners may well initiate such sexual activity. And as Phelps does with Nynee Mell and Irish Jim, Atherton suggests that working women have more reason than their middle-class counterparts to expect sex as pleasure, as leisure activity. Even as middle-aged women were enjoined to reach out to the community and to motherless children, as Emma Drake counsels they should do to drain their restless energies (107–8), Agnes's witnessing of youthful sex power stimulates her own forgotten sex drives. Rather than reforming her youthful workers' sexual impulses, Agnes's settlement work leads her to reverse the charge: Agnes cannot reform because she is too distracted by her own sexual needs.

Atherton contrasts the middle-class woman's self-possessed but alienated sexuality with the working woman's sexual ownership. The middle-class woman's effort at reforming her sexual sisterhood fails when her youthful charges bring the middle-aged woman's sexuality to consciousness or, at least, to what Pamela Haag describes as the "dispossessing notion that women's sexuality constituted an unruly and internally alien entity" ("'Real Thing'" 577). Thus, women prove to be bifurcated by their conscious and unconscious sexual drives as much as by their class status. Or perhaps class is again being redefined here by the female's lack of consciousness of sexuality, its repression, in opposition to the fully conscious choices the settlement women make for themselves.

Ultimately, Mary Zattiany is unsympathetic to Agnes's plight as a "debauched gerontic virgin" (264). This ambivalent encounter with the spectacle of frustrated female desire frames the heroine's decision to reject sex expression with her youthful lover in favor of the greater political legitimacy of relief work in postwar Austria. In the end, then, Mary's political commitment has the same function as Agnes's settlement social work: both keep them from expending sexual energy on younger men.

The novel ends with Atherton's affirmation of Mary Zattiany's political power, which she gains only when she abandons her engagement to her thirty-four-year-old lover, Lee Clavering, and resigns herself to a political marriage with Prince Hohenhauer, her Austrian lover of sixteen years ago and her political partner now. With that marriage, she must repress the "sex-imagination," which "often outlives the withering of the sex-glands" (262). In doing so, she regains her "will to power" (240), just as she had regained her youthful looks with the Steinach treatment. "Sex-magnetism" and sex expression distract women from real power. Atherton can support neither the "feministics" (156) of women searching for personal autonomy, unleashed by sex expression, nor the values of psychoanalysis as a way to unhinge repression: "No soft feminine seductions. . . . No damned sex nonsense. . . . [Clavering] knew barely another woman who didn't trail round to sex sooner or later. Psychoanalysis had relieved them of whatever decent inhibitions they might have had in the past" (62). While Clavering blames psychoanalysis for unleashing women's sexual impulses, he finds the fifty-eight-year-old Mary to have transcended these unconscious desires for decidedly conscious ones. Thus, every chance she gets, Atherton denounces youthful and middle-age sex expression alike as destroying women's reputations and importance in the public sphere.

Atherton's novel denigrates midlife sexuality, which, by the end of the twentieth century, also reinforced the general distrust of middle-age competence. Precisely at the moment when the culture was exploring and celebrating youth as it never had before, it was creating, under the force of generationalism, an unbreachable rift between white heterosexual productivity and everything else, especially middle-aged white women's sexuality. Midlife sexuality was contained or rechanneled because the culture did not have a use for middle-aged women. If middle-aged women were pursuing younger men, then those younger men (as Atherton shows) were not pursuing younger women and, hence, were not reproducing the culture. As Gullette notes, the force of generationalism, such as the creation of Generation X, only deepened the rifts between age and youth, setting off competition and "youthful arrogance" (240). Yet the greater nervousness at the turn of the century was not about women's sexual power, or "competence," but about women's unchanneled power altogether. Pitting middle-aged women against younger women, thus setting off generational battles for power, was one destructive strategy for restricting women.

In "Sex in American Literature," Mary Austin declares this Atherton novel an "advanced" treatment of American sexuality: "The whole institution of marriage is built up out of this subconscious conviction of women that the common life of husband and wife, what they may achieve by way of offspring, by conquest of the maternal environment, or on the plane of perceptive consciousness, is more important than what they feel for one another" (391). This larger goal for sexuality in American life can only be accomplished, Austin writes, when mature women have the ears—if not the hearts—of younger men (392). Austin worries that American male novelists and men in general "are, as a matter of fact, a little inclined to be shocked at the notion that a woman who has reached the years in which she is definitely recognized as 'older' has any love life which should intimately concern them, or, in view of the general refusal of the mature American woman to use her knowledge for the purpose of creating sex 'situations,' that she has any knowledge that needs to be taken into consideration" (393). These men are not concerned with the "love life of any but extremely young women." As much as Austin admires Atherton, however, she claims that there is no better writer on "the range of sex experience which our varied American makeup offers" than Willa Cather (391).

LOST SEX

I started this chapter with Freud's argument against the power of older women to attract younger male partners, but it is an argument that Atherton, Wharton, and Cather all advance. Perhaps another version of this story is the worn-outness of the older men whom these heroines first marry and then outlive or outlast, since there is something to be said for seeing the turn-of-the-century naturalist writing of Dreiser and Wharton, as Fleissner does, as dramas of "Old Men and New Women." But there is also something to be suggested about Young Men and Older Women. And for that story, we turn to Cather. Cather's novel *A Lost Lady*

(1923) contends that women without children will go after younger men, thereby linking the issue of middle-age sexuality with childlessness.

Published the same year as *Black Oxen*, Cather's *A Lost Lady* filters a woman's sex expression through the eyes of a teenage male narrator, Niel Herbert. He falls for the heroine's "long-lost lady laugh" (68); "it was a habit with him to think of Mrs. Forrester as very, very young" (72). In fact, he imagines her as about his age, although she figures to be significantly older than his twenty when he heads off to school at MIT. He is willing to erase her age for himself, but not for other men. In that regard, he judges Marian Forrester for her habit of drinking "too much French brandy" (101) and her extramarital affairs, in which she exercises her choice for men the teenager sees as decidedly inferior. At times, her sexual choices outrage Niel, and at others, he is offended by the idea of a female capable of choosing sexual partners and acting on her desire. Neither romantic love nor contracted marital obligation, this freely expressed sexuality disturbs Niel precisely because no one seems to understand it. It is beyond a father's control, a husband's power, and an adolescent admirer's prescriptions, although seeing Marian Forrester's sexuality as part of her "self-possession" means acknowledging women's desire. In that way, the novel really has more to say about the boy's alienation from sexual culture than about Marian Forrester's reckless-ness. That she doesn't get to tell her own sexual story is commonplace enough, as we know from a history of male writing on female subjec-tivity. Even so, Niel decides he "knew everything; more than anyone else; all there was to know about Marian Forrester" (111). In short, he can possess her because he knows her secrets, thereby laying claim to a symbolic sexual ownership that he sees her exploit in her liaisons first with Frank Ellinger—a bachelor of forty who leaves her for the wealthy Miss Ogden—and later with Ivy Peters—an "unscrupulous," per Niel, local businessman.

Yet Cather's story refracts that sexuality through her age. Once Captain Forrester dies, she is a widow and measures her power to live in terms of how many years she has left: "Perhaps people think I've settled down to grow old gracefully, but I've not. I feel such a power to live in me, Niel" (119). And that power emerges from youth and sexual attraction through her own assessment of her sex power: "I always know how I'm looking, and I looked well enough. The men thought so. . . . I wanted to see whether I had anything left worth saving. And I have, I tell you" (119). What does she measure in herself to keep going, a quantity or commodity worth "saving" in her and later "spending" in California? Her sex power turns into a measurable force, decreased by the number of years she has been using it. Her vision of self-possession is embedded in how much sexual power she has left, after her marriage to Captain Forrester and her affairs have diminished it. For Cather, this is not just a throwback to older models of explaining sexual energy through metaphors of electricity. Instead, she equates sex power with youth, diminished by each year she spends taking care of her invalid husband. As Niel imagines, "When women began to talk about still feeling young, didn't it mean that something had broken?" (120). After her husband's death, she is called the "Merry Widow," a woman "after the young ones" (148, 146). Yet all she intends to do is to teach younger men some sophistication.

By the end of the novel, these very young men have lost touch with Marian Forrester, except through the gossip that two men exchange about her. She is living on a ranch in Argentina, remarried to a British husband whose previous wives included a Brazilian woman. Once again, Atherton's reference to the "equatorial sisterhood" comes into play: these Brazilian women are the sexual standard against which U.S. women are compared. Deep in their nostalgic cups, her former male acquaintances romanticize her. Her sexuality is not irrelevant for it still maintains some sort of nostalgic power over them. But she is not irrelevant, even in aging, to their sexual desires; she is an enigma to them.

Whatever narrative of decline—sexual or national—was in place by the 1920s, Cather's *A Lost Lady* protests it. Living in South America, where she wears plenty of makeup, "like most of the women down there," and dyes her hair black, Marian Forrester is married to "the kindest of husbands" (165). While she had " 'pretty well gone to pieces' " before she left Sweet Water after the death of her husband and her affair with Ivy Peters, life in South America revitalizes her. Cather suggests that women don't age "down there," and whether this is her crude joke, the reference to South America or to female genitalia is telling. Whether through the remarriage or the new South American geography, "the lost lady" is no longer beyond the pale of sexuality. Challenging the prescriptions of her time, Cather's suggestion is that age doesn't change Marian Forrester much.

Her life after Sweet Water does alter her future. Some people speculate that Marian Forrester finally made it out West, to California, in order to "see whether [she] had anything left worth saving." Yet Niel sees her new marriage differently: that her new husband takes care of her and that her newfound comfort has little or nothing to do with her own definition. In any case, Cather suggests that middle-aged women must leave the country in order to pursue any vestige of sexual power, just as Atherton's Mary Zattiany must go to Austria to regain hers. Once Marian is in South America, she is no longer lost but revitalized.

Niel has no way to make sense of Marian Forrester's adultery, no symbolic frame for it except as a literal act of betrayal of her husband and his friends, insofar as he cannot recognize her desire except as it is symbolized through her marriage to Captain Forrester. Nor does Niel have language to articulate what that desire might mean. U.S. culture may have understood youthful sexuality as instinctual, perhaps even unself-conscious; what it could not understand, as Atherton's and Cather's novels show, was a middle-aged woman's drive for sexual fulfillment. By the 1920s, as Pamela Haag argues, "the unconscious" and "instinct" "emerged as keywords for understanding and categorizing sexuality" ("'Real Thing'" 557). But middle-aged women who sought sexual partners belied conventional wisdom and even newfound Freudian theories. Haag explains, "Whereas popular psychoanalytic theories tended to affirm the male subject's self-possession, assuming an alliance between his conscious action and unconscious instincts, the same theories when applied to female subjects tended to replicate and exaggerate their *lack* of self-possession—a woman's alienation from sexual desires claimed by an internally alien unconscious" (557; Haag's emphasis). In large part, Atherton's and Cather's novels come to terms with their heroines' refusal of sexual alienation, even at the cost of social alienation and ostracism. Once again, we return to the idea of fantasy, a term that Fleissner effectively glosses as "conceived not as another word for sentimentalism, but as an open-ended orientation toward the future that sentimental realism finds itself wholly unable to conceive" (191). In these terms, fantasy refers to the possibility of women finding work or self-expression as a "middle ground *between* abject need and mere frivolous desire" (191; Fleissner's emphasis), confined either to domesticity or to the consumerism that marked therapeutic culture. For me, however, these fantasies are about different sexual possibilities and the invention of a language that might express them. This is not some fantasy of linguistic fulfillment but one about the satisfactions of a female sexual imagination, a sexual imaginary.

As the next chapter will show, some American women writers such as Austin, Wharton, and Parker capitalized on these fantasies of sexual power. This sex power emerged not from class or age but from women's intentional use of sexuality: what they could get from a self-conscious deployment of "sex magnetism" or attraction. Sometimes the cost of such sex power is self-alienation, since self-expression and sex expression prove—for Stowe and Wharton—to be antithetical. So far, too, women writers discuss sexuality as a natural impulse, or even compulsion (as Fleissner notes), but not an act of will. While writers such as Gilman suggested that women needed to refrain from their impulsive sexual acts for the good of the race, other writers seemed to suggest that women needed to will themselves into sex power. What was to happen if women could *will* themselves into sexual control? A new generation of American women writers thought of sex as a conscious power, not an unconscious drive or impulse. Sex was not a compulsion so much as it was a resistance to overwhelming male control. As such, sex expression could be harnessed for women's independence.

Unlike earlier generations of religious women who believed that "a complex negation of the sexual self" would lead to increased spiritual and social power (Thurman 72), no such negation would be widespread or generally acceptable. Instead, many women saw the equation of sex with social power, a power that only needed fine-tuning in order to benefit most women universally, without race or ethnic, class or age distinctions. As it happens, the lines of sexual normativity broke down between the ugly and the beautiful, and then the young and the middle-aged, as well as between white normative sex and racialized otherness. And, Bruce Burgett argues, "the pressing historical question is not how 'sex' and 'race' have intersected in various historical conjunctures, but how, to what ends, and in what contexts we have come to think of the 'two' as separable in the first place" ("Mormon Question" 94). How, then, did sex power come to be the domain of white/beautiful young women—and not a promising liberation available to all women?

#

CHAPTER FOUR

POWER

Why did American women writers like Louisa May Alcott, Harriet Beecher Stowe, Mary Austin, Edith Wharton, and Dorothy Parker start imagining sex as power? Ugliness and beauty, youth and age were once considered determining factors of sexuality, but now I turn to the question of how women writers imagined sex as their own power. These writers explored sex power as an implicit historical argument about their choice of sexuality. As I have been arguing, sex power emerged out of sentimental culture's preoccupation with self-expression, sometimes as sentiment's corollary but more often as its antithesis. In this chapter, I explore how some women writers recuperated or repudiated sex power —and why they did so. For instance, Edith Wharton, one of the most vocal of sex power's detractors, distrusted sex expression as alienating, while one of the most pro-sex writers of the 1910s and 1920s, Mary Austin, was also anxious about women's uses of sexuality. Wharton's and

Austin's characters reject their moral repugnance to sexuality and accept their psychological ambivalence about sex expression. Given their doubts, sex power became a mode of retrenchment from social change and liberation.[1]

This "modern love," as critics like Nina Miller define it, was the new dispensation for women to seek sexual pleasure. As Ann Douglas writes, sex became "It," which was "a pop version of Freud's id, an undefinable voltage of openly sexual energy"—what the age called sex power (*Terrible Honesty* 47). Yet how was this voltage to be channeled, given the demands of the social world? The question of sex power is much more settled for Miller, who argues that "modern love" was predicated on gender inequality, an assumption that heterosexual relations were "permanently and intrinsically flawed." This recognition of heterosexual inequality led to "cynical detachment" from love, even as modern love fictions treated "readers as sophisticates" and involved them in a complex irony (109). Miller describes this posturing as an urbane "response to a newly problematized heterosexuality" (110), by which she means that more and more women writers took it upon themselves to explain love as an ironic force rather than a romantic ideal. For Miller, these writers—including Dorothy Parker—write from an "*irony of embeddedness*" (245; Miller's emphasis), which did not give them an escape from or an end to the complex tensions of modern life.

Part of this embeddedness meant that women writers like Austin, Wharton, and Parker struggled with the effects of sex power and the new uses of it as part of women's cultural agency. Not surprisingly, this power to choose sexuality came hand in hand with the rise of birth control and the power to choose contraception. The debates about sex power led to a new ethical dilemma for women writers, one dependent upon the ideas of choice and consent.

As I will show, Parker, for one, offers a bitter sentimentalization of sexuality in stories like "Big Blonde" (1929), but that sentimentalization was meant to be taken with a wink. Another response was Anita Loos's *Gentlemen Prefer Blondes* (1925), whose humor—too broad to be accompanied by a wink—capitalized on the heroine's willingness to talk about sex without ever seeming to understand its consequences. Such urbane writers are the memorable few; as a rule, American women writers had to address the inequality of modern love by defining sex power rather than exploiting the confusion about what made "It" so powerful. Miller and Douglas notwithstanding, it may be that we have written literary history significantly wrong. Reading the times through their new focus on sexual ambivalence offers a new history that gives us a deeply divided sexual culture.

Dorothy Parker's bemused acceptance reflects the mark of an upper-class sexuality, perhaps most vividly purveyed in magazines like *Bookman*, *Vanity Fair*, or even the *New Yorker*, insofar as irony did not circulate generally in the middle and working classes. While Sharon Ullman in *Sex Seen* and Helen Horowitz in *Rereading Sex* have surveyed the crucial prehistory of the transformation of private into public heterosexuality at the turn of the century, too many stereotypes about New Women, flappers, and the Jazz Age still distort our understanding of how American women writers came to distinguish between sex expression and sex power. As Ullman explains, "The inclusion of desire into female identity, a central focus of the heterosexual vision, was not a triumphant process." The subjects of Ullman's historical study, she recounts, "did not wake up one morning and march through the streets, ushering in a world of sexual 'liberation' " (43). While elites might have triumphed over their newfound sex expression, it is unclear how most women lived their sexuality; sexual liberation was always a relative measure of social equality, but it does not speak to how women embraced sex expression as their own power.

In fact, at the end of the second decade of the twentieth century, well-known authors Edith Wharton and E. M. Hull, author of *The Sheik* (1919), directly confronted the issue in their novels. Instead of being a source of celebration or liberation, sex power remained a problem for most middle-class and working women. As much as these women would soon be supposed to embrace their heralded sexuality, a generation of American women writers had already helped to teach them how *not to hate* sexual power and sex expression. By the 1910s, Wharton already represented what was gradually becoming the view of an older generation: that sexual freedom subjugated more than it liberated. Through her heroines, Wharton expressed her own uncertainty about how women were to feel about and use the newfound sexuality they were purported to wield. Wharton's women disdain their sexuality because they come to understand its power as illusory. This sort of antipathy was characteristic of the decade. Even in the best-selling romance of 1919, E. M. Hull's *The Sheik*, the heroine's beauty vexes her because it makes some men crazy for her, but not the Sheik, the only man she wants: "She had never been proud of her own beauty; she had lived with it always and it had seemed to her a thing of no consequence, and now that it had failed to arouse the love she wanted in [Sheik] Ahmed Ben Hassan she almost hated it" (154–55). It seems that sex power cannot be trusted because women cannot control its effects or consequences. Despite this ambivalence, the heroines in Wharton and Hull move—however slightly —from hatred to "almost" hatred of their sexual power. It is clear from these popular novels that rather than being of "no consequence," youth and beauty empowered women, though they might distrust the effects of that empowerment.

Consider Joseph Hergesheimer's best seller of 1919, *Linda Condon*, which treats the impressions of the mother's sexuality upon the daughter. Horrified that she has become "middle aged," most notably after receiving a bad permanent wave, Linda's mother marries a Jew, thus corroborating the mother's decline and scandalizing the daughter. Equally horrified, the daughter decides never to accept middle age and, thus, never to love. Because of her mother's rantings against men and her subsequent capitulation to them, Linda grows up detached and unable to conjoin love and marriage. To her death, she remains beautiful but sexless: there is no possibility "which might give her, for a day, what even her mother had plentifully experienced—the igniting exultation of the body" (282). The daughter's "famous coldness" is her defense against the "change . . . in women themselves" (286), a transformation that allowed women to accept as fact, "in unequivocal scientific terms," what Linda Condon had considered "a nameless attribute of women, or, if anything more exact, the power of their charm over men" (287). The novel documents the daughter's fear of "modern love," an anxiety that leaves her without feelings and without a language of desire. It gives voice to the generational transformation in sex expression. What was once sex power for the mother becomes sex anxiety for the daughter.[2]

The difficult transition from hating sex power to welcoming it became the subject of a host of American women's novels, many of which
dealt with sexuality only indirectly. On the one hand, some articulated
what had heretofore remained inchoate in working women's sexuality;
others depicted a fantasy of black women's sexual power; still others
rejected sexuality for white middle-class women altogether. Sex power
was even more complex when considered in light of women's work since
working women had greater access to sex in the workplace. On the other
hand, middle-class women were defined by their association with domesticity. How were middle-class women to learn about sexuality at
home? Did sex power make these women ever more eager to enter the
workforce? When did sex power come to equal social power?

From Harriet Beecher Stowe to Dorothy Parker, women writers contemplated the value of sex power and introduced their worries about its
price, especially its emotional costs and how it could be co-opted as a
traditional and harmful pattern of women's subservience. Many men,
they argued, still had the desire to interpret sex expression in old regressive ways, regardless of how clarifying women wanted modern sexuality
to be.[3] Yet many women writers used sexual power to generate a language (including terms such as "It," "desire," "varietism," "magnetism")
as a conscious strategy for achieving their ends in the world. Not reform
but reformulation, much of this new writing was a struggle to redefine
"good women" as sexualized beings and to divorce sexual agency from
its previous associations with prostitution. Some women writers—like
Edna Ferber and Kathleen Norris—worried that women could not control the effects of sex power: in their works, characters exert sex power,
but readers could still interpret sex expression according to well-worn
cultural grooves, usually associated with bad women and prostitution or
sexual disgust (which marks the boundary of what was considered sexual normalcy or health). In this light, many American women writers
examined sexuality with a healthy dose of ambivalence, acknowledging
the emergence of sex power as a significant new manifestation of personality and later style. But they debated its ethics in novel after novel.

Like Stowe, Louisa May Alcott was one of the first of a new generation of U.S. women writers to explore the ethical dimensions of women's

use of sex power—variously termed "attraction," "magnetism," "chemistry," "It"—as a resource against male narcissism and what Alcott calls "insolence" (238). Challenging received sexual norms and believing in sexual liberation both require overcoming sexual disgust, along with accepting the potential failures of intimacy. Women had analyzed sex power before but had always associated it with prostitution, seduction, evil; now they sought a way to appropriate it and distinguish it from disgust. Yet once that disgust was overcome, women writers did not find it any easier to negotiate the expectations of how they were supposed to perform.

What would respectable sex power be?

To answer this question, I examine the moment when women writers conceived of the novelty of sex consciousness and the ambivalence with which these writers came to terms with that new female sexual openness. As we will see, Austin committed herself to sex power as a form of genius. Once considered a form of "liberation," sex power became a new envisioning of women's sexual labor; women achieved sex power through a conscious set of exchanges and manipulations of desire, what Austin calls "sex consciousness."

SEX POWER AS SEXED LANGUAGE

Angela Heywood's unbridled enthusiasm for candid sex language begins with a definition of sex power. Married to a free-love reformer, Angela Fiducia Tilton Heywood maintained that sexual frankness would lead to sexual equality.[4] Describing herself as "the product of a sunny and beautiful life, well worthy of examination if ye would know a good woman," she called for for a new recognition of women's sexual expression ("Grace and Use of Sex Life" 3). Eschewing sexual disgust as a form of dishonesty, Heywood advocated a linguistic sexual openness. Until Heywood, women reformers had often separated sex and power; after Heywood, sex and power would be conjoined.

Publishing in the 1880s and 1890s in *The Word*, Ezra and Angela Heywood defined "sex power" as the force that results when the truth of sex is revealed through "the Human Crotch Fact" ("Human Sex-Power"

3). Denouncing mere "penis-action" as "irresponsible," Heywood hopes that sex power will be available to men and women alike: "In creative sex-power resides the *central matter-of-fact* of social endeavor. It is insipid *falsehood* for woman to pretend to man that the sex-fact is not as much to her, as it is to him; of the confluent contracting parties she is an equal unit, able to give, as to receive, good" ("Sex Service" 2; Heywood's emphasis). Women need only have the courage to speak about the "vibrating Womb unduly craving the natural offices of our Savior, the Penis" ("Woman's View of It").

Heywood recognizes the inextricability of sexuality and female financial independence. "Nature, ever exactly just and beneficently retributive, visits on children and children's children the sins of restrictive irrationalism; lecherous, treacherous irresponsibility in men, acquiescing, dead-level servility in women, frightful prevalence of secret vice in minors and adults of both sexes—loveless homes, syphilis, gonorrhoea, clap, pox, idiotic sterility, and premature death are ghastly fruit of inattention to Sex-Laws of Life I inculcate" ("Penis Literature" 2). As Caroline Levander argues (43), Heywood maintained that women must seize the language of sexuality and make it their own in order to avoid "*heistic usurpation and sheistic-slave disease*" attending the unnatural division of the sexes ("Ethics of Sexuality"; Heywood's emphasis). "She-dudes and he-dunces think they can afford to neglect" such social revolution, Heywood claims, and she foments this revolution herself in "Creative Dualism—Motherhood":

> Woman now is in the van of intuitive thought, she now stands on the threshold of the mechanical world asking better tools, better skill in making and *using* tools, the penis-womb-power of human beings. Man's irreverence, his crudity, sex-wise, is not manly; woman in frenzy would run her womb through with a sword if she could think that extant, legalized "morality" was man's ultimatum; he now blushes at mention of sex-questions; when wiser he will blush that he ever blushed in the presence of these pregnantly interesting themes. The wholesome, timely odor of barns precedes milk in its sweetness, butter in its neatness; so generative, excrementive experience precedes the flower of life in human beings. Walking this eth-

ical street between the spiritual and the mundane who is unworthy
to say "I came here through the personifying end of man's penis";
typically God has us not only on the hip but in our generative-sex
power. (3; Heywood's emphasis)

Passion, along with the urge for equality and explicitness, fuels this
generative-sex power. Revitalizing sex language would lead, as Jesse
Battan argues about Heywood's intentions, to a rejuvenated American
sexual culture.

Yet the very language that Angela Heywood uses to extol the virtues
of "sex-power" can be turned against it: as she explains, "sex-power
rightly used is beneficently serviceable; what one lacks another supplies;
minus here is plus there" ("Marriage Moloch"). "Sex-power" eventually
becomes "service"—a renewed form of women's work devoted to cultural change, far from the kind of sexual democracy she envisioned.
"Sex-Love" and "Sex-Mutualism" are her terms; by the 1890s, those
terms are transformed into the more colloquial "sex magnetism" and
"sexual attraction," a new form of the gender division by which women
do the cultural work of sexuality—making the terms of intimacy and
providing physical solace to a new generation of men.

Concerns about finding sex power and channeling it into a career or a
passion dominated much of women's writing about sexuality. As the
culture increasingly emphasized self-fulfillment rather than mutual intimacy, sex power seemed like a good investment of energy. Greater
frankness about sexual expression did not lead inevitably to a culture in
which intersubjectivity was possible or mutual fulfillment was inevitable.
Rather, as Wharton suggested, sex expression often resulted in one
individual serving another. So for Wharton, sex expression was about the
survival of the "couple" when sex power was wielded by one member for
the self-fulfillment of the other. Women's sex power resulted from the
merging of women's power to choose (based on commodity consumption) with men's entitlement, an arrangement that seemed to create a
new service economy based on sex and romance. With this economy,
men were entitled to sexual pleasure, while women had the right to use
sex power to negotiate for social freedoms. One source of women writers'

ambivalence turned on how much sex power was compulsory (men demanded it of women) and how much it revealed women's own exhilaration (women's greater consciousness of female sexuality).

Mary Austin did not assume that sex power would necessarily equal personal or self-fulfillment; rather, as an exercise of choice or even self-advancement, it proved to be a great literary strategy and a force for change. Sex power is always a means of achieving an end; but by the beginning of the twentieth century, U.S. consumer culture emphasized women's "psychological" power, a manifestation of their inner selves that was not a social or economic power. The new realm of sex power is intimacy; its mode is relational. As cultural wisdom (or mythology) goes, women use power to attach themselves, while men use power to individuate. Sex power does not necessarily concern change or achieving equality, but it does offer a certain leverage for women to use in negotiating modern sexual exchanges.

For writers like Heywood and Wharton, sex power became another way for women to tap into their interiority in order to work toward and advance sexual equality. Sex power did not revolutionize social relations, but it did serve effectively to lend elements of consumerism—for better or worse—to heterosexual romance. Sex power evades the question of social power and redirects it to the quantity of "It"—magnetism, attraction, desire, even antagonism—that a woman can generate to attract a partner. It also assumes that women have a reservoir upon which to draw and from which to balance sex and power; in this way, a female's sense of personal pleasure cannot be greater than her desire for power. Hers is a power emerging from her sense of relational dynamics; she is rewarded for these sexual qualities, but with what? This is the question —whether sex power is voluntary or a coerced practice—informing the fictions I discuss below.

LIKING SEX POWER

After the Civil War, women's investments in sex power were closely linked to the much-documented turn from women as producers to women as consumers. Harriet Beecher Stowe especially was concerned about how the drive for "things" would affect women's desire for sex. Would consuming power contribute to a desire for other powers, namely sex power? In her *Pink and White Tyranny* (1871), Stowe posits women's beauty as a tool for control over husbands and lovers, but not as women's desire for their own sexuality. The idea of sex power emerges from a general confusion about how women could best express themselves, whether through the secondary narcissism of devotion to family or the primary narcissism of self-expression. The power of saying yes to sexuality took a great deal longer for American women writers to establish.

Pink and White Tyranny features Lillie Ellis Seymour, an antisentimental woman who devotes herself to bad French romances and turning her husband's small-town mansion into a fashionable showplace. With her desires for clothing, Newport society, and redoing his house, not to mention her insistence that he neglect his factory charities, she comes close to ruining John Seymour's business. Only on her deathbed does she repent and acknowledge her use of sex power on her husband to get the goods she wanted. She first lies about her age, claiming to be an ingenue of twenty rather than twenty-seven. Yet Stowe celebrates middle-age power, that venerable deference and respectability which comes with matronliness.

In Stowe's novel, sex power serves as a warning. John attempts to rein Lillie in once he "heard and overheard much that made him uneasy. He heard her admired as a 'bully' girl, a 'fast one'" (123). Such talk of "fastness," let alone "bullyness," undermines his sense of his wife's innocence. Lillie finds pleasure, her husband discovers, in "smoking" and "painting." Painting is a form of self-expression, which is supposed to take place in the home or, more centrally, *as* the home. Lillie's desires run counter to the sentimental attachment to things that Lori Merish argues characterizes Stowe's materialism. As Merish writes, "Like Hawthorne— and like Warner and Cummins—Stowe designates the interior domestic space as the space of human fulfillment and the satisfactions of intimacy" (160). John's ideal of such intimacy is shattered by his effort to fulfill Lillie's adamant wish to be in Newport society. For Stowe, women's feelings are bound up with the things they nourish within themselves and tend to in the home, but Lillie forms no attachment there. Instead, she substitutes a sensational publicity in which her actions—smoking, painting, holding court—become sex expressions, desires turned outward rather than symbolic or domestic virtues.

Smoking and painting are symbolic codes for Lillie's sex power. These are desublimated acts, modes of action no longer harnessed to the home or its decoration. Rather, smoking is an eminently social act for Lillie, just as painting is a less sublimated desire for expression than house decorating. As she explains to her mentor and friend, Mrs. Follingsbee, " 'If a woman falls in love herself, there's an end of her power' " (168). The trick is to find " 'a man you can get any thing in the world out of' " (169). A woman's power, then, comes from purchasing and exchange, not from reciprocal intimacy. But sex expression is also about controlling a man's feelings: "The only way was to keep him as uncomfortable as possible without really breaking her power over him" (206). Her sex power has to be flexible. "The difference between Lillie in good humor and Lillie in bad humor was a thing which John soon learned to appreciate as one of the most powerful forces in his life" (218). Here, following Lauren Berlant's dictum in *Queen of America* that "sexuality is the modern form of self-intelligibility" (17), I am showing how sexuality became a "force" and, therefore, became central to Stowe's dismissal of sex power as a failure to develop a moral identity. For Stowe, Lillie's sexual identity negates her moral one.

This realm of sexual display in Newport is a creation of Lillie's own sexual fantasy, by which she gets to revel in her sex power. Her husband is forced to bring her home, if only to domesticate that sex power. As Stowe's narrator moralizes, "There comes a time after marriage, when a husband, if he be any thing of a man, has something else to do than make direct love to his wife. He cannot be on duty at all hours to fan her, and shawl her, and admire her. His love must express itself through other channels. He must be a full man for her sake; and, as a man, must go forth to a whole world of interests that takes him from her. Now what in this case shall a woman do, whose only life lies in petting and adoration and display?" (110). Stowe forgoes sex power for men, claiming "other channels" as their main interests.

But if he's not there to see it, does she have any sex power? She moves her venue to Newport in order to fulfill her "longing" and to demonstrate her "prestige" as "a rich young married lady." "Had she not jewels and gems to show?" (111). In one of Stowe's famous direct addresses, she asks the reader: "Now, dear friends, don't think Lillie a pirate, or a conspirator, or a wolf-in-sheep's-clothing, or any thing else but what she was,—a pretty little, selfish woman; undeveloped in her conscience and affections, and strong in her instincts and perceptions; in a blind way using what means were most in her line to carry her purposes" (110). To get what she wants, Lillie uses what Stowe indirectly names her sex power—"what means were most in her line." In turn, John must try to keep her sexual displays and sexual power under control, even as his own expression takes "other channels." The heroine has no other channels for her expression except display, while John finds an outlet for his self-expression in work and charity, in perpetuating his family's good name and in upholding its standing. By default, her outlet is sex expression, which she must abandon if she is forced to return home from Newport. Stowe's is one of the first sentimental texts about privatizing sexuality, and it details the effects of sentiment on women's sexual fantasies. John's own sentimental fantasies of charity and domesticity take precedence over his wife's cosmopolitan ones.

Lillie Ellis personifies American narcissism played out through sex power. She wants to go to Newport—and later to Manhattan—in order to be seen, to exercise her ego and power over men. There is no end in sight for these occasions, nor does she seem to want a conclusion. In fact, she backs away from someone who shows serious interest in her as a potential sex partner. What's important here is that her sexuality is public, not a privately expressed or an intimately performed act or set of practices. She finds her sexual satisfaction outside of the home, in a decided move away from domesticity and, more important, domestic interiority. In this way, sex expression quickly becomes imagined as woman's interiority, where sex is figured as the corollary performance of the inner life that, as we will see, so occupied writers like Austin and Wharton.[5]

Louisa May Alcott's notably feminist story of 1866, "Behind a Mask: or, A Woman's Power," not only prefigures Stowe's moral disgust but also posits a more self-conscious, self-reflexive sex power. In it, Jean Muir—an old maid of thirty—pretends to be a young governess of nineteen in order to seduce the master of the house, Gerald Coventry. Alcott describes sex power as follows: "In that moment Coventry experienced another new sensation. Many women had smiled on him, but he had remained heart-whole, cool, and careless, quite unconscious of the power which a woman possesses and knows how to use, for the weal or woe of man. Now, as he knelt there with a soft arm about him, a slender waist yielding to his touch, and a maiden heart throbbing against his cheek, for the first time in his life he felt the indescribable spell of womanhood" (394–95). The question for Alcott's women is this: How can women bring to consciousness that which remains "unconscious" in a man? It is not just that women have power and can use it at will. They must make men go from unconscious recognition to conscious response. Thus, men's self-fulfillment remains buried, while women's fulfillment is all self-conscious, all motivated by an explicit desire.

Moreover, women's sex power here is "indescribable," beyond men's description; it is a form of unknown or unspoken language all its own like Coventry's unconscious. Gerald reads one of Jean's letters in which she refuses another man's offer of love and marriage. In doing so, he recognizes her ability to express passion, a sex expression seemingly unavailable to him: "[Jean's letter] was evidently an answer to a passionate appeal from the young lover, and was written with consummate skill. As he read, Gerald could not help thinking, If this girl writes in this way to a man whom she does *not* love, with what a world of power and passion would she write to one whom she *did* love" (404). Gerald imagines his own self-fulfillment in the will to submit to Jean's power, her power to express the sexuality that was previously indescribable, but also unconscious, for him. In other words, Jean teaches him the sensations by which he can translate unconscious impulses into conscious desire. And she is forced to erase the sexual labor she does even as she performs it. For Alcott, the unconscious is also at odds with instinct: Gerald expresses his unconscious love for Jean even though his instincts warn him against her.

The recognition of women's sex power increased the general anxiety about the authenticity of sex expression: How much was sexual attraction an effect of a will to power, and how much an effect of authentic or "true" desire for intimacy? That sex power could be feigned—a mask for power—led to the growing sense that desire could deceive and that both men and women had to guard against its ill uses.

LOVING SEX POWER

As Mary Austin describes it in her 1912 novel, *A Woman of Genius*, "sex attraction" occurs when a woman becomes conscious of her sexual desire and imagines the stirrings of "the wings of power" (164). Austin's novel is told as an autobiography of Olivia Lattimore and documents a woman's "obligatory" marriage and her refusal to let it tie her down to a conventional life as a housewife in a small midwestern town (51). Instead, she leaves her husband for months at a time in order to pursue an acting career; after his death, she struggles to fulfill her acting talent in the midst of her grief and finds that gift in sex expression.[6] The novel also depicts Austin's version of how women "stumble on the grown-up consciousness of sex," but without mature judgment of it (51).

As a teen, Olivia has one passionate encounter that gives her a feeling of "power." Throughout her life, she imaginatively reconstructs this event, a kiss that—in recollection—inspires her as "a woman of genius" on the stage. In contemplating this sex power, the heroine Olivia walks the streets of Chicago trying to isolate and recapture the source of her sexual excitement: "I would come back from these excursions beginning to faint with the day's heat, to wear through the afternoon with books and long drowses, and then in the cool of the evening it would call me again, and I would seek It until late at night, sometimes in the lit streets, fetid with the day's smells, sometimes on a roof garden or at a park concert, where the lights, the gayety, and the music served merely as a drug to my outer sense, which went on busily at its absorbing quest" (165). Perhaps what makes it difficult to analyze sex power in U.S. women's writing can be discerned in Austin's tendency to dodge naming "It." For writers such as Austin, the very elusiveness of this power also promised the expansion of roles possible for women. Sex, as Austin's heroine here experiences it, is an attempt at self-expansion and self-development; in this sense, self-expression and sex expression are one in the same.

Austin addressed several key questions about "sex consciousness" (5), transforming sex expression from the biological to the social. Was sex an instinct or a consciousness, and if a consciousness, how self-conscious would women become about their own sexuality? If sex was a conscious choice, then women could perform it as a kind of power. If sexuality was a biological urge and women lost power by acting upon it and losing control, then it was in their best interests to eschew the biological idea about sexuality for the self-conscious strategizing about how to use sex power (see Haag, *Consent* 138). In order to create a literature of sex consciousness, Austin uses metaphors of the body and the exchange of bodily fluids in sexual congress. The answers to these questions necessitated Austin's creation of a new sexual style, figured through a bodily materialism located in her heroine's new awareness of sex expression.

The novel vacillates between the first person and the third person, sometimes in the form of an autobiography, less often as a report by an omniscient narrator about the success of an actress. Key to the development of sex consciousness in her heroine is the movement between the "I" and the character "Olivia." Does one move from innocence to knowledge, or is this exactly what Austin calls into question by shifting between the first person and the third? Here is one of the first examples in the novel: "The chief difference between Pauline and me had been that she had lived all her life, so to speak, at home; nothing exigent to her social order had ever found her 'out'; but Olivia seemed always to be at the top of the house or somewhere in the back garden, to whom the normal occasions presented themselves as a succession of cards under the door" (70).

Here an autobiographical account suddenly switches to the third person. Or more telling, the following passage captures just how split the narrative voice is: "My baby was born within ten months of my marriage and most of that time I was wretchedly, depressingly ill. All my memories of my early married life are of Olivia, in the mornings still with frost, cowering away from the kitchen sights and smells, or gasping up out of ingulfing nausea to sit out the duty calls of the leading ladies of Higgleston in the cold, disordered house. . . . With Olivia in a wrapper, half hysterical with weakness—all the young wife's dreams gone awry!" (77). Olivia sees herself as though from the outside, in contrast to her inner self. It is the housewife who is acting, while the actress lives out her interiority on the stage. Austin thus makes evident the split between the personal self and the social self, a split that leads to the development of the third self: the sexual self, neither entirely private nor entirely social. If sexuality was becoming increasingly "personal" rather than social, Austin drives a wedge between these ideas by suggesting a third self, though not a third sex.[7]

Austin's unconventional novel tells the story of the rise of Olivia Lattimore's acting career. Born in a midwestern town, she marries an unimaginative local boy and attempts to lead a traditional life with him. Their child is born prematurely a mere ten months after their wedding and dies some eight months later. The deaths of her child and subsequently her husband compel Olivia to find other reasons to live than conventional marriage. A chance to act gives Olivia the courage to go on the stage, and then on the road, with an acting company. She tries her luck in Chicago but nearly starves before a Jewish agent finances her career and her New York debut. Polatkin's investments in her acting begin with a contract that contrasts with Olivia's ideal of a "pure" relationship, where sexuality would not be subject to exchange but simply spontaneous. She comes to respect Polatkin insofar as he lives up to his side of their contract, more imaginatively than her dead husband had. He "orders her corsets" and sizes up her figure, a symbolic act of assessment that characterizes the sexual-economic terms of their bond as well as Austin's stereotypical depiction of the interests of a Jewish investor.

Acting was a suspect profession because it suggested that women's emotions could be feigned, just as their self-commodification onstage might be a prelude to sexual commodification.[8] Austin dispels this stereotype by insisting that Olivia is a "good woman." All sorts of assumptions about her sexual nature are bandied about, and her husband dies defending her honor against the gossip he hears about her at a local men's club. As Betsy Klimasmith argues, "the figure of the actress allegorizes capitalism's dangers" when Olivia acts as a form of "self expression" (130, 131). Rather than self-expression, I would argue, Olivia Lattimore's acting represents a transitional move to her sex expression, bolstered by the access that the stage gives her to various men who represent the spectrum of traditional to unconventional masculinity. While she befriends fellow actress Sarah, Olivia recognizes her own ascendancy, even as Sarah recognizes the limits of her acting powers. By the end of the novel, Sarah chooses heterosexuality and motherhood, while Olivia eschews another conventional marriage for life on the stage. Given the weightedness of pleasure toward men in sexual exchanges, as Austin's heroine figures out, pleasure is to be found more on the stage and in public than in any relation based on private intimacy.

Thus, in confronting the myth of intimacy as social equality, Austin's novel assesses the contemporaneous status of women's sex power against the social ideal of women's sexual innocence. During the week of her wedding, the heroine asks her mother for information about the wedding night; horrified and vexed, her mother responds with fear: "Almost before the question was out I saw the expression of offended shock come over my mother's reminiscent softness, the nearly animal rage of terror with which the unknown, the unaccustomed, assailed her." Eventually, her mother apologizes and confesses, "'I can't help you. I don't know. . . . I never knew myself'" (75).

Crucial to Austin's understanding of sex power is her challenge to the culture's disgust—or plain ignorance—about the sexual act. Olivia overcomes her mother's revulsion and her own internalized resistance to sexuality. In order for her heroine to tap into sex power for acting (which Austin celebrates over sex as survival), she must also overcome the internalized disgust over what sexuality signifies to her peers. When Olivia sees her stage manager leaving a colleague's room at one in the morning, she first realizes that some actresses use their sexuality to secure parts. Sickened, she takes to bed in a fit of moral paralysis after what she describes as her "first actual contact with sin of any sort" (112). More to the point, she realizes that others in the company have suspected her of having an affair with the manager: "I lay on the bed and shuddered with dry sobs; other times I lay still, awake and blazing"

(112). Her friend Sarah counsels her to "'take no notice. It is not that these things are so much worse with actors, but it is more difficult to keep them covered up. You must know that a great many people do such things'" (113). Olivia once assumed only "wicked" people did them, not people she liked. Yet she moves beyond this ambivalence and anxiety.

Overcome by her realization of the stage's different morality, Olivia leaves the company and returns home. She learns from one of her colleagues that sex is the payment for star treatment: "In Cecelia's opinion this was the quintessence of art, to attract males and keep them dangling, and to eke out her personal adornment by gifts which she managed to extract from her admirers without having yet paid the inestimable price for them. Married woman as I was, I was too countrified to understand that inevitably she must finally pay it" (95). In Cecelia's own words, "'You gotta get a hold of some rich guy and freeze to him'" (156). Conventional modes of sexual exchange and barter do not work for Austin's heroine. Instead, her gift for acting leads her on a quest to determine another metaphor for sexuality besides "freezing."

But using sex power is not just saying yes to sex. Austin was concerned that sex might mean subjugation. As her heroine explains, "Depend upon it, the subjugation of woman will be found finally to rest in the attempt visibly to establish, what the woman herself concurs in, the inward conviction of possession" (240). For Olivia, the derepression of female sexuality—unmooring it from its association with freezing and frigidity—starts with dissociating from this "inward conviction of possession" by men. She must be sure that sex is mutual, more than giving pleasure as payment for her survival or career. This exchange does not count, according to Austin, as sex power; it counts as contract. "True love" must be more than a contract, beyond the mystification of modern liberalism. While Olivia falls in love, she does not consent to the social ideal of love as a fulfillment of her individual needs. She still needs work. She refuses to equate her private self with her sexual self, a transformation in modern intimacy that was demonstrated throughout the early decades of the twentieth century. Austin thus opposed sexuality as conscious choice with the irrationality and all-consuming tendencies of "true love." True love was a cover story for the willingness to subsume the self in some dreamworld of longing and belonging, what Austin calls the "inward conviction of possession."

Relying on her "gift" of genius, Olivia goes far in her acting career. After many years, she meets again the first man who kissed her, Helmeth Garrett, now a widower raising two young daughters. They fall immediately in love, but just as he cannot give up his architecture and mining ventures in Mexico, she won't give up her acting career: "And now you know what I meant when I said in the beginning that the social ideal, in which I was bred, is the villain of my plot" (266). While she manages to keep her acting gift—which she distinguishes from sexual power—and her sexual interests separate, refusing to see the interanimation of libidinal power and acting talent, she cannot attain the "social ideal" of marriage. The height of Olivia's acting powers eventually coincides with the intensity of her love affair with the man who first ignited her passion when she was a teenager.

By the end, they give up on each other, and Olivia contemplates marriage to another man, the playwright with whom she has been friends for the duration of her career. It is a career marriage for them both, based on mutual comfort and self-knowledge, not on passion or sex. From the playwright, she learns how sexuality plays the muse. Jerry McDermott cannot write unless he is "interested"; that is, unless he has a sexual muse or is having an affair with one of his actresses. In short, sexual tension fuels his creative genius, allowing him to write passionate plays and earn success on the stage. Finally, however, it is Olivia's younger sister Effie who sustains her, seeing in her stage success a model for "'women everywhere getting courage to live lives of their own'" (261). Olivia stumbles into a suffrage parade, a symbol of the very social experiment her choice of career over marriage comes to represent, a parade that measures the equivalent progress of Olivia's internal independence.

A Woman of Genius marks a transition from the old way of seeing sex power—as a dangerous and instinctive mode of women's actions in the world—to the new way of seeing sex power as instrumental in attaining women's possibilities. Austin shows the heroine's transition from seeing sexuality as a sin or moral blight to seeing it as a force for vitalizing passion; eventually, Olivia Lattimore Bettersworth becomes a famous tragedian who employs her sex experience to increase her emotional range on the stage. Yet Austin's heroine does not move from innocence or ignorance to awareness only to invest in a new companionate or intimate ideal. Her sexuality remains self-focused insofar as Austin refuses the conventional move from sex to heterosexual exclusivity, and Olivia refuses intimacy when it will cost her the career she has nurtured ever since her baby died. Rather, the novelist focuses on Olivia's anxiety and aggression as sexual impulses, ones that allow her to act. Austin's novel seeks to find room for the female aggression in this model of heterosexual intimacy.

No wonder this novel has not been recovered: its signal strength lies in the layers of aggression undergirding female sexuality. Austin neither celebrates nor condemns this greater consciousness about sexuality but sees it—unlike Stowe and Alcott before her and Wharton and Cather after her—as a means to a professional end. Hence, this is a novel not only about genius but also about the necessary link between sexuality and art. Eschewing the Protestant link between sex and sin, the novel foregrounds instead the modernist link between sexuality and creativity, the flow between the currents of work and sex.

As Muriel Dimen argues about intimacy, "domesticating desire" is like taking the aggression from sex and leaving a diminished state, a deadness where the aggression used to exist as an animating force (288). Women substitute "pseudomutuality" for aggression, an identification based on likenesses rather than competition (191). So much the better, some may argue, but the aggression is displaced nonetheless. From this displacement emerges the anxiety that fosters confrontation and change. Olivia finds her most exciting moments of passion—those that sustain her acting career—from the sexual rebellion she enacts. She refuses sexual conformity in order to create an alternative to it, a passionate relationship to self. She is sorry for the aggression she feels, but she cannot imagine relinquishing it.

Austin's novel is a thoroughly anxious book. Its fundamental anxiety emerges from the heroine's ambivalence about heterosexual sex and the greater pleasure she feels in acting, in play, on the stage. Olivia's apprehensiveness about sexuality leads to her first sexual encounter with

Helmeth, an intercourse that occurs during a storm after a lightning bolt ignites a fire. Until this point, they had just kissed, a mutually pleasing eroticism, but her anxiety about loss and destruction moves them to the genital act. The storm is associated with the fluidity of female sexuality: "His arms were around me and all my life up to that moment was no more to me than a path which led up to those arms. I remember that . . . and the world dissolving in the wash of the rain outside . . . and the lift of his breast; and deep under all, old, unimagined instincts reared their heads and bayed at the voice of their master" (238). Austin equates Olivia's anxious submission to "instincts" as some sort of atavism, a mastery that leads to a momentary erasure of self. The author, however, is careful to suggest that this runs counter to the fashioning of a sexual self that Olivia has been undertaking since she first met Helmeth. The original ellipses in Austin's passage above indicate the absence of speech for this sexual encounter. She cannot describe this passion but can only become subject to it. Hers is a physical response, atavistic in its passion, yet it does not count as the kind of psychological intimacy she has been searching for. It is, by her account, "a profound, exalted intimacy of passion" (259); nevertheless, it is also "shut out" from the rest of the world.

This submission leads her to think of marriage and abandoning the stage, but not for long since she has developed "a man's attitude toward work," which for her means "com[ing] unconsciously to the man's habit of keeping love and my career, in two watertight compartments. I found I was not able to think of them as having much to do with one another" (247–48). Her sexuality with Helmeth is predicated on her anxiety about loss, which prompts her sexual submission. While Olivia wants to believe in the idea of pure choice as motivation for sexual intimacy, the actual motivation is anxiety. A "subconscious knowledge of [a couple's] unfitness," Austin ventures, sustains affairs (293). The failure of this affair is based on the assumption that the sexual self and sexual fulfill-ment are sufficient as a basis for authentic intimacy. Rather than choos-ing sex, Olivia is driven to it by the storm. For Austin, choosing sexual agency is at the crux of modern women's sex expression, though she offers no positive example of such choosing. Instead, Olivia channels her sex passion into her acting.[9]

Austin works through her culture's view of sexuality's moral indeterminacy by testing out the dimensions of Olivia's sexual self-representation. Her character's illusion about pure intimacy, beyond the market, belies this anxiety. Olivia sustains a belief in spontaneous affection and pure love, in contrast to those sorts of exchanges she has seen between pretty women and their lovers or husbands, their directors or bosses. Olivia ends up with a man with whom she rationalizes a marriage, with whom her connection is not anxious but deliberate.

In this novel, Austin reconstitutes "the relation of Art to Passion" by showing how a subtler interpretation of passion is even more necessary than the finer acknowledgment of unconscious instincts (272). If sexuality expresses subliminal urges or unconscious drives, then only the repression of these urges creates the "good woman." If the technology that saves her sister's premature baby had existed at the time that Olivia gave birth, she imagines that her life would have been different, perhaps less of a struggle with the "social ideal" and more of a negotiation rather than an aggressive sexual rebellion. Austin's novel raises anxieties about the efficacy of sex power, insofar as it tests Olivia's ability to sustain her independence against the social ideal of the good woman.

That Austin's novel ends by endorsing sexual (and social) experimentation is consistent with her later fictions, such as *No. 26 Jayne Street* (1920). In that novel, Neith Schuyler moves out of her aunts' apartments and into her own, on a street where radical intellectuals agitate for workers' rights and celebrate the Bolshevik Revolution while awaiting Trotsky's New York appearances. Neith's fiancé, a radical leader, has had an affair with another activist, but he breaks it off when he grows tired of her. Confronted by the woman, Neith cannot stand the fact that her fiancé broke off relations without acknowledging the depth of his lover's feelings and commitment, crying that his "abominable" behavior did not yield her "justice." Refusing to become one of the "scab women" who marry men no matter what their sexual pasts, Neith decides to postpone her engagement and remain single (297). Thus, Austin echoes Emma Goldman's 1910 essay, "The Traffic in Women," in which she warns the middle-class woman—borrowing from Havelock Ellis—that she, not the prostitute, was the real "scab" if she married for money and respectability (26).

Austin argues here for the democratization of sexuality, an ideal of democratizing sex expression that challenges conventional sexual norms of middle-class white women. The young idealist Neith Schuyler comes to terms with "Anarchist" radical sexuality by contrasting her great-aunt's maidenly reserve with the power of sexuality in the radical intellectual movement, which Austin represents through Neith's fiancé's Bolshevism. Austin pushes the boundaries of sexual experiment by leveling out its effects, showing that new technologies to save premature babies are of a piece with the sexual experimentation of radicals, just as suffrage parades contain the sexual, libidinal energies of women in public. The novel questions, in Austin's own words, whether "sex feeling" can be "democratized" (135). Austin associates the radical movement with sexual relations; her critiques of militarism and capitalism serve as the background for the larger and more foundational critiques of feminism and sex equality. (One Austin character launches the argument that "one in five" underfed children become "unstable, oversexed" as a result of malnutrition.) Austin's characters wonder whether "'men *as* men'" are even "'capable of Democracy'" since women are better exemplars of "lived" sexual expression than men (313; Austin's emphasis). As Austin sees it, men compartmentalize their feelings, while women use passion to fuel their politics. Greed, power, sex: Neith comes to see these as the "bourgeois" trappings of patriarchy (328), and her last act is to commit herself to the "new feminism" that refuses to "scab" other women (342, 297). This last image—drawn from the radical workers' movement that Austin followed and celebrated—is her alternative to "freezing" onto men and speaks to her desire for women to form a kind of sexual sisterhood.

HATING SEX POWER

In "Regionalism in American Literature" (1932), Mary Austin declares Edith Wharton's *House of Mirth* and *The Children* as representative regionalist fiction. However, in "Sex in American Literature" (1923),

Austin does not identify Wharton at all, claiming that Willa Cather, Gertrude Atherton, and she herself have been the originators of sex novels in American culture. Perhaps Austin ignores Wharton because in her novels, from *House of Mirth* (1905) and *Fruit of the Tree* (1907) to *Summer* (1917) and *Age of Innocence* (1920), the heroines declare that they hate sex power.[10] Wharton has no faith either in women's homosocial alliances or in the "new feminism" Austin describes—a change in patriarchal personal relations commensurate with the radicalism that *No. 26 Jayne Street* espouses—and she resists the democratizing of sexuality. Wharton's reluctance to support sex power as liberating for women informs her most infamous book, *Custom of the Country* (1913), about one woman's disposition for what Austin, in her series of essays on cultivating intellectual gifts, *Everyman's Genius* (1925), calls "the genius for sex provocation" (233). Austin defines that talent as the "art" that became necessary for women once "marriage had become thoroughly identified with economic support" (234). But while Austin calls the sexualization of American culture "genius," Wharton calls it failure.

What is often taken as dismissal or disapproval in Wharton's fictions is part of a very complex analysis of the hatred of sex power, or if not hatred of sex power itself, then hatred of the self-alienation associated with sex power. Wharton's attitude toward sexuality has defied scholarly consensus because she seems to embrace passion even while she distrusts its power.[11] For Wharton, sex expression registers a struggle with her culture's promise of intimacy, and she offers her sense of that intimacy as an addiction, even literalizing that metaphor. To that end, Wharton argues that the deadening of feeling cannot be relieved by the drug of sex: in *Fruit of the Tree*, she celebrates the time when "love was not a deadening drug but a vivifying element that cleared thought instead of stifling it" (534). Whereas younger women writers embraced sexual freedom as liberating, Wharton asserts its moral terms: she hates how women internalized the effects of this cultural ambivalence over sex power. That ambivalence about modern sexuality surfaces in her social critique of alienation, which she understood not as repression or absence of passion but as passion misdirected toward objects and ideas or, worse, as passion degraded to desire-driven consumerism.

By focusing on the failed desires of one woman after another—first Lily Bart; then Justine Brent, Mattie Silver, and Zeena Frome; from Anna Leath to Undine Spragg to Charity Royall and Ellen Olenska—Wharton shows how women become estranged from themselves. Sexual power, for Wharton's heroines, gradually becomes the only way to protest the forces of cultural oblivion or invisibility. Wharton negotiates this sentimental/sensational divide by focusing, instead, on the unspoken term between them: the sexualization of American life that produces her revulsion from modern culture.

For Wharton, that passion is dangerous since it marks "the ascendancy of youth and sex over . . . subjugated judgment" (*Fruit of the Tree* 533). Indeed, in *Fruit of the Tree*, Justine "began to hate the power by which she held [her lover]" (534). This is the same language that Charity Royall uses in *Summer* to describe her sexual dominion over Royall: "Charity ruled in lawyer Royall's house. She had never put it to herself in those terms; but she knew her power, knew what it was made of, and hated it" (23). Wharton's heroines hate their sexual power, especially when it is associated with youth and beauty, because that power cannot be rationalized. Sex expression as the source of that power is thus made to seem temporary or merely conditional since such power is circumstantial rather than intrinsic, accidental rather than chosen. Sex "subjugates" judgment, a power that comes too close to addiction and evasion; these women despise that power too since it seems to undermine any purer basis for intimacy. In this complex formulation, middle-class sexuality is distinguished from "impulse" by its clarifying—"unsubjugated"—judgment. The propinquity of sex and power unsettles Wharton's vision of a world of tempered desire. She wants her intellectual pleasures to remain distinct, an unalienated wish for unalloyed passion.

Thus, the changing forms of passion in the twentieth century disturbed Wharton's sensibility. If she viewed sex in turn-of-the-century America as an amalgam of the older Protestant ethic of repression with mass cultural images, psychosexual impulses, and new urban mores, Wharton introduced in the 1910s and 1920s even more improbable, tortured metaphors for the condition of American sex. She worried that sex seemed too much like recreation or, worse, addiction, that sex was

becoming not a means to pain or pleasure (she experienced the possibilities for both) but an avoidance of intimacy. Consider Wharton's resolu-
tions for disclosing the consequences of passion: suicide in *The House of
Mirth* and *Custom of the Country*; euthanasia in *The Fruit of the Tree*;
paralysis and disfigurement in *Ethan Frome*. Starting with *Summer* in
1917, symbolic incest figures in and contorts novel after novel, including
The Mother's Recompense (1925) and *Twilight Sleep* (1927), and actual
incest occurs in the "Beatrice Palmato" fragment (either 1919 or 1935,
depending on the critic).[12]

Against the critical tendency to read Undine Spragg as aggressive, I
find Wharton's *Custom of the Country* just as anxious about female sex
expression as Austin's *A Woman of Genius*. The source of that anxiety over
sex power is my concern, as well as why critics often read Undine's
power as aggression.[13] In one of the most quoted of *Custom's* passages,
Charles Bowen explains that the real "custom of the country" is buying
off American women in order to leave men alone to do their business.
The emotional equivalent of the "big steal" in business is the exercise of
sex power. According to Bowen, "Where does the real life of most
American men lie? In some woman's drawing-room or in their offices?
The answer's obvious, isn't it? The emotional centre of gravity's not the
same in the two hemispheres. In the effete societies it's love, in our new
one it's business. In America the real *crime passionel* is a 'big steal'—
there's more excitement in wrecking railways than homes" (207). The
psychological ramifications of this big steal, the cheat, the con, and who
was defrauding whom interest Wharton. Wharton is careful not to confuse sexuality with relatedness and intimacy. For Wharton, sex power
divorces women from authentic intimacy, which she idealizes as the
true goal of sex relations (even as she recognizes, as Austin had, how
much intimacy is undergirded by aggression). Sex power thus seems an
exclusively female domain. Reading *Custom of the Country* in this light,
we might risk assigning blame to Undine for her misuse of sexuality
since for Wharton sex power is a form of self-aggrandizing or self-
anesthetizing. Wharton presents us with the double bind of analyzing
without moralizing or pathologizing Undine Spragg's (U.S.'s) sex power.

One example of this double bind occurs with Undine's sexual identification with prostitutes. Twice in the novel, the heroine gets pleasure from imagining that she will be taken as a "bad woman" when she appears with Peter Van Degen in unseemly places. Her pleasure is part of this blurring of good and bad women, just as Austin's novel took pains to expand the realm of sexual pleasure for all women and to imagine a respectable sex power. Like Olivia Lattimore, Undine takes pride in claiming to her friend Indiana Rolliver that "she was not 'an immoral woman'" (353). Reading Wharton is like being pulled into the vortex of Undine's pleasure, of the undifferentiated categories of experience that Wharton delivers through Undine's reactions. Ralph Marvell's experiences are too differentiated, too precisely counterpopular, for Undine to find them interesting and engaging. Ralph is the exception; Undine, the exemplar. Ralph is disturbed when Undine resets her engagement ring, "destroying the identity of the jewels" (214). While he believes in the jewels' identity, he does not believe in Undine's, preferring to think of her as malleable under the pressure of his more serious values, which—like the stones—he imagines to be more lasting. He wants to celebrate his own uniqueness, while Undine sees him resolutely altered by his pretense of unmediatedness.

On the contrary, Undine is quite assured of her identity and doesn't believe the Parisian demimonde threatens her being. Being mistaken for a prostitute is such an unmediated pleasure for Undine because it suggests that her value—like the reset jewels themselves—does not change according to its new setting. Undine enjoys "the midnight haunts where 'ladies' were not supposed to show themselves, and might consequently taste the thrill of being occasionally taken for their opposites" (282). Consider what the prostitute does in helping men to feel their own sexual power. In using sex power, prostitutes profit from their own sexual agency by conferring sexual interest onto others. So too Undine, who increases her power the more she exercises it. So ladies *in* the night get their thrill from being in proximity to ladies *of* the night: the prepositional difference is key, for it indicates just enough distinction between ladies and prostitutes to fend off moral resistance.

Wharton makes clear that Undine is not "consciously acting a part" (266). Perhaps Undine's "nervous breakdowns" are not some pretense, further instances of her not "consciously acting a part," but real anxiety attacks. In short, we need to take Undine at Wharton's word: that is, we need to see her as a creature of impulse. Her nervous condition is a symptom of the constriction of her world (just as any sex power is always a symptom): the pale countenances, her lassitude and irritability are signs of real distress. While it is easy to demonize Undine or to read her from her son's point of view, it is less easy to take her seriously as a case study, even though Wharton employs the language of Undine's "case" herself (430), exploring the psychic consequences of using sex power: "It was instinctive with her to become, for the moment, the person she thought her interlocutors expected her to be; but she had never had quite so new a part to play at such short notice" (386). This is an interesting case itself since Undine is not "consciously acting" but "instinctively" playing a part: such unconsciousness is a problem of impulse that leads, for Wharton, to subjugated judgment and will.

The languages of impulse and instinct and even the "call" of Ralph's passion for Undine are Wharton's tropes for sexual desire (217–18). When Undine runs off with Van Degen for two months, she sees herself as "proclaim[ing] the sanctity of passion and the moral duty of obeying its call" (365). Undine responds to "the close contact of covetous impulses" (224), which for Wharton signals a move toward the impulsive and the unconscious. In Undine's own words, Ralph has "got over being crazy about me" (241) since her effect upon him has been only unconscious, primitive. Ralph loses his "craziness" for Undine when he makes a more conscious assessment of her character. Undine's marriage annulment, "by cutting the last link between them, seemed to have given him back to himself; and the mere fact that he could consider his case in all its bearings, impartially and ironically, showed him the distance he had travelled, the extent to which he had renewed himself" (433). This move from unconscious libido to conscious will is Wharton's assessment of modern love—a move from impulse to choice.

It is no less a "call" to passion when Ralph decides to commit suicide, and alas, it is too easy to blame Undine for the crisis. Undine responds to his death with a fair amount of guilt, increasing her rage against de Chelles, her third husband, whom she comes to see as much like Ralph.

From rage to recognition, her transition is a sign of psychic growth: "The sense of having been thus rendered invisible filled Undine with a vehement desire to make herself seen, and an equally strong sense that all attempts to do so would be in vain" (408). Undine feels the lack of space for women's sexual aggression or rage except through the exercise of her sex power, which Wharton figures as a dangerous substitution. Undine is desperate to be recognized, with all of the psychic coherence that such validation offers, since she equates her ambition with the acknowledgment of her sexual power.

She is especially anxious with de Chelles. Her anxiety manifests when she reveals herself in an unconscious slip about her husband's repayment of his brother Hubert's debts. Undine deeply resents his repayment of these losses given that they are not hers. When Hubert and his new American bride take over the premier rooms at the Hotel de Chelles, she is especially incensed and must thereafter repent her rashness: "'Of course you can do what you like with your own house, and make any arrangements that suit your family, without consulting me; but you needn't think I'm ever going back to live in that stuffy little hole, with Hubert and his wife splurging round on top of our heads!'" (503). Undine's dream of being buried alive, with her brother- and sister-in-law dancing on her head/grave, indicates her not-so-buried fear of the unconscious into which she may slip. Her "old weapons of aggression" elicit de Chelles's uncomprehending response: "'You don't understand'" (527). Her response to Hubert's extravagances and gambling debts is symptomatic of Undine's neurosis.

Above all, Undine has anxieties about space and the spatial restriction of being "made small," just as Frank Norris's McTeague half-articulates the fear of being trivialized, compressed, and dismissed. For Undine, this fear takes shape in her refusal to identify with her mother, a washed-out and anxious woman, stuck in hotel rooms and unable to venture out. In Europe, "Mrs. Spragg's shrinking from everything new and familiar had developed into a kind of settled terror," but even in New York, Mrs. Spragg has to screw up her courage to venture out (382).[14] Undine projects her own psychic traumas onto her material reality. Her sexuality is the only power she has to move her from a small space to a bigger, safer space. Propriety dictates that she rein in her monstrous desires, but her sexual energy also creates the juggernaut of her desire, which in turn generates new anxieties. For Wharton, sex power is a symptom of a much deeper, perhaps even national, neurosis. Undine is full of rage—and Ralph almost as much so (437)—especially in the last third of the novel, when her customary responses to the world yield little power at all. And her rage and aggression are matched, Wharton suggests, by the current of self-loathing that subtends her anxious use of power.

Like Olivia in Austin's novel, Undine has a deep disgust of immoral women, as she reveals when the Princess Estradine drags her along to Nice on a pretense: "A sincere disgust was Undine's uppermost sensation. She was as much ashamed as Mrs. Spragg might have been at finding herself used to screen a clandestine adventure" (395). Undine's emotional reaction emerges from her ties to her mother. To maintain her ties to respectability while also forming useful ties to society, Undine must create her own branding, what Wharton calls "Apex dash and New York dignity" (386)—a version of aggression exercised through sex power. (That Undine and Elmer had originally married in "Opake, Nebraska," is actually one of Wharton's tells: its opaqueness is much closer to Wharton's ideal of authentic intimacy.)[15]

The novel ends with a vision of lonely, bereft Paul Marvell, Undine's nine-year-old child, yearning for some of his mother's time. Paul embodies the figure of grief, first over the dead father and then over the absent mother. It is not surprising that Undine has little time for her son since Wharton could never reconcile sex expression and maternity; the author would routinely admonish her culture for being too easily persuaded that women could negotiate both. Undine may not be able to grieve for her dead husband, but their son can and does mourn his father. But she is no less melancholic than he is, and she is restless because of that failure to grieve. Paul's dejection allows us the pleasure of loathing Undine without the responsibility of renouncing the desires that Undine embodies.

That Wharton keeps returning to the efficacy of sex power in novel after novel indicates her deep ambivalence about it. Undine's sex power inclines to aggression when she is not awash in her own anxiety; her disconnection from her spouses and son signals an anxiety about sex power and its concomitant aggression that Wharton could not ironize or parody. It would take a writer of Dorothy Parker's wit to assess what Wharton could only lament.

"WHAT EARTHLY GOOD CAN COME OF IT?"

The last line of Dorothy Parker's poem "General Review of the Sex Situation" (1926) provides the best way to consider her view of sex power and its costs: "What earthly good can come of it?" Like her poetry, Parker's O. Henry Prize–winning "Big Blonde" (1929) assesses the dark side of sex power, for as much as sex power is presumed to be "fun," it proves exhausting to keep up. Often linked to the story of Parker's first marriage, "Big Blonde" details Hazel Morse's rejection of the conventional division of sexual labor. Hazel is kept by one man after another, engaging in a series of relationships that depletes her psychic energies and leads her to a suicidal melancholy, even if she has no remorse. If Undine embodies the aggression and anxiety that undergird sex power, Hazel is the obverse, exhausted by the psychic energy it takes to keep up sexual passion.

When noted sociologist David Seabury examined "The Bogy of Sex" in the pages of *Century* magazine in September 1927, he found that everyone spoke of sexuality "casually either as a right or a joy; a release from crushing inhibition or a necessity for health. Yes, even more than this, many believe it to be the single motive of the human being, the dynamic of life" (529). So matter of fact had sexual debate become by the end of the 1920s that, Seabury suggests, "by the age of seven most children are sophisticated" (528), articulating details and nuances that would have once made adults blush in shame. Seabury took pains to suggest that the 1920s mark the loosening of sexual inhibitions, just as a "flood of sexuality" would follow the breaking up of an "ice jam" of human emotions (531). Ubiquitous as this flood imagery is as a trope for women's release, the embrace of sex power was much more deliberate and gradual than the irrepressible "flood" image suggests.

Hazel's "laughing at [men's] jokes and telling them she loved their neckties" reveal how her sex power works (105). As a result of her gaiety, "men liked her, and she took it for granted that the liking of many men was a desirable thing. Popularity seemed to her to be worth all the work that had to be put into its achievement. Men liked you because you were fun, and when they liked you they took you out, and there you were. . . . She was a good sport. Men like a good sport" (105). After a "couple of thousand of evenings of being a good sport among her male acquaintances," she tires out, becoming "more conscientious than spontaneous about it" (106). This is the move to be found in many of these sex-expression fictions: from unself-conscious sexuality to a studied, determined use of sex power and, finally, to sex exhaustion. Hazel chooses the "aching . . . melancholy" over the insistence on fun and being a sport that her sexual relationships demand (114, 115). Being a sport is about women's compliance, being someone who understands sex as a game. She prefers the "privilege" of sadness (115) and the pleasures of the "voluntary dead" and of "never again putting on tight shoes, of never having to laugh and listen and admire, of never more being a good sport. Never" (117). This exhaustion is the end of the sexual self that Nina Miller argues is part of Parker's plan to "deflate the romance of heterosexuality" (131, 140). Parker's deflation of female sex power, however, is accompanied by a startling revelation.

Being married gives Hazel license, she thinks, to "relax"; she finds peace in isolation, but "Herbie was not amused" (107). "In the first months of their marriage, she had given him all the passion she was ever to know" (106). While she had given passion, it was not shared. Drinking Scotch together leads Herbie to think she might regain her "high spirits," a coded phrase for her sexual jocularity, but these efforts don't last. Drinking only briefly drowns her melancholy, the central emotion that reappears in Parker's stories (see "The Little Hours"). Melancholy is the price to pay for sex power. When Hazel can't or won't exercise her sexual power, Herbie becomes aggressive, resulting in slaps, a black eye, and ultimately abandonment. Once Herbie leaves, Hazel befriends her neighbor, Mrs. Martin, fortyish, and spends time with "the Boys" (110), curiously infantilized men in their forties and fifties. She goes through one man after another—Herbie, Ed, Charley, Sydney, Ferd, Billy, Art—

each nearly indistinguishable from the others and ultimately fungible. When she can no longer sustain the joy that her lovers require of her, she attempts suicide.

Sex power works, and that it does so makes Hazel depressed. Her suicide attempt results from her dejection about the efficacy of sex power, not its failure. That the serial repetition of this sexual formula—laughing and loving, good sportsmanship—gives no pleasure is less Parker's lament than a call to arms, for sex power uses so little of the self that it creates emptiness rather than intimacy. When sex power becomes obligatory, it can only deliver pain since the privilege of choosing whether to use sex power is denied women. Sex power, then, is no longer a choice but a requirement of female sexuality.

That Hazel takes veronal to sleep—like Lily Bart's chloral—signals her sexual exhaustion. To alleviate the "slow, grinding wretchedness so horrible" (119) attached to the idea of sexual gaiety or the "slow, saturating wretchedness" (123), Hazel chooses suicide. Having a genius for sex provocation, in Austin's terms, means also having a wider range of pain—the depths of despair, along with the possibilities for irony. Sex power, perhaps inadvertently, gives women's deep emotional range its radiating possibilities. Sex power cuts Hazel off from other parts of her self, and only by relinquishing her "gaiety" and good sportsmanship can she explore these other emotions. Thus, Parker sees the relinquishing of sex power as a gain, though it is an exceedingly painful transition from gaiety to irony and then to emotional depth. The story, however, stops short of being a narrative of recovery or therapy; it will be left to Fannie Hurst to create narratives of sexual therapy (see chapter 6).

Parker's revision of these codes of female suffering are part of her legacy to American literary history, which was originally cast in terms of sentimental rather than sophisticated discourse. Parker revives suffering as a legitimate female complaint, intertwining female pain with the pleasure of sexuality as the opposite of the female "good sport." Parker locates pain at the heart of women's exercise of sex power. How much of this was cynical sophistication and how much a debate about the sex power of modern women may be a matter of interpretation, but as part of a history of women writers dealing with sex power, Parker's doubts about women's security with intimacy—across sentimental, sensational, and sophisticated styles—make an important contribution to the sex-power debates.

Perhaps Parker rejected the celebration of the power of another "big blonde" in her contemporary Anita Loos's *Gentlemen Prefer Blondes*, which Wharton lauded as the great American novel when it appeared in 1925, imagining it as the sequel to her own *Custom of the Country*. The gold-digger comedies of the 1930s would continue the ironizing of sex power that Parker and Loos made famous. In *I'm No Angel*, Ellen Tremper argues that without sexual equality, there can be no true comedy (170); according to Tremper, Parker's stories about melancholy suggest there is no sex equality. Hazel seems no match for the string of men who want good sportsmanship from her. In the gold-digger comedies, women were characterized as both sexual and ambitious, opening the door for sex and humor in a new fantasy of pleasure and comic relief. The comedic sexuality in *Gentlemen Prefer Blondes* is matched by the desire to take women's sexuality seriously, not as barter but as pleasure. Recognizing sexuality's foundation in active female aggression made sexuality easier to joke about since pleasure had nothing to do with the mere passive-aggression with which women found their first footing in sex power. The funniest women are the most aggressive, and poor Hazel's internalized self-loathing, her sexual exhaustion, is a comment on her misplaced aggression and self-destruction. The difference is between internalized and externalized aggression, a distinction that makes all the difference for the female.

This chapter has charted the move from the "good woman" and her sex power to the "good sport" and her sexuality. Starting with Heywood's sex power and ending with Parker's sexual sportsmanship, I have shown that women writers used the same terms and layered them with alternative meanings. What looked like liberation to Heywood in the 1870s came to seem like a new form of repression and sexual labor in the 1920s—sexual liberalism but without the liberation. Of course, sex power as a rallying cry resurfaces from so deep an underground that it looks new in the 1960s and 1970s, when radical feminism claims it as a liberating force. Yet by the time sex power reappears in the 1960s, linked to the idea of a sexual revolution, critics mistake sexual liberalism for the more hopeful sexual expression of the 1920s.

Much of that hope was invested in the promises of the democratization of sexuality. By the 1920s, women's sexual expression in fiction appeared with the racial ideologies of modern liberalism: the attempt to erase race and eradicate racialism. We now know this to have been a wish of liberalism, but at the time, many women writers hoped for sexual equality—as a concept or an experience—across racial and class lines. Positing that sex expression cut across identity categories (that there existed a sexuality that was not marked as black or white, Irish or Jewish), these novelists argued that sex was cultural and thus adaptable by all. My aim is not to document this claim's objective truth but rather to demonstrate that women writers across the spectrum believed or hoped this vision to be true. They invested sexuality with the potential of furthering liberal equality, though they came to doubt and critique exactly these premises.

Middle-class women's work—getting out of the house and out from under the economic tyranny of patriarchal marriage—enabled a new emphasis on heterosexual intimacy. As George Chauncey argues, "The new complexity—and restrictiveness—of sex/gender roles was epitomized by the flapper, who was at once both sexually precocious and profoundly heterosexual" (144)—and profoundly young since such sexuality was reserved for women who were expected to grow out of sexual desire upon marriage. But it wasn't just the flapper who exercised this new sexuality, as the next chapter shows. Rather, the democratization of sex was in full swing.

CHAPTER FIVE

INARTICULATE  Sex

Sex power was still double-edged. As the debate over who could claim sex power shows, confusion about the norms of American sex created a problem. Although sexual identity was no more articulated than sexual practice, sexuality became part of one's identity, something one *was* rather than something one *did*, given the complex intermingling of the languages of sex previously stratified by race and class.[1] In this identification of the self as sexed, one question remains: Is women's sex expression unconscious instinct or sexual self-consciousness? That is, can women claim sexual desire as part of their identity, and if so, what sort of sex expressions will result?

One way to answer these questions about the state of sexuality is to return to V. F. Calverton's *Sex Expression in Literature* (1926). Calverton starts by analyzing Elizabethan England (which has the "utmost freedom of expression") and ends by giving his views of contemporary American and British literature ("newer freedom for literati and laymen will come only from the freedom of a newer society") (13, 309). As Calverton writes, "Where sex expression is not dealt with, it is because there is no sex expression—because it has been subdued or repressed, castrated from literature"—at best, a "eunuchoidal gesture" (vii). This thwarting of sex expression risks occlusion, despite the ongoing decay of the bourgeoisie and the inevitable contemporary sex release in literature that follows (276). In the bibliography, Calverton lists writers whose works signaled the rise of sex expression insofar as their treatment of sex realities and sex practices helped to bring about the decline of genteel literature: Sherwood Anderson, Sholom Asch (Polish-born American novelist), Randolph Bourne, Theodore Dreiser, James Joyce, Judge Ben Lindsey, H. L. Mencken, Harvey O'Higgins (author of *The American Mind in Action*), and Eugene O'Neill, along with two women—Beatrice Burton and Elinor Glyn (283). Burton had just published *The Flapper Wife* in 1925 (about a newlywed wife who misguidedly takes the flapper as a model); Glyn was famous for her "It" girl references in her 1920s books.

Calverton blames the lingering force of sex repression on those "vestigial Howellsians" who follow Comstock's censoring of sexually expressive books. The New York Society for the Suppression of Vice condemned "*Jude the Obscure, The Damnation of Theron Ware, Hagar Revelly, Homo Sapiens, Trilby, Edna, A Summer in Arcady, Susan Lenox*—all were victimized in one way or another by the virtuosi of virtue" (295–96). The authors of these books are all men: Thomas Hardy, Harold Frederic, Daniel Carson Goodwin, Stanislaw Przybyszewski, George Du Maurier, Guido Bruno, James Lane Allen, and David Graham Phillips, respectively. Despite the success of writers like Burton and Glyn, Calverton in 1926 sees sex expression in literature as a masculine domain. Yet this masculinist "new morality" ignores the extent to which women writers in the 1920s use sex expression both as an end in itself to counter bourgeois domesticity and as a means of dramatizing women's recently emboldened moves in the workplace.

What sort of "final emancipation" would occur for Calverton if the literature of new sex expression was written by women without the conventionality of Burton and Glyn (307)? Glyn's "It," for example, was

amazingly ubiquitous: a way both to pleasure and to self-despair, con-
founding rational fantasy with chaotic female desires, as Haag observes
(*Consent* 177). Glyn had identified "It" with the girl who embodied
sexuality and eroticism, but "It" "is not ambiguous," even if it could not
be articulately defined, as Michael North observes in his excellent *Reading 1922* (197). A new "purposeful vagueness" cloaked the references to
sexuality, leaving "it" and "that" to stand as powerfully inflected pro-
nouns or "an absent referent" of sexuality (North 197). More often than
not, vague references to "it" or dashes, ellipses, or asterisks represent
what cannot be expressed, due to some fear of explicitness. North argues
that modern literature was believed to "popularize the unconscious"
(67) by bringing into the public various concerns that were as yet unarticulated. Thus, he questions whether American writers could offer a
vision of sexuality predicated on choice rather than on unconscious
urges. To meet this challenge, these novels aim to establish a new kind of
normative heterosexuality based on the overcoming of sexual ignorance
and the emerging hope that modern love would lead to social and racial
transcendence.

In Victorian literature, signs of female sexuality might be read upon
the body—a blush, a gesture, a tear—that betray an absence of speech
and the reluctance or refusal to admit desire. Those plots focus on
domesticating that desire once it is expressed, and the construction of a
sexual style, at first associated with immigrant and racial others, was
readily appropriated for the novel-reading middle classes. But this modern sexual style came with a twist: the new sex expression was based on
a dimension of "purposeful vagueness," the inarticulate. Instead of being
an explicit language or lexicon, this inarticulateness reencodes women's
sex power. Inarticulateness is a complex reaction to sexual practice,
given that it suggests how, in exchange for women's silence about these
acts, women might accept the new norms of female sexuality. Readers
learned the codes of bourgeois sex expression that had heretofore eluded
speech, such as the terms of exchange in "hot loving," the idea of a
sexual sisterhood, and the means of achieving an oppositional sexuality,
one that undermined the usual association of sexual power with hatred
and loss, as in Wharton. Whatever sympathy there was for "bad girls"

came from their inability to discuss sex, saving the heroine from the worse accusation of being articulate about sexuality or using sex consciously as a power rather than as an unconscious motivation.

"Inarticulateness" becomes a virtue because it acknowledges that sex can be expressed without necessitating explanation or elaboration. Women's sexual inarticulateness might then prove to be a screen for their innocence. If they were less intuitive and more calculating—like Undine Spragg in *Custom of the Country* or Lorelei Lee in *Gentlemen Prefer Blondes* —they would lose their redemption. For the 1920s, the pattern is set: the more inarticulate the heroine, the more popular the novel.

This chapter studies four representative authors of "It" fictions from the 1920s—Anzia Yezierska, Viña Delmar, Julia Peterkin, and Jessie Fauset—for their literary strategies about women achieving sexual pleasure rather than using sexual power for modern love. In creating a mode of sex expression that their characters share, these four women writers assumed that sex expression was beyond race or ethnicity, "as neither a coin of economic exchange nor a possession to be claimed only in marriage" (Haag, *Consent* 170). By exploring what happens to girls who defy sexual restrictions, Yezierska's *Salome of the Tenements* (1923), Delmar's *Bad Girl* (1928), Peterkin's *Scarlet Sister Mary* (1928), and Fauset's *Plum Bun* (1929) all focus on variously eroticized or exoticized characters who attain sexual pleasure and repudiate social restrictions and protest against sexual repressions. These novels, as we will see, legitimate sexual liberation, making visible and articulate the dynamics of sex expression and the profits that accompany it.

Those profits came in the countertradition of inarticulateness. These four writers operated within or in sympathy with the sex expression of marginalized social identities and were rewarded for their efforts. By 1923, Yezierska was the celebrated author of *Hungry Hearts*; she was paid $10,000 for the film rights and subsequently went to Hollywood to write the screenplay for her work. Viña Delmar, daughter of a Jewish vaudevillian and a Catholic chorus girl, grew up in the Bronx, Brooklyn, and Harlem. Only twenty-three when she published *Bad Girl*, Delmar later moved to Hollywood, where she too wrote screenplays. South Carolina writer Julia Peterkin was heralded as the representative of the

New South, devoted as she was to exploring and preserving Gullah plantation life. When she won the $1,000 Pulitzer Prize in 1929, she was celebrated as a southern realist who tried to make women's pleasure a secure subject of serious fiction. Finally, Jessie Fauset, editor of *Crisis* from 1919 to 1926, spelled out her program for sex as a new politics in her four novels about black women's ambitions.

Different as their circumstances were, each found a way to create a symbolics of pleasure. Their novels explore the politics of sex expression as the transformation of what their characters once hated—or lost—into something they could love. As Sharon Ullman explains about sex expression in 1910, "This new public sexuality was as yet a language under construction. Its syntax and grammar remained undesigned, and its vocabulary still lay encoded in the conversations of the past" (38). Even without a language in the matrix, it is no empty gesture to turn disempowerment—coded here as inarticulateness—into a lesson for women about how to work and love in the world. Their inarticulateness signals a new kind of literary subject, women who live with pleasure.

CODING PLEASURE

These novels describe how the threat of sexualization, which once created "bad girls," is transformed into the promise of self-advancement, not self-erasure. Pleasure comes where these characters show up. Female sex expression is a movement, even an aggressive one, between the self and the lover. For example, in *Salome*, John Manning—the scion of Protestant privilege and expression—imagines that Sonya Vrunsky embodies an "irresistible attraction": "Now, the woman beside him was a flame of life—a vivid exotic—a miraculous priests [*sic*] of romance who had brought release for the ice of his New England heart" (106). Sex expression depended on a woman's ability to perform her self-interest, drawing on the "flame of life," an aggressive move that showed individuality in sexual terms. The other novels also offer an enabling sense of women's sexuality, though perhaps they don't offer the same comprehensive sense of women's power that Yezierska envisions.

Instead, their disidentification with respectability—what Yezierska calls the "the grey fog of smothering respectability on Madison Avenue" (133)—leads to a reevaluation of female possibility and bodily pleasure. Unlike the narratives in the previous chapter, those that create each character as a function of her own sexual power, these heroines pitch their sex expression as action. That is, heterosexual romance may or may not change class status, but it does open up possibilities within culture for more pleasure; one set of urgent desires opens up another set in the social world. Finding themselves ambivalently between female self-consciousness and pleasurable unconsciousness leads to both a startling freshness and a disturbing dislocation.

Encoding working women with this kind of sexual feeling—one that brought them pleasure rather than exploitation—met with some cultural resistance. Sexual modernization elicited social aggression against women —aggression not only against their sexual frankness but also against their unconsciousness about sexual subjectivity. While such modernization brought women access to desire, it may also have unwittingly returned them to their submission to it. They might own the desire, but it owned them, too. In Sonya's transformation, she comes to realize that she and Manning are the same: "So at bottom we're all alike, Anglo-Saxons or Jews, gentlemen or plain immigrant. . . . When we're hungry, we're hungry" (183). The countertradition that I see proceeds out of the convention that sex power moves from its association with race and ethnicity (often viewed as "ugliness") to a transformative power, one that became crucial in a visual culture where beauty could be marketed and sold as both a personal and a public trait. As Haag argues, "If economically secure men created a female subject out of love and its inseparable language, young women had the more daunting task of generating an authentic sexual identity or subjectivity through tools of narration, style, and self-embellishment" (*Consent* 183). Haag's point is well taken: women's sex expression had to be refashioned through a creative imagination. Narration, style, and self-embellishment were crucial to how women's sex expression reimagined how American sex would work for middle-class women.

This new sexual climate demanded an account of urges too powerful to ignore but too transgressive to put into conventional expression.

Finding a new code was key. The less verbal the characters, the greater the symbolic vocabulary of sexuality: as we have seen, talking of sex often introduces anxious plots. To configure sex through, say, "love charms" rather than speech allows women "pleasuring," as Peterkin writes, for her heroine "to laugh and dance and sing again" (190–91). Such sexual pleasure occurs without pathologizing the sexuality of the characters involved. Once women writers could articulate sex power, they could decide how to transform that power from its ambivalent beginnings to either economic or personal empowerment. While sex may be complicated, these heroines' sexual interiority allows them to work as mother, artist, dressmaker, or plantation worker. And that work is an affirming enterprise, worth the values encoded once these women command their sex expressions. In short, these novels configure, in condensed form, the desire to have pleasure but without the articulateness to talk about it.

Unlike Dorothy Parker, who was teaching *New Yorker* sophisticates an ironic, double-voiced discourse about sex power, Yezierska, Delmar, Peterkin, and Fauset instruct their mainly middle-class readers in the much more quotidian sexual practices of Jewish immigrants, working-class women, whites, and blacks. In an interview with W. Adolphe Roberts in *The American Hebrew* in August 1922, Yezierska announced her intentions to "[disregard] the taboos against these four things: tragedy, religion, sex and dirt," claiming that "sex is a universal fact. Its manifestations, however, are ignored in the pages of respectable magazines. For myself, when I write about the Oriental woman, I cannot depict her as being as sterilized as the Anglo-Saxon" (342). If sophisticates and elites practiced ironic detachment and sexual ambivalence, Yezierska describes a posture mostly available to the middle class, which perhaps lacked cosmopolitan worldliness and cultivated neuroses as alternatives. Instead, these writers offered antisentimental assessments of modern love in novels where heroines move from loss and grief to commitment either to careers or to a renewed vision of domesticity.[2]

The primary lesson that writers like Yezierska and Peterkin taught their readers was how to celebrate the female body as the repository of pleasure in order to counter social discipline. Writing in the July 1930

Forum and Century, Peterkin rails against her conventional upbringing: "Girl children were thought to be better off when kept ignorant of certain matters which men—certainly men who were doctors [like her brother] must inevitably know. I was encouraged to turn my attention toward more graceful interests, such as music or pictures or literature. Ignorance concerning the fundamental facts of life was believed to be better for me than knowledge" ("What I Believe" 49). Peterkin wrote so effortlessly about passion in order to overcome her distrust of the new powers of sex expression, a kind of sexual inarticulateness that paradoxically enabled a new frankness. Peterkin's Sister Mary felt her pleasure keenly: "For to save Mary's life she could not keep her mind fixed on the joys of Heaven, but sought her pleasure right here in this world, where pleasures are in such easy reach. She believed in God and Satan and Heaven and Hell too, and she had no doubt that sinners fed Hell's fires, but the rules of Heaven's Gate Church made the Christian life very difficult for a young, strong, healthy woman" (*Scarlet Sister Mary* 219). In a culture rife with sexual innuendo and ironic implications (especially in films prior to the Hays Code in the 1930s), these "young, strong, healthy" heroines teach readers how to find pleasure in the world. Despite all of the deflections, indirections, ironies, and double-voicedness, the newly wrought sex expression transformed troubled, disappointed, wayward, or "bad girls" into modern lovers.[3]

This subtle change about modern love represents a major shift for women. If, as I have argued, the "ugly girl" was sexually active in the 1860s and 1870s, when beauty signaled sexual purity,[4] then by the turn of the century, beauty was divested of its moral suasion and invested instead with sexual power, a characteristic that was newly imagined to denote—and even promote—sexuality. After 1900, "ugliness" came to represent repression; in contrast, beautiful women acted on "It," their own sex expression. Beauty symbolized a degree of strength (what Yezierska called "the resistless magnetism—feminine mystery" [35]) and outstripped the ugly girl's previous claim to the authority of sexual pleasures. And what happened to ugliness? It got targeted by consumer capitalism as something to be fixed and reconstituted for the new sexual arena, insofar as the cosmetic industry arose as a way to tackle the new

American meaning of ugliness. "Going the limit" and "pleasuring" came to define women's embrace of sex power, even as they were enjoined from discussing either sex or power. Those desires were to remain unvoiced, suppressed, unarticulated, for as soon as women voiced them, they became "ugly"—common in a minor key but monstrous in a major one. Thus, in Delmar's *Bad Girl*, the naive heroine's sexually active friend —ugly by Dot's own measures—wasn't a "bad girl" (36): "she hadn't a frightened, persecuted expression" after sex at all (84). No wonder that women read voraciously about how to use their sex expression.

As I explore inarticulateness in the rest of this chapter, I am not claiming that such a universal sexuality exists, only that writers like Yezierska, Delmar, Peterkin, and Fauset postulated a utopian hope for a code or symbolics that allows women to reach across barriers. The conflicted, multiple sets of these writers' desires are not constant or always coherent but are no less powerful for being complex, fluid, and surprising. Of course, white and African American middle-class writers and readers still stereotyped ethnic women, as Wharton did throughout her career, and I do not aim to excuse the use of racialized or classed sexuality as their way to navigate their own middle-class terms. For instance, in *Plum Bun*, Fauset describes the young Jewish girl, Rachel, as having "some faint hint of an exotic voluptuousness": she "was like a fresh breeze, a curious mixture of Jewish conservatism and modernity" (211). Fauset's ethnicizing of the Jew mirrors the white racializing of Fauset's heroine, a comparison that Fauset won't make explicit, for the illusion of inarticulateness that these women writers employ was the hallmark of middle-class women's sexual style.

REPRESENTATIVE SEX

How readers could see beyond the ethnic or the immigrant, the working class, or the plantation-bound to the sexual is key to this chapter. How did characters adapt this frank sexuality for their own purposes, namely, to voice the unconscious or repressed urges of U.S. culture? These novels, I argue, changed the codes by which we read bad girl sexuality as an *essential* quality of identity. Rather, readers approached these texts, as their reviewers suggested, to discover how to democratize sexuality, like the democratizing of beauty that Sonya imagines in *Salome of the Tenements*.

While we might read *Salome's* Sonya Vrunsky as totally impulsive, *Bad Girl's* Dot Haley as tactically naive, *Scarlet's* Mary Pinesett as naturally responsive, and *Plum Bun's* Angela Murray as intentionally clueless, the contemporaneous reviewers of these novels reveal the most significant connection among them: their inarticulateness, particularly about matters of passion. The reviewers addressed the extent to which these novels confronted the most searching questions of the day: Was sex a swindle, a bribe to make women forget other sorts of freedoms once they had won the vote? How much did the sexual bohemia of the 1920s extend to different parts of the city and, indeed, the country? How was sex playing in Peoria?

In her day, the responses to Anzia Yezierska's novel were less about Jewishness and more about sex. In the *New York Times*, Sonya was considered "an illiterate, hot-blooded little savage" (22). The same reviewer calls her an "unconscious" and "instinctive" courtesan and blackmailer. The *New York Tribune* reviewer underscores Sonya's "inarticulate spirituality," a corollary to her "incoherence," which is "racial," though he "would hesitate to call it typically Jewish" (26). Given this disclaimer, one wonders whether the reviewer's comment is really anti-Semitic or actually a charge against the heroine's sexual inarticulateness.

Anti-Semitic as the reviewer might be, it is no coincidence that the reviews of Delmar's, Peterkin's, and Fauset's novels also denounce their heroines as inarticulate. As another review of Yezierska notes about the Jewish/Protestant divide, "The Oriental and the Anglo Saxon cannot find a mutual language, even the language of love" (*Boston Evening Transcript* 5). The force of the word "even" in the review gives us a clue about how Yezierska's protagonist was read in her time. Sonya cannot speak across the divide to her WASP husband, though she readily can communicate with Jaky Solomon, the Jewish dress designer. The Anglo-Saxon world lacks the same language of intimacy, while Sonya's expressiveness eludes speech: "I got no language," Sonya claims (30).

The reviews of Delmar's *Bad Girl* also suggest the incoherence of the heroine. In virtually all of them, the "young people" are called "inarticulate" (*Saturday Review of Literature*). The *New York Herald Tribune* announces: "The principal novelty of 'Bad Girl' is that it succeeds in making articulate and comprehensible the experience of people who are neither articulate or reflective, and this, no doubt, will constitute its chief interest to many readers" (8). Readers identify, the reviewer posits, with the sexually unreflective couple. Hence, the reviewer quickly dismisses sexual "badness" to get to the middle-class joys of sexual practice, insofar as the last half of the novel accounts ironically for how the heroine outfits her new apartment and buys all the accoutrements of middle-class domesticity, including layettes, furniture, and baby toys. Instead of sexual power, Dot has commodity privilege, giving her a new purchase on life as a mother.

The reviewers note the heroine's inarticulateness, even as they celebrate the couple's indirection about sexuality. Delmar's novel was popular precisely because it gave affect to the inarticulate, as one reviewer puts it:

> In the world of Dot and Eddie marriage is often determined by seduction; and seduction, despite its guise of casual accident, is the inevitable outcome of a love too inarticulate to express itself otherwise than as desire. Mrs. Delmar makes this inarticulateness very moving; the yearning of her young people for one another is no less lovely or wistful because they know neither words nor gestures with which to communicate it; and their incapacity for communication is what gives their subsequent fortunes the qualities of pathos and irony. (*New York Herald Tribune* 7)

According to this reviewer, articulate love might be sophisticated, but it has no pathos. Instead, articulate love shows both a psychological depth and an interiority that Delmar's characters lack: "Eddie and Dot have no history, and they have no destiny; this, in the last analysis, is what makes them representative and significant." Sex power, as this reviewer sees it, is transformative and eschews desire. Delmar's power, on the contrary, is to show sex expression as beyond communication. Dot and Eddie fall quite accidentally, even wordlessly, in love.

As the *New York Times Book Review* explains: "Mrs. Delmar recognizes the very patent fact that at least one-half the world is inarticulate" (8). The reviewer points to a new category of sex and class distinction: between those who talk about sexuality with sophistication and the rest of the readers, presumably those who are too inarticulate to recognize irony. Hence, the rejection of sophistication is also an acknowledgment that "one-half the world is inarticulate," not so much because of race, class, or ethnicity but because of their newly voiced sexual desire.

It will come as no surprise, then, that even the 1929 Pulitzer Prize winner, *Scarlet Sister Mary*, was heralded for the heroine's inarticulateness, a debility sometimes ascribed, as it was in reviews of Yezierska's work, to the heroine's "primitive" passions. Peterkin was considered, at least by her reviewers, one of the strongest artists of her time. In the *New York Herald Tribune*, she was lauded for mastering the "mysticism of the primitive" (6), and in the *Saturday Review of Literature*, she was called an excellent "interpreter of negro character." "But whether she be black, white or scarlet, she is an amazingly vital and brave hearted woman" (*New York Herald Tribune* 318). Each reviewer sees the heroine Mary as "universal," as an "earth mother," just as reviewers see Yezierska's and Delmar's heroines as transcending race and class (*Boston Evening Transcript* 5). As one of Peterkin's reviewers claims, "Her book is real because she realizes that people, be they black or white, are fundamentally alike" (*Outlook and Independent* 1212). Peterkin's reviewers assess the universality of the heroine: "In her fecundity, kindness, health and happiness, as well as in her indifference to social stigma, she embodies many essential qualities of all strong women, more frankly because more primitively than would be possible for her sophisticated white sisters. How many of the latter would admit even in secret that 'men are all alike,' good only for 'pleasuring,' while work and children are woman's realities?" (*New Republic* 172). The key phrase here is "sophisticated white sisters," whose cultivated sophistication does not allow them to express or embody the frank sexual power of Peterkin's heroine.

Not unlike the reviews of these other novels, reviews of Fauset's *Plum Bun* rarely upheld it as a race melodrama or naturalist tragedy. Surprising as it seems, many of the reviews ignore race altogether or make a point of the novel transcending race. The *New York Evening Post* claims that Fauset writes "with a simple fidelity to character which has nothing to do with race or creed or color. Jessie Redmon Fauset's people are individuals first and members of an oppressed race afterward" (10). And like *Plum Bun, There Is Confusion* (1924) was hailed as a novel in which her characters strove for expression and became "articulate" (*Literature Review* 661). In these assessments, Fauset is likened to Wharton, since they share an "impersonal" art (*International Book Review* 559). For *Plum Bun*, the editor emphasizes Angela's ordinary desires for luxury and love rather than any particular attribute of black sexuality.

These reviewers erase the difference among women of Jewish, African, and American descent; plantation-worker, working-class, and sweatshop heroines feel the same desire. The true difference for these reviewers is between the ironic, seductive, articulate elite and the sexually inarticulate. In fact, these reviews show us that we need to take the widespread inarticulateness about sex as a starting point of this new sex expression.

SALOME AND SEX EXPRESSION

Yezierska invents a new term—"resistless magnetism"—to describe Sonya's "feminine mystery" (35), which, like similar constructions, critics saw as a veiled reference to Sonya's Jewishness. Yet how much was the confusion about sex power vectored onto a generalized ethnicity? Clearly, sex power promoted a general anxiety in the middle class. In one of the most compelling readings of this novel, Michael North argues that, "more overtly than the most confirmed nativist, Yezierska associates the unconscious with the immigrant, with a young woman who continually does things for reasons even she cannot understand" (99). North links her revolt from her husband John Manning to the stereotype of the anarchist, who is willing to destroy order for impulse. For Yezierska's Salome, this impulse is sexual, and as we learn, there is no racial or social order that can stand up to sex expression.

The racial nationalism of the time vigorously exoticized Jewish women. As E. A. Ross claims, Jewish women were especially short, "just over five feet, and the young women in the garment factories, although well developed, appear to be no taller than native girls of thirteen" (*Old World in the New* 289). Ross's description suggests just how confusing Jewish women's sexuality might be to a WASP male: they were physically mature but no different from young "native" teenagers. For Ross, the exoticism of Jewish women lay in their barely pubescent or adolescent appeal, and the equation of sexuality with young Jewish women came to represent, Ross would argue, a refusal of the demands of assimilation, especially the demand of sexual repression, which was generally an implicit requirement of Americanization. Thus, the notion of assimilation is bound up with sexual seduction. But who, this novel asks, is being seduced: the Jewish woman or the WASP male?

For Yezierska, sex expression is inextricably linked to fever, arguably the same contagious illness linked to Jewish immigrants. For Sonya, love is "only a sickness like smallpox or typhoid" (93), though it is Manning who is obviously contaminated, not Sonya (his family blames her for this contagion). As Sonya cries, "If I had the law in my hand . . . I'd confine love-sick fools the same as lunatics and dangerous criminals, for you never can tell what harm love-sick madmen can do to themselves or the people they love if let loose" (93). This guilt by association led to the 1924 National Origins Act, which excluded some immigrants in part because of myths of their contamination. By recasting sex expression as a form of contagion, as she does in Sonya's speech about love-sick madmen, Yezierska distances her Jewish characters from the charges of their inferiority and degeneration, and she indicts Manning instead as a carrier of such sexuality.

Manning's friends see Jewish women as " 'mere creatures of sex' " (128). He speculates that he and Sonya are "the mingling of the races[.] The oriental mystery and the Anglo-Saxon clarity that will pioneer a new race of men" (108). This sort of assimilation is exactly what eugenicists feared when they argued that such intermixing could only lead to a failure of society. Forsaking her dream of intermingling for the passionate desire of Jewish identity, Sonya also ultimately rejects this assimilation. While Manning sees their union as eliminating all "artificial class barriers" (120), Sonya comes to understand it as a violation of her self since her urges are for creativity and spontaneity.[5] Is this spontaneity Jewish or artistic? Yezierska uses this symbolic slipperiness to her own ends. After all, Manning becomes less articulate as the novel progresses, while Sonya becomes more so.

Yezierska's language of sexuality disavows an eroticized assimilation. Sonya's expression of passion resists the Americanization process that turns love into reason, coldness, and clearness; yet she aligns herself with assimilation in describing that passion in terms of its power to consume, to burn, to propel her out of the masses and the lower East Side into a new world of individual distinction. As Mary Dearborn argues in *Pocahontas's Daughters*, "One is reminded of the paradox of melting-pot rhetoric: de-eroticized by its proponents, re-eroticized by racial purists" (126). Caught in this divide, Sonya refuses to American-ize, though she has a vague desire to assimilate: she is stuck somewhere between the Protestant Manning and the Jewish entrepreneur, her men-tor Jacques Hollins (the former Jaky Solomon). For Sonya, sex expres-sion is not the way to "her deepest self-expression" (165). Sex and self are opposed since female sexuality is language that eludes her essential self, which she imagines as Jewish. She finds that being with Manning is a violation of self, however sexually vitalizing it might be to escape the East Side ghetto.

But what happens if we divorce sexuality from ethnicity and im-pulsivity from the immigrant? That is, how Jewish is this Salome? As I have been arguing, Yezierska realizes the identifying power of desire, the way it can locate and classify women's relation to power. In doing so, desire as an identity marker overturns more stereotypical identity cate-gories such as race and ethnicity. Susan Glenn notes in *Female Spectacle*, "Before Fanny Brice took Salome in hand [in 1910], the Jewishness of the character had not been prominent in American public discourse. . . . Americans emphasized her more amorphous Oriental associations. If they identified the image of Salome with Jews, it was more to the remote Hebrews of the Bible rather than to recent Jewish immigrants from Eastern Europe" (118). Yezierska's Salome may be linked to Fanny Brice, a canny revision of the "Sadie Salome" that the comedienne made popular on the stage by turning "the legend of Salome's threatening sexual perversity into a scene of comic incongruity" (119). Yezierska is invested in redeeming her Sonya from comic dismissal without turning her into an ethnic stereotype. The author plays one stereotype against another: the Oriental exotic against the "awkward ghetto girl" and her relative powerlessness (120), all designed—as Glenn argues—to explore the individuating desires of modern women (123–24).

Most important, Sonya sees her desires as oppositional, challenging the genetic discourse, related to the criminality and transgression that her ancestors in Russia were presumed to possess. While Yezierska adopts the narrative frame of the cultural legend of Salome, only when she moves beyond the cultural script of repression that Glenn uncovers does Sonya gain sex power. Just as Peterkin, Delmar, and Fauset will do, Yezierska pitches Sonya's sexuality as a desire to undo repressive history and create a sexual sisterhood.

As a paean to modern women, Yezierska repeats the phrase "consuming passion" to describe Sonya Vrunsky's desires. Salome is a cultural myth, refigured by Yezierska to focus on women's "unvoiced dreams." In a culture not ready for sexual revolution, Sonya's inarticulateness is her redemption. Sonya confesses: "I am a Russian Jewess, a flame—a longing. A soul consumed with hunger for heights beyond reach. I am the ache of unvoiced dreams, the clamor of suppressed desires. I am the unlived lives of generations stifled in Siberian prisons. I am the urge of ages for the free, the beautiful that never yet was on land or sea" (37). Sonya is all desire—no restraint or repression—but without a cultural language to name her "urge." Her expressions for desire suggest the undoing of past repression: unvoiced dreams and suppressed desires. These aren't individual or spontaneous desires but a reaction to the "unlived lives" of her ancestors: not self-made or ready-made but inherited from the "ages." Her urges are not standardized or Americanized but emerge instead from a history of desires being stifled. Sonya's metaphor historicizes her sexuality without reverting to the language of genetic indebtedness that plagued most claims about ethnic sexuality.

Eventually, like Jaky Solomon before her, she turns to designing dresses as a way to escape the settlement work she shares with Manning and the ghetto. Like Solomon, she creates style for Protestant women, the goyim, who are still too repressed to find even a language of fashion for themselves. She rejects the "marriage metaphor" of assimilation for another—that of "dress" or "dressing" the other. Sonya finds completion in the work of making beautiful dresses, "the released passion of creation" (170). She falls in love with work: " 'Is there anything in the world so real, so thrilling, as *real* work?' " (175; Yezierska's emphasis). Sonya thus layers "Jewish" style onto the passionlessness and blandness of American Protestants. She identifies with Protestant women since they too must make sex power work for them with the bloodless gentile male.

Perhaps more significant than identities—Jew versus Protestant—is the fact that Sonya displaces her sexuality from her body onto her dress. First, she models the dress that Jacques Hollins makes her, then she begins dressing herself. Leaving Manning and marriage, she opts for dressmaking with Hollins; that is, she trades Manning's sexual connection for Hollins's business tact. Failing at intimacy with Manning, Sonya chooses the self-gratification of clothes and, even more important, making clothes. Yezierska's idea of sexual style supersedes the idea of assimilation by marriage through suggesting that ethnic "style" can be tried on and adjusted, fitted to the figure of the woman. Fashion is predicated on both desire and impermanence or change, and it is here that Sonya can work her magic, giving credence to the "consuming passion" that had defined her sexual relation with Manning. Attention to dressing other women is attention to the body—to physicality—which the culture otherwise disdains. This is Yezierska's version of sex expression: if Sonya can make gentile women her canvas, she has mastered the codes of sex expression. If she can fight off the alternatively bland or savage male WASP, then she can reclaim her own sex power.

But that sex power is really the power of work. As she tells Manning, " 'Didn't you hammer it into me that work is the *only thing real*—the only thing that counts—the only thing that lasts?' " (104; Yezierska's emphasis). By the end of the novel, this is the lesson that sticks, for Sonya has turned herself from a Salome into the "Sonya model," the creator of the dress ("a poem in silk") that makes her fame and presumably her fortune. Hence, Yezierska transforms the doctrine of sex expression into the gospel of labor by way of democratizing the beauty that she so admires. Perhaps this has to do with the modernist preoccupation with authenticity, and clothing is more authentic than sex because it is material rather than ideal. Perhaps only American capitalism can transform sexual appetite and pleasure into the love of work. When Yezierska has her heroine call for a "democracy of beauty" (26–27), she also claims the rights of ethnic women to the powers of sex expression available to "It" girls like Clara Bow.

Published two years after *Salome of the Tenements*, Anita Loos's *Gentlemen Prefer Blondes* stands as an important counterexample. Loos presents a less ambiguous portrait of sex expression as capitalist engine: the Aryan bombshell, Lorelei Lee, succeeds by carefully controlling her passion. John Manning is the gentile version of Loos's Gus Eisman, the Button King; Loos's male is a Jew whose sexual gregariousness paves the way for Lorelei's sexual education with diamonds. The male Jew is exploited for all he is worth, for Loos, happily. Both Yezierska and Loos train their sights on the uses of beauty, which sustains women's power in the social world.

BAD GIRL AND URBAN SEXUALITY, OR INTIMATIONS OF IMMORALITY

There is something of what Jessica Burstein calls the blasé in Delmar's *Bad Girl*, although the novel's seeming indifference to sexuality may actually belie that nonchalance. For Burstein, the "blasé" is a new category of modern writing in Dorothy Parker, as I see it in Delmar: "The specific kind of boredom at stake . . . is jadedness, the artfully arranged ennui that comes from the weariness of seeing the same old thing over and over" (243). In these terms, Delmar's blasé dealings with female sexuality set the tone of *Bad Girl*: there is nothing interesting about Delmar's heroine—she calls herself "so darn dumb," and she's right. She is interesting only insofar as she expresses a vague naïveté and disbelief about everyone else's sexual waywardness (33). Why was Delmar's book—so thin in plot and so thick with inexpressive dialogue—such a popular success? Why toy with the idea of sexual wantonness only to have the novel end with a celebration of family and heteronormativity, consumption and procreation? This is a story about a set of friends—Maude McLaughlin, Pat Macy, Pat and Sue Cudahy, Edna Driggs, Dot Haley, and a Scottish Eddie Collins—that demystifies sexual badness and celebrates sexual inarticulateness.

The novel begins when Dot and Eddie meet on an excursion boat and size each other up: "The limit? No she would not go the limit. She would lie against his shoulder, moist-lipped, panting, but ever alert lest the purely physical barrier that guaranteed her self-respect be taken from her." In his thoughts are vaguely conscious expectations about "how far one could presume on the somewhat vulgar virginity of the lower middle-class girl" (7). They sleep together after thirty dates (45), after which Dot becomes a "bad girl," fearful that everyone will know her sexual exploit, so they get married the next day (54). Dot's brother kicks her out of the house the night of her first sexual encounter because he suspects that sex preceded the decision to marry. After a month or so of marriage, Dot becomes pregnant, and the novel charts the couple's refusal to admit to each other their happiness about the baby. They pretend displeasure but are secretly thrilled to become a family. Hardly the stuff of scandal, even for its day.

That's the point. *Bad Girl* sets out to dispel a host of stereotypes about sexually active women, even as it reinforces the domestic realm as the place where women—and men—really live, according to Delmar. The novel resolves the sexual confusion of the working-class heroine by celebrating reproductivity. Delmar includes some birth control rhetoric —should Dot have an abortion, given that she doesn't know whether her new husband wants the baby?—but she quickly dismisses birth control as the refuge of the lazy and of women afraid to be mothers. And, of course, Jews are both, as the conversation in the lying-in hospital reveals: "The Jewess [in the next bed] had a sister-in-law who had had eleven abortions. Dot was promised a glimpse of her; she was coming to visit that very evening. Dot would know her by the big diamond she wore" (233).[6] Reproductive control is associated with the abortive Jew, as well as the bourgeois Jew, who is financially rather than physically reproductive. With ethnic sex came a certain "mystique," a question of how much sexuality was linked to ethnicity and race and how much it was purely cultural or even a purely personal choice. In posing the question this way, middle-class Anglo-Saxons could try on the idea of sexuality but distance themselves from it if it turned out that sex was indeed racial, not cultural (just as the Protestants try on Sonya's dresses in *Salome* to see how well they fit). Perhaps that is why the sexuality is so blasé, even for Dot's more risqué girlfriends. There is no talk of bodies, pleasure, noises, disgust, or sweat, as though Delmar responds to the culture's desire for sex without discourse, providing as she does a clear leap from "hot loving" to family values. Delmar doesn't have to give details since the path of heterosexual intimacy is already laid out for her readers.

This plot is so standardized that Dot and Eddie's sexual intimacy proceeds without much talk or comment. Their flirting is done in "Movie"-speak (75), a language of sexual innuendo they inherit from popular culture. Their conversations reveal nothing, neither interiority nor emotional intensity. Thus, the dramatic tension of the novel results not from their sex but from their refusal to speak to each other, except in code. And this code reveals that, by 1928, the culture had absorbed the kind of sexual discourse of promiscuity that had inflamed movie audiences—via *The Sheik* (1921), for example—earlier in the decade. Delmar's chapter 12 begins with exactly such inarticulateness: "It wasn't possible to face nine months cooped up in a three-room apartment with a person so depressingly silent as Eddie. She knew what his silence meant. He was sore clean through. He didn't want a baby" (126). Like Eddie, Dot takes a vow of silence about the baby herself, ashamed to be so domesticated, so they spend the nine months outguessing each other.

Dot's friends, however, are more versed in sexuality than she is, giving her intimations of their sexual lives. Dot's best friend Edna abandons her affair with Dot's brother once he suggests that Dot is a whore for having slept with Eddie before marriage. She cannot stand his double standard, given their own sexual relations. Maude McLaughlin tries to scare Dot into having an abortion with stories of her own labor. Sue Cudahy mocks Dot's naïveté about premarital sex: "'Sue!' Dot was startled. 'You don't mean that you slept in the same place alone with Pat!'" (84). Upon Sue's response, "the room whirled before Dot's dizzy gaze. So Sue had let Pat go the limit, and no one had known it. Pat hadn't told anyone. Maybe Eddie wouldn't have, either. Sue wasn't considered a bad girl. She hadn't a frightened, persecuted expression" (84). The novel's drama revolves around Dot's becoming aware that alternative sexualities exist and that her friends don't wear the mark of their sexuality on their faces. Delmar argues that sexual desire need not mark the heroine. Dot discovers that sex expression has no expression at all.

Not understanding about adultery or promiscuity herself, Dot believes all her friends are virgins, without sexual histories or abortions. On Maude's advice, Dot goes to see a lecherous abortionist, Dr. Griegman, who fondles her during his examination (114)—an experience that makes her opt to have the baby. Her second encounter with open sexuality occurs at the lying-in hospital, which is near "New York's Congo" (162); Delmar openly associates sexuality with the geographical space of Harlem. When Dot goes into labor, she hears "The St. Louis Blues" coming from a party in a house behind the hospital: "The shades of their windows were drawn. Dot could only see the silhouette of two figures melted into one as a couple, in beautiful rhythm to the music, wiggled by" (220). Dot's labor is played out against a backdrop of more open sexuality, some "beautiful rhythm" other than the excruciating rhythm of labor pains. As she lies postpartum in her bed, she hears the all-night parties in the "Congo" and the "husky, deep voice of a dusky woman" (266) singing: "If I ain't gave you lovin' / It's your own darn fault." The women and men in the "Congo" speak the language of sexuality in songs, a medium that Delmar's heroine and hero lack. While Delmar highlights Dot's familial love as the most central passion, she does provide—quite literally— African American and Jewish American sexuality as the background to Dot's lying-in. Yet her heroine's sexuality is more about bourgeois possibility and geographic location than it is about racial stereotypes of black promiscuity and Jewish greed. In short, the "Congo" and the Jewish aborter are cover stories for middle-class whites' desire for sexual illumination and a deflection of their own sexual aggression.

Yet this misplaced aggression does not mitigate the complex sense of sexual othering that takes place in Delmar's novel. Delmar engages in all sorts of projections of sexual fantasies, not the least of which is the potential for liberation in racial and ethnic others. There is more hope than shock in the heroine's glimpse of the nearby beds and windows outside of the lying-in hospital, whether in terms of the Jewish women's acceptance of abortion or the African American blues tradition. After all, these women have what Dot lacks: a discourse of sex expression adequate to even the most blasé or banal of heterosexual experience, like her own. The novel ends with Eddie's silencing of his wife, "Shut up!" (275)—a clever ending for a novel about sexual inarticulateness.

ANOTHER SCARLET LETTER

As critics have noted, African American women writers cautiously resisted providing such illumination for white readers. Both Ann duCille and Deborah McDowell explain that black women's sexuality was virtually off-limits for black women writers of the 1920s, although sex was *the* subject for blues singers of the decade, as Delmar dramatizes in *Bad Girl*. The new morality about sexual pleasure, however, curiously became a topic for white writers—such as South Carolinian Julia Peterkin— writing about black women.[7] Peterkin's writing was hailed as realistic, especially concerning the struggle between the conflicting calls of religion and sexuality.[8] The novel begins on Mary's wedding day when she dances, a sin; she gives birth just seven months later to a full-term son, a scarlet sin. Although she renounces sin in order to join the church, she has sex with her fiancé and dances on her wedding night heedless of her renunciation of physical pleasure. The rest of the novel negotiates how she reconciles her scarlet desire with her status as Church Sister. When her husband leaves her, Mary eschews sexual fidelity and takes many lovers—some married, some not—in the plantation community. Later, Mary raises nine children, all by different fathers, and also raises her own daughter's illegitimate daughter. Nothing bad happens to her, even though others attribute the death of her first-born "Unexpected" to her own sin. Mary agrees to be baptized yet again after testifying to a vision of her redemption, but she refuses to give up Daddy Cudjoe's love charm, which has kept her young, vibrant, and happy (195). Sex also keeps her slim: already the equation of sex and slimness has become part of American sexual lore. "Ugliness" is associated with sex repression, such as in the depiction of Mary's sister-in-law, Doll, who is both "fat and stupid" and sexually repressed.

As I have been arguing, the sexually inarticulate cannot say what the middle class *will* not say or doesn't know how to express. More urgent, I see this inarticulateness as working in close conjunction with white middle-class women's desire to appropriate a language of pleasure.[9] One way to explain the attraction—enough to earn a Pulitzer Prize—of Peterkin's novel about a black woman's fall from grace into "sin" or what the heroine calls "pleasuring herself" is through the language of pleasure it offers. Does this characterization rely on racist primitivism or Peterkin's desire to come to terms with sex expression?

Sister Mary negotiates this social conflict between sex expression and religious discipline by having pleasure and forgiveness, too. One of the first of the sex-expression novels to provide an index of "pleasure," Peterkin's work was praised for the sexual frankness that its reviewers wishfully insisted transcended race. As one of the deacons remarks, Sister Mary is "a good 'oman . . . even if . . . de wickedest sinner Gawd ever made" (241). The novel specifically associates sex with cultural beliefs that ensure Mary's psychological and sexual survival. (Like Min in Ann Petry's *The Street* [1946], Mary seeks out the root doctor's medicine—the conjuror's love charm—to keep her husband in love with her.) The novel finesses Mary's sexual relations by having her repent them without renouncing her Gullah superstitions. She wants both church and sex, and Peterkin gives them to her.

Scarlet Sister Mary ups the ante for sexual pleasure. Mary's sexuality is related to the love charm—made up of blood, toenail, armpit hair, and conjure root—she gets from Daddy Cudjoe, her sexual power buoying her beliefs in hoodoo. Mary must save her husband July from another woman's predations, which are themselves associated with magic and witchcraft. In order to attract a man, a woman must have enough sexual magic or magnetism to seduce him; to keep him, a woman must rely on her own sexual magic or conjuring. In this way, her sexuality is deflected onto the idea of magic (not religion), thereby giving her more leeway in exercising guilt-free pleasure. Mary dissociates religion from pleasure, just as Peterkin dissociates sexuality from innate desire, or blood, and puts it directly in a belief system or ideology. In this language of pleasure, there is also oppositional sexuality at play. (The movie theaters and chop suey joints in the white Harlem of *Bad Girl* and the lower East Side of *Salome* correspond to the conjure rituals of the South.) Throughout the novel, Mary formulates her sexual policy. One man is as good as the next for "pleasuring"; Mary may be "scarlet," but scarlet sin keeps her young:

> If getting men, taking them from their rightful owners, had been hard work, she would never have bothered about it; but it was such an easy thing. All she had to do was call them with a look, or a smile, or the wave of a hand. Sometimes with no more than a glance. Whichever man she wanted came running, whether he was old or young, sinner or church-member. All she had to do was wear that little charm on a string around her neck as it was to-day. (248)

Peterkin's complex portrayal of Mary's oppositional sexuality corresponds to Sonya's and Dot's equally forthright sexualities. Based on Gullah history, the novel juxtaposes African religions and the power of heterosexual desire. Peterkin doesn't rehearse the history of the folk "brown girl," the "natural" woman. Nor is this the portrait of a lady kept repressed by Christianity. Mary's sex expression, like Salome's, is borne out of the social circumstances in which she is abandoned and outcast. Like Salome in the ghetto and Dot in white Harlem, she uses her sexuality to determine her place on the plantation.

When her husband leaves, Mary complains that "she never had any pleasure" (107); without pleasure, she was "withered and ugly with no way to stop being so" (110). Beauty and vitality are not possible without sexual pleasure. As Mary grieves, her only friend tells her she's "pure old an' ugly" (165). She decides to "learn to rule herself and her feelings, too," thereby cheating ugliness and poverty and plantation life (169). After this decision, the other women fear her power over men (221), and they respond by demanding money from their men to compensate for their sexual dispossession. Mary remarks: "Women have got to be strange things these days. They don't need book reading to make them act crazy. All they want is enough money to buy themselves cake and candy and bottle-drinks and stuff to sweeten their mouths and rot out their teeth. They were not satisfied to ruin their feet wearing shoes every day, but they wanted irons to straighten their hair and grease to lighten their skins" (245). Compared to Doll's new material desires for sweets and shoes and makeup, Mary's pleasuring looks more reasonable, less restricted. She rejects beauty culture for sexual expression as a more immediate and less painful mode of pleasure. Immediate pleasures ruin the body, leading to damaged teeth, feet, and hair; Mary's pleasure, on the contrary, keeps her focused and young.

That Mary treats her husband and lovers as easily fungible results from the social conditions of the male workforce on the plantation. July leaves the plantation because of its endless round of hard work; June, his twin brother, becomes Mary's lover after July leaves but eventually abandons her after he can no longer earn money on the plantation. Mary's first-born, Unexpected, also leaves to find work. If Mary's choice of man after man for pleasuring herself seems random (or magical), it is determined by the economics of the plantation: one man replaces another as the former leaves to search for viable work. Her sexuality is neither individual nor political but a choice that is actually a social necessity. Which is to say, Peterkin gives women pleasure in a culture determined by the plantation economy. In terms of conjuring, magic, love charms, Peterkin expresses a desire for what women lack, a sexual control in the context of a social order beyond their control. In this way, Peterkin and Yezierska mirror each other in their treatment of local economics.

Mary's pleasuring is set against her Aunt Maum Hanna's preservation of tradition and church doctrine. Besides Mary's sin, Maum Hanna's biggest fear is the change in the midwifing policy on the plantation that is replacing the black midwives' tradition with new white medical practices. Despite her resistance, these new white medical policies transform traditional practice by regulating black midwives.[10] Maum Hanna worries that the "birthing lesson" given by the white instructor is "sinful": "I'll tell you dis much; de lady had a razor wid em. E took em out an' showed em right in de house o Gawd" (264). According to Maum Hannah, "White people try to be too smart. . . . They ought to be careful with their laws and projects. The old way to birth children has its drawbacks, but it is plenty good enough" (210). To the extent that the medicalization of childbirth is meant to change the daily practices of the Gullah blacks on the plantation, it signals the profound discontinuity between the practices of the plantation and the outside representations of experience: whether from hell or the hospital, the outside world threatens the world of "pleasure" constructed on the plantation.

Peterkin refuses to reconcile any of these intrusions. What prevails, then, is the notion of "pleasuring" that is directly opposed to the visions of hell and medical progress that intervene in the last chapters. Spoken in Mary's internal voice, this ethos represents the novel's most vigorous endorsement of women's sexuality: "If she had stayed a good Christian girl, as she started out to be, then God might have listened to her prayers. But she sinned. She was a fallen member. She would have to depend on magic now, the only power that will work as well for a sinner as it does for a Christian" (116). Peterkin sees magic and conjuring as an ideological mechanism that guarantees her heroine Mary personal sex power against the religious and economic systems that would imprison and repress her. One could argue that sex expression doesn't do much for Mary; it's no great liberation, after all. Nevertheless, sex does stave off the ugliness that Peterkin associates with Christian repression and church sisterhood. Mary's love charm betokens her desire to control such urges and impulses, for "it is a hard thing to keep a man satisfied. A hard thing" (127). The love charm suggests that sex power resides outside the body, in some magical power other than biological impulses or psychological urges. To attract or seduce a man means to use the power of magic, and by magic here, Peterkin suggests an unconscious/conscious desire, a bridge between the two.

Christianity and hoodoo are not antithetical or contradictory. As Theophus Smith observes, it is possible to see them in tandem since religion and magic channel human passion even as plantation labor channels physical work. Thus, in their own ways, both Christian repression and love charms contain excess passion so that the plantation system will work efficiently, forcing passion to become the surplus value that must be controlled either through repression or magic. This is why the double-voiced Mary is the heroine: Sister Mary in the church and Scarlet Mary in the realm of hoodoo re-create a double-voiced perspective of the sex expression of the late 1920s. That is, Mary is both the sister and the scarlet woman, refusing to choose one or the other as her own mode of sexual identity.

Whether in dancing or in sex, Mary's idea of pleasure is immediate and physical, opposed to the delayed gratifications of Christian renunciation. Some of Mary's desires even arise from their opposition to Christian repression; she is commanded not to dance, but she does so anyway on her wedding night. Most of her sexual pleasure comes as leisure, for what else is a woman to do after a day on the plantation? Sexual pleasure remains when all else fails or leaves or dies. Peterkin, like Delmar, makes sex seem quotidian, as common as making or trying on a new dress.

PASSING, PASSION, AND PROFESSIONS

In the decades after the Civil War, consumption of tasteful fashion was a way to cite a sentimental attachment to white middle-class values since creating dresses for the white middle classes was an accepted ambition. Yet when does making clothes for oneself—as Jewish dressmaker or African American modiste—indicate a move from self-expression as ambition to sex expression as sexual desire? Dressing oneself indicates the erotic creation of a self, one available for contractual relations. In the age of ready-made fashion, choosing to buy from one maker or another signifies class loyalty. Making one's own fashions is a sign of something else entirely, about owning the means of seduction. Seeking clothes outside of mass production might allow for another kind of sexual expression altogether. As Lori Merish and Nan Enstad have shown, for late nineteenth-century women, fashion was a sentimental rhetoric, and particularly for working-class women, fashion (like consumption) was a political and class rhetoric. Several decades later, fashion became a sexual rhetoric, a rhetoric of style, that helped women make the transition from bondage to contract relations. As duCille argues, "Ostrich feathers, beaded satin, yards of pearls, hats, headdresses, and furs are among the accoutrements black women blues singers donned in constructing their performance personas and staking out their sexual ground" (94). When would middle-class women do the same? When would clothes, especially self-made clothes, become signs of a self-fashioned sexuality for the middle class?

Could sex power be used by African American women writers in the same way that Yezierska, Delmar, and Peterkin used it to signify a new modern style? Respectability is a key factor in white woman's novels of sex power insofar as "good" women can also be sexual ones. Given the stereotypes about black women's sexuality and Jewish women's exotic otherness, as well as the myths about plantation and working-class sexualities, could writers use the same tropes of sex expression without reinforcing those erotic stereotypes? Sex power perhaps had its limits.

Most critics say no. Hazel Carby exemplifies this critical consensus in "Policing the Black Woman's Body" when she argues that black sexuality was contained as part of the opposition between working-class and middle-class sexuality in urban culture. Sexual promiscuity threatened middle-class respectability, and certain professions—such as laundress and maid—were particularly suspect because of their seclusion within the home. (Carby cites van Vechten's *Nigger Heaven* [1926] and McKay's *Home to Harlem* [1928] as examples of such policing.)[11] Ann duCille, on the contrary, argues for a more coded expression of black sexuality in novels that attempted to rewrite the course of racial sexuality or to venture into "the forbidden realm of female sexual desire" (86). By the 1920s and 1930s, Fauset's writing says yes to the possibilities of sex expression.

Focusing on the legacy of slavery and the possibility of integration, Fauset's novels treat sex expression as a bellwether of cultural change. Gayle Wald has argued that passing mediates Fauset's attitudes toward sexuality (29), yet passing is only one such strategy; professionalizing is another means to sex expression. Fauset struggles to define American Sex as a function of bourgeois assimilation, distinct from racial identity, so that American Sex can only be "American" when it is raceless.[12] As Fauset envisions it, sexuality then serves as an ambition in this bourgeois landscape of desire, and in her fiction, she tests whether sexual equality will emerge as a corollary of middle-class black life. Yet even as she does so, she condemns the restraint of bourgeois sexuality for the pleasure-killing stultification that accompanies embourgeoisification.

Some critics consider Fauset an accommodationist; instead, I argue that her fiction offers an analytical assessment of the state of American Sex, in which she argues that sex is defined less by plot or character than by profession or ambition. Her characters achieve symbolically inflected professions: they are dancers in *Comedy, American Style* and *There Is Confusion*; modistes in *Comedy* and *Chinaberry Tree*; artists in *Plum Bun*; doctors in *Chinaberry Tree* and *There Is Confusion*. Sexuality accrues to each profession more than to any identity category itself. As duCille first argues, dressmaking is crucial in Fauset's symbology because sexuality is something one tries on and discards at will, a mark of deliberation rather than instinct. When sex expression becomes impulse, for Fauset, it becomes dangerous. The author repeats a pattern of professions and redefines sexuality and respectability through her characters' ambition to achieve bourgeois status. For instance, when Fauset's characters pass for white in her novels, their sexual desire takes a nosedive since they cannot pass and be sexually expressive. Sexuality accompanies professional status, not performance or passing.

The political rights that Fauset claims also include sexual rites. Consider Fauset's first novel, *There Is Confusion* (1924), which is the story of Joanna Marshall, who learns the African American cultural tradition of the "barn dance" and becomes a famous singer and dancer in the review, "Dance of the Nations." Her fame is "the big handsome extra wrap to cover her more ordinary dress,—the essential, delightful commonplaces of living, the kernel of life, home, children, and adoring husband" (274). Sexuality is tried on, like the profession, and replaced with respectable marriage. Sexual experimenting comes first, as Joanna exercises sex power as a way to advance in the world. Sex, like Joanna's ambition, is an experiment of building the self but not an end in itself.

Fauset repeats this pattern in *Comedy, American Style* (1933), the plot of which is driven by one woman's obsession for her family to pass as white: Olivia Cary wants to pass and wants her children to marry whites. Her youngest child, Oliver, is too dark. Embarrassed by his color, his mother urges him to dress up as a Filipino butler when she entertains her white friends. Once he realizes how much his mother despises him, he kills himself. Her daughter passes and marries a French professor, without his knowing of her race. The novel ends with the estranged mother, Olivia Cary, destitute and alone in France. The mother's goals for her children's passing and intermarriage fail: one son commits suicide and the other is alienated from her, while her passing daughter has nothing to do with her because of the husband's disgust over African Americans.

The daughters in this novel—Phebe Grant, Teresa Cary, and Marise Davies—have more hope. Phebe becomes a modiste and marries a doctor; Teresa marries a white professor at the University of Toulouse and struggles as a housewife while passing; and Marise becomes a famous dancer and marries a man from their old neighborhood, one whom she controls with her passive-aggressive eroticism. Marise has sex power, which she uses onstage, but she has no intimacy with her husband. Only Phebe's marriage turns out well. Phebe's mother herself had once been "gay, even to recklessness," having an interracial baby out of wedlock (282). This sexual recklessness had "disciplined her so severely" (283), and her daughter Phebe internalizes the mother's lesson. "Phebe knew all the pitiful details of that early disastrous love-making of her mother—such a child she was!" (290). She takes this lesson about impulse and choice to heart, forgoing choice and recasting love as part of concerted ambition. When Llewellyn Nash proposes marriage, Phebe confesses that she is passing. He is appalled, and his shock occasions their exchange about what constitutes "color" and "whiteness." After four months, Nash propositions her, sending her $5,000 and urging her to run away with him to France. She sends the money back and rehearses her sexual history. First, "she was a colored woman loving a colored man. But her skin was too white for him. So he had given her up. . . . She was a white woman, deeply interested in a white man. But for him her blood was too black. So he offered her insult" (295). She then marries Christopher Cary and becomes the primary caretaker for her mother and her in-laws; exhausted by this work, she is tempted by an old suitor into adultery. Overwrought from taking care of her depressed father-in-law, her color-struck mother-in-law, and her own mother—all in the same household—she welcomes her former suitor's invitation to meet him in New York for an assignation. At the last moment, before entering their trysting-place, she runs back home to her husband, in-laws, and mother. The novel ends with her relief.

In *Chinaberry Tree* (1931), Fauset chooses fashion as the means for women to meld self-expression and sex expression. Laurentine Strange is a dressmaker, which serves as both professional and creative expression.[13] Grasping the relation between fashion and contract, Laurentine also understands that she cannot make dresses for black women for fear that her valuable white women customers will no longer hire her. But she does dress herself and, in so doing, aligns herself with white women's sexuality and taste. Dressmaking for black women might have been a passage to middle-class status, but it also bore the stigma of bondage relations. That dressmaking symbolizes sex expression and exchange also complicates this history of the move from sexual bondage to contract.

By the end of the novel, both of the Strange girls marry, but not without the specter of sexual trauma: Laurentine's cousin Melissa marries Asshur Lane and becomes a farmer's wife. She had come dangerously close to having incestuous relations with her unrecognized half-brother before someone revealed that his father had had an affair with her mother that had resulted in Melissa's birth. Here Fauset deals more directly with the legacy of slavery—the possible incest that haunts women who don't know their fathers and can't recognize their brothers. Fauset's work registers a loss of the ideal of intimacy. Over the course of Fauset's career, she meditates on the contradictions of sex expression; she still dismisses the idea of authentic sexuality and refuses to accept the politics of respectability surrounding bourgeois sexuality.

Thus, Fauset illustrates the dilemma of the woman writer struggling to create the lexicon of sex expression (or borrow it from white middle-class heterosexual dramas) in the face of such sexual contradictions within contract relations. To that end, *Plum Bun* deliberates on the consequences of passing for the heroine, Angela Murray, and her sister Virginia, who "shows color" and cannot pass. Angela Murray takes instruction first from her mother in how to pass and then from her sophisticated friends in how to use sex power to gain social standing in New York City. In doing so, Angela must renounce her former identity as a "white coloured woman" from Philadelphia and re-create herself as "Angèle Mory," an artist studying in New York City (named "The Market"). At the crux of the novel is her refusal to acknowledge her sister when Roger Fielding, Angela's white lover, comes upon them in the train station. Differentiating herself from her sister by disavowing Jinny completely, Angela faces an ethical dilemma in what Fauset calls the "sex morality" issue. Angela Murray uses her sex power to compensate for her social inequality, which suggests that passing is both a racial and a sexual strategy. She must repair her offense and be reunited with Jinny in order to fulfill her needs with Anthony Cross, an arts school colleague who is also passing. Fauset's novel poses this question: If passing can produce a satisfying social equality, why can't it produce a sexual equality, too? Fauset creates this trade-off for ideological reasons, though her conservative response is ungratifying for readers seeking some sort of sexual revolution: sex equality works only if one abides by the rules of social *inequality*, which Fauset upholds as antagonistic to sex expression.

In large part, Angela Murray confuses her needs with her desires, mistaking sexual desire (her affair with Roger) for need (social and financial security). Educated by her friend Paulette in the uses of sex power, Angela happily pits her sex expression against Roger's economic privilege. According to Paulette, " 'A woman is a fool who lets her feminity [sic] stand in the way of what she wants. I've made a philosophy of it. I see what I want; I use my wiles as a woman to get it, and I employ the qualities of men, tenacity and ruthlessness, to keep it' " (105). Later, Angela's friend Martha Burden has to spell it out for her: " 'It depends on (A) whether you are strong enough to make him like you more than you like him; (B) whether if you really do like him more than he does you you can conceal it' " (145). These instructions lead to Angela's sexual experimentation, in which she achieves a "curious intimacy" with Roger (192) that is based on pleasure, not power; hers is a level of sexual experimentation that, interestingly, Fauset links with her characters' shame.

Angela realizes that "power, greatness, authority, these were fitting and proper for men; but there were sweeter, more beautiful gifts for women, and power of a certain kind too. Such a power she would like to exert in this glittering new world, so full of mysteries and promise" (88). To accomplish her ends, Angela decides to trap Roger in marriage in order to lead a useful life and to atone for her suppressed rage over having to pass (162). She recognizes her self-betrayal even as she wants to use Roger's freedom, money, and power for her own purposes. At first, Angela rejects Roger's offer of a "love-nest" (182), preferring to take nothing from him in exchange for their sexual relations. While she realizes that "men paid a big price for their desires" (183), Angela imagines her commitment as beyond contract relations, choosing instead to embrace her own "treacherous impulse" for sexual pleasure (189). While "power, greatness, authority" were men's desires, hers are cast as "pleasure, protection, and power" (200). What constitutes pleasure for Angela must be found in "protection" and proximity—her closeness to Roger. So she exchanges sex power for protection, or white male power. Hers is thus a contractual relation after all. As Fauset shows, there is nothing beyond contract, no intimacy without power and exchange. The difference between social equality and sexual equality is not, then, a matter of purity or distance from contract. In Fauset's terms, her heroines cannot achieve intimacy—true intersubjectivity and respect—because of the social alienation that black women face.

Angela is desperately afraid of her needs, in large part because she realizes that they conflict with the code of color and social inequality. Her disastrous affair with the white racist Roger Fielding leads her to dissociate her needs from her desires: she achieves social equality but at the expense of sexual intimacy. Later, after Roger leaves her, she fears intimacy with Anthony Cross despite the promise of sexual equality because she must relinquish passing. Angela develops a "deep anger," a rage against the social circumstances of race that force her to choose between social and sexual equality: "A sick distaste for her action, for her daily deception, for Roger and his prejudices arose within her. But with it came a dark anger against a country and a society which could create such an issue" (162). The problem may be a national one, but Fauset works out a solution for the individual character, not the culture. Angela is reunited with her lover Anthony only in France, outside of the confines of the United States' social inequality.

Angela lives by the diminishment of desire, by trying to constrict her needs to the most minimal fulfillment. Her desire for social equality conflicts with her deep drive for sexual equality—for intimacy and recognition. Roger represents social equality (Angela's want), while Anthony represents sexual equality (her need). To get Roger, she has to hide her race; to achieve intimacy with Anthony, she has to reconnect to her race and her work, to her ambition to paint. The way to intimacy for Angela is to individuate herself all the more, even to lose herself in her painting.

Thus, desire is disorganized, out of alignment with the passions of each character. At one point in the novel, Anthony is engaged to Angela's sister, but he loves Angela; they deny their love in order to maintain social respectability. Anthony stays engaged only because he feels sorry for Jinny, who doesn't really love him anyway. Jinny loves her old Philadelphia boyfriend Matt Henson, who is afraid of pursuing her because he once loved Angela. This plot represents the chaos of desire against the social rationalization of racial hierarchies: white over black, white over Jew, Jew over black. Angela's Jewish friend, Rachel, claims that she " 'wouldn't marry a nigger in any circumstances,' " although she is engaged to a Catholic (313). As Rachel says, " 'My parents are orthodox—they will never consent to my marriage. My father says he'd rather see me dead and my mother just sits and moans' " (312). Rachel's fate scares Angela, who realizes that she must forgo social equality for sex expression.

In a novel primarily focused on racial equality, Fauset's concern about "sex morality" is grafted onto the individual woman who chooses to use her own sex power (66). Sex power thus works as an individuating act, one that employs what women can use to level the playing field, but Fauset is ambiguous about the efficacy of this kind of sex expression. Because Fauset equates sex power with embourgeoisification, sex power is too respectable to be radical. Thus, the very sexual energies of the novel—which are designed to overcome racial inequality—prove inadequate because they cannot be racial powers. As Fauset argues, sex power is too middle class, too conservative. The question that Fauset has such a hard time resolving is whether sex power can be used for the benefit of the individual (social power) as well as the race (social equality).[14]

Just as Angela returns to self-expression (37) and relinquishes sex expression as a mode of being, the novel boldly announces that there's no such thing as "free love" for black women, any more than free love exists for white women (204). Sex power for women is an intermediate step, and it inevitably results in sex exhaustion, or what Fauset describes as the desire to be alone, making women "sick of men and their babyish, faithless ways" (230). She banishes sex power because of its inability to break the deadlock of white racism.

Fauset keeps testing the radicalness of sex power, first by having Angela desire Roger (as morally vexed as this may be) and then by having her fall in love with her sister's fiancé. She thus highlights the conventionality of desire, what duCille calls a "bourgeois version of the copulating blues" (100). Despite the hope for a democratized sex expression, Fauset—like Yezierska, Delmar, and Peterkin before her—reveals a deep skepticism about the potential of sex expression to liberate women. For each author, work, not sex, liberates women.[15]

WHEN SEX IS REALLY POWER

These novels variously seek to reclaim the "ethnic Salome," the "bad girl," the "scarlet sister," and the "tragic mulatta" as symbolizing modern womanhood rather than signaling fallen women. Gradually, almost imperceptibly, they move from hatred of sex power to inarticulateness to ambivalent acceptance. In doing so, they show how desire emerged from oppositional resistance to repression, as well as how the fallen woman is redeemed by the code of sex power, a plot of incorporation, or a rejuvenation of a girl's virtue. These novels make the route to power through work articulate.

Unlike Wharton, who wanted a singular or reigning passion, these 1920s novels are characterized by the desire for "passions," as though "passion" in the singular had already burned out as the engine driving New Women's lives. Being a "bad," "scarlet," or "fly" girl ends not in disaster but in newfound territory. Delmar's novel barely mentions "hot loving" and quickly goes on to discuss the result of sexual passion—motherhood. Delmar invests no dramatic tension in the sex itself but focuses only on its consequences. Yezierska and Peterkin also invoke the risks of sexuality, but only to let their heroines find themselves creatively. Fauset dismisses the radicalness of sexuality in favor of equality. Instead of portraying sexuality as posing dangers to women, these novels affirm sexuality as a way for women to flourish on the lower East Side, in white Harlem, on the plantation, and in the Bronx.

My point is that these novels—from Yezierska's to Fauset's—do not call attention to the difference between Jewish or African American or working-class sexuality. Rather, they obscure the difference between ethnic sex and sex in white Harlem or on the plantation. "Ethnic sex"—or what is also termed "primitive passions"—is really no different from 100 percent American Sex (one reviewer calls the leads of the theatrical version of *Bad Girl* "two young Bronx morons" [*Outlook and Independent* 314]). All of the protagonists are, finally, sexually naive. Sonya's passion may be based on her ethnic heritage, Dot's arguably on class, Mary's perhaps on race, Angela's on her racial ambivalence, yet their inarticulateness redeems them.

The series of heroines I have examined here embody the new sexual freedom. Although they live by their desire, they cannot articulate its value, either as power or as resistance. They distinguish sexuality from sentimental caring—for the home, for objects, for their dependents. In doing so, they define sexuality as a universal, even normative, desire for women, not part of ethnic inheritance, racialized experience, or class resistance.[16] This sexual psychology emerged to explain women's sexual complexity and their sexual desires, which were distinct from the predations of the street or their sexual obligations in the home.

How sex power went underground after sex expression took its final turn as a form of sexual liberation is the subtext of Fannie Hurst's eighteen novels, which are explored in the next chapter. Why Hurst? Hurst understands the ever-widening gap between what the culture allowed and what women felt. Her repeated concern in each of these novels is to figure out how women could come to terms with their sexuality without using sex power. In reimagining sexuality in terms of therapeutic psychology, American women writers like Fannie Hurst came to see sexual interactions as less an assertion of self than a claim to rights, preparing reasons for a modern heritage. Unlike the previous chapters, each of which deals with a range of different women authors on the same topic, I treat Hurst's long and impressive career in my next chapter as representing how the social changes of the 1920s and 1930s had an intimate correlation to what Hurst's heroines want.

CHAPTER SIX

Is Sex

EVERYTHING?

In a 1919 article entitled "American Family Life in Fiction" in *Catholic World*, Maurice Francis Egan claims that "Miss Hurst is frankly, but never coarsely, vulgar—that is, she makes no pretence of standing apart from the very vulgar people she describes, and this is a sign of the sincerity of her art and the fine quality of her work" (295). That "sincere vulgarity" opened up many doors for Fannie Hurst, a Jewish American novelist whose eighteen novels and eight collections of short stories represent her contribution to sex expression. Hurst showed the new dynamics of women's sexuality by dealing with a range of subjects, from rape and sexual blackmail in *Star-Dust* (1921), to a husband's past sex addiction and "burn out" on women in *Hallelujah* (1944), to a woman's own sexual "itch" in *Anywoman* (1950).[1] Following what Jackson Lears calls the "hegemony of the normal" in place by the 1950s (*Something for Nothing* 238), I will show how Hurst figures sex expression as a compulsory element of women's psychology. How were American women writers to normalize sexual relations so that "anywoman"—Hurst's code for the woman suddenly struck by the sexual itch—could feel free to pursue her sexual desires? Gone were the days when writers such as Gertrude Atherton could describe sexuality as a force of magical proportions and sexual potency, insofar as sexual magnetism provided an alternative to the regulation of sex lives. Such sexual magnetism allowed readers a fantasy of sex power beyond control, a force so great it could disrupt the regulated lives of even those surviving the Great Depression. For Hurst, however, women's sexual desires had to be explained in more rational and psychological, even psychoanalytic, terms (see, for example, *Hallelujah* for the heroine's analysis of her husband's alcoholism and her own father fixation). Irresoluteness about love and marriage, romance and intimacy, defines Hurst's heroines. She easily enough diagnoses men's dysfunctions and thus allows her heroines the self-awareness denied to their male counterparts. Yet Hurst is no social realist (the closest she comes may be in her early novels, *Lummox* [1923] and *Mannequin* [1926]); instead, she psychologizes women's sex expression and demonstrates the individualized "sexual choice," however it is prescribed, that women feel compelled to make.

This chapter's title comes from Hurst's 1942 *Lonely Parade*, in which one character—the niece—announces to the heroine: " 'Sex isn't everything.' " Her aunt counters with her own declamation about the truth of sexuality: " 'Perhaps not. But try living a life in a world that has everything but sex' " (269). This is the question that animates almost all of Hurst's novels over four decades—from the earliest *Star-Dust* in 1921 to her final *Fool—Be Still* in 1964. In a culture fixated on codifying sexuality, Hurst poses alternatives to the possibility that sex was becoming "everything," thus making her career by challenging the centrality of sex. More than any other writer of the 1920s, 1930s, and even 1940s, Hurst offered an amazing range of popular fictions devoted to the same topic: negotiating the demands of sex expression within liberal contract ideology. The public female display of the 1920s gave way in the 1930s to various forms of sexual indirection and redirection that Hurst's novels invariably dissect.[2]

So why is Hurst (1885–1968) remembered, if at all, principally for *Imitation of Life* (1933) or the huge popular success *Back Street* (1931)? She was a prolific and popular novelist and short story writer (one of the highest paid of her generation), and her interests were in various social-ist and feminist causes, in addition to the race politics of passing for which she is mostly known. Yet *Imitation of Life* is something of an anomaly in her career, a novel distinct from her lifelong interest in the psychology that animates women's success and sexual life. As *Back Street* especially illustrates, Hurst had a feel for melodramatizing the dilemmas of female need.

Hurst's model of therapeutic sexuality predicated on purity of motive takes precedence over her interest in either socialism or racial and gender equality, for Hurst's career represents a four-decades-long bul-wark against the sexual changes that occurred over the course of the twentieth century. Hurst's novels register the greater economic possibil-ities for women—Bea Pullman creates a restaurant empire in *Imitation of Life*, and Nella in *Fool—Be Still* invents her own cosmetics line sold door-to-door, eventually making her a millionaire. Meanwhile, the psy-chological possibilities of sex expression remain constant for Hurst. From *Star-Dust* onward, Hurst imagines female sexuality to be therapeu-tic rather than liberating.[3] In her first and last novels—and pretty much every one in between—women do not want security in exchange for their sexuality (in short, the liberal contract); they might compromise in marriage or in engagements and attachments, but they inevitably hold out for passion on their own terms, and failing to achieve that, they want nothing to do with sex expression, particularly any kind of sexuality that can be mapped onto contract. Her obsession with the sexual contract can be most clearly seen through her reading of the relation between the mistress and her lover, a relation that ostensibly bypasses the contrac-tual nature of marriage.

Thus, while the culture registered the liberation of women's sexuality from conventional norms, Hurst's novels—read together—do not. In her first novel, *Star-Dust*, for example, the heroine leaves her husband of two weeks for a life on her own in New York City, unaware that she is already pregnant with his daughter. She raises her daughter alone, teaching her to flaunt all conventions and to pursue her dream of singing opera. The mother's love for her daughter is pure, despite the fact that she had to sleep with her boss in order to secure a safe home for her daughter. The mother is in love with her boss's brother, who loves her in turn but falls for her daughter by the end of the novel. In much the same way, *Fool—Be Still*, a slightly altered version of her *Anywoman* (just as her 1960 *Family!* replays virtually the same plot as *Hallelujah*), depicts the widow's sexual desire as no more developed than that of the heroine of Hurst's first novel, despite the opening up of sexual norms (or what one neighbor describes as her need for a "kick" or a "cyclone" instead of the "breeze" she married [41–42]). According to Hurst, female sexual drive is inevitably bound up with social need, and a woman's sexuality is always a reaction, or even opposition, to the cultural changes around her. Hurst's insistence on sexual purity is not about having sex or being sexual, as sexual purity was defined in the nineteenth century; it is about the motives involved in sexual object choice.

Hurst's numerous portrayals of sex power revolve around the consequences of a new high standard for heterosexual intimacy. Women circulating in the culture could connect with men in the promiscuous, anonymous spaces of the city. Given that such sexual communication was beyond observation, intimate contact could transcend racial, class, and (hetero)sexual boundaries. Sexual contact begat sexual contact, spreading—as many commentators noted—like contagion. In contrast to this contagion theory, Fannie Hurst was one of the first modern women novelists to imagine female sexuality as a sort of antidote or therapy for male failure, an increasing need once the Depression took hold. Her therapeutic sexuality is modeled on the idea of absorption, in which her heroines internalize and keep everyone's secret sexual lives to themselves. They gain nothing economic or social by their sexual power but instead use it as a force for healing. By therapeutic intimacy, I mean a sexuality based on the belief that sex expression liberates and heals, especially through the talk that is supposed to cement intimacy (see Illouz, *Oprah Winfrey* 161). A woman's sexual identity is rendered meaningful through its effects on others, not as an end for her pleasure. Hurst's therapeutic orientation resists, and sometimes refigures, the demands of standardized intimacy, the kind of intimacy that wives and mistresses demand from their men: the business-contract-as-intimate-partnership. Instead, Hurst's heroines compartmentalize sexuality so that its diffuse force retains its meaning and potential power. This sexuality liberates some pain or emotional depth but cannot repair the structural inequalities undergirding modern relationships. For Hurst, sexuality is less a physical than a psychic phenomenon, as if her mantra were less soma, more psyche.

FROM SEX POWER TO SEX EQUALITY

Floyd Dell, once editor of *The Masses*, defined bourgeois American Sex as patriarchal and diagnosed modern sexuality as too mired in the past. Managing sexual desire, the socialist argued, was possible and desirable for the mental health of the nation (while only an occasional novel of "sexual luck" suggested that some people escaped the general pattern of mismanaged or disappointing heterosexual relations). As Dell argues in *Love in the Machine Age* (1930), sex is a swindle offered to the young as a bribe to get them to settle into an outmoded and bourgeois "patriarchal property-marriage" (156–57). For Dell, "the ultimate aim of the offer of 'sexual freedom' is to restore the segregation of the sexes." His tract explains how modern lovers could process their desires before settling down to "normal" heterosexual relations. Dell believed that modern women should explore sexuality by following "sexual instinct" "through a series of delays and experiences and half-matings to its immediate goal of love-choice and sexual union—not stumbling into it by accident nor trying it in casual experiment, but leading up to it as an emotional finality" (329). An argument for sexual experimentation, Dell's study of modern love and his dramatizations of it end in the same way: a rejection of "patriarchal tyranny" in favor of a "middle-class revolution" that will result in a new kind of mental hygiene or psychic and sexual health (403, 201). Even E. A. Ross wrote about his own "sex starvation" in "Positions and Attitudes" in 1935, claiming that his "big and husky sex thirst" nagged him until his marriage. He wrote, "If, for all that [i.e., efforts to whet it "by low company or erotic reading"], unappeased desire was an intermittent torment to me, how this 'thorn in the flesh' must mar the happiness of young men required by our mores to live celibate for years after manhood has touched its zenith! *And* the young women! Confessed to me a prominent society woman, 'Before my marriage I went through hell'!" (17). So Ross's hell needs Dell's sexual mental hygiene to liberate it.

Dell celebrates Owen Johnson's 1913 novel, *The Salamander*, in which a girl " 'played with' fire and was not burnt by it!" (170), as the harbinger of modern sex relations. As Johnson announces in his preface, "Precarious the lot of the author who elects to show his public what it does not know, but doubly exposed he who in the indiscreet exploration of customs and manners publishes what the public knows but is unwilling to confess!" (1). Refusing sex expression in favor of sexual "mental health" is central to this plot. Instead of falling, such heroines redeem themselves by accepting conventional heterosexual relations, enthralled with the men who domesticate them. They are women who escape punishment for sexual transgressions, but they are the exceptions, not the rule, of sexual conduct.

Johnson gets his title from the mythical animal that can endure fire without harm, a figure he offers as an exemplar for modern women. He exhorts women whose "rebellious ideas sway them," especially in the city, to exercise their "undisciplined and roving imagination" (2). Yet Johnson insists such women must maintain their sexual innocence. They should venture to the city to "examine everything, question everything, peep into everything" and then return to discreet life: their "passion is to know, to leave no cranny unexplored, to see, not to experience, to flit miraculously through the flames—never to be consumed!" (4). Johnson creates a new heroine, one of the modern women who "are determined to liberate their lives and claim the same rights of judgment as their brothers" as long as they remain virgins (7). Yet what begins as the "daughter's" right to claim her "brother's" privileges ends up as a return to conventional sexual norms.

Thus, the heroine (self-named Dore Baxter) of this 500-page novel, a would-be flapper *avant la lettre*, decides to marry and give up her life of sexual escapades, all conducted while she maintained her virginity until the age of twenty-three. Throughout the novel, she has vowed never to become a conventional "hausfrau," but by the end, she decides to become "a conventional member of society,—rather extreme in her conservatism" (529). Johnson's heroine gives up her life as a "salamander"— the creature that could endure fire, as well as a reference to young women's flashy but empty careers as various types of adventurers—and chooses to reform a young, rich male drunkard instead (a plot Hurst will revive five decades later); she attends to his needs when he goes on a bender and then, after his reformation, settles down with him rather than with her married admirer. Johnson's idea of "modern love" demands a kind of ethnographer's imagination, a willingness to observe but not participate. Johnson ushers in a new heroine, one who doesn't care about sexual desire at all but instead wants to experiment in the social world.

Dell's own *Janet March* (1923) also leads the heroine through various New Women roles, only to end with her pregnancy and upcoming marriage at age twenty-one. Dell explores the effects of feminism, sexual experience, abortion, orgies, patriarchal relations, and "modern love" on his heroine and her future husband. They both gain sexual experience, which is Dell's prerequisite for "mature" love, until they are ready to commit to each other. Such commitment seems to augur the regulation of heterosexual relations, for Dell shows how early sexual indulgence can lead to a life of managed or healthy relations. In "Sex in American Fiction" (1948), Dell complains that "as an elderly person" who once wrote fiction himself, "I sometimes shocked people by its frank treatment of sex" (84). He is now disgusted by the influence James Joyce and D. H. Lawrence have had on American literature, making sex expression "the dull sickening subject that it is today in so much of American fiction" (85). Dell argues for a return to the sexual frankness he advocated over the "sour neurotic notes of contempt for sex and hostility toward women" that current fiction delivers. Dell looks back to his hopes for sex expression: "I used to look forward, as a young idealist, to the time when American fiction would be free to deal frankly with the sexual side of life. I believed that our fiction would be, as a result of that freedom, gayer and sweeter, healthier and saner. The results of the freedom, so far, have not come up to my expectations. I suppose I should have realized that when the lid was lifted from that seething cauldron of repressions, what would emerge first in fiction would be the neurotic fantasies of guilt and fear" (89). Dell's young idealism allowed him to revere sex expression, which he rejects as a "seething cauldron" when he is in his sixties. And Dell ends by discounting the neuroticism of current authors: "I expect to be bored, disgusted and shocked by humorless, unkind, crude and incompetent accounts of the sexual behavior of slobs and louts and loons" (90). Yet Dell holds out for the mental and sexual hygiene of great literature.

Unlike Johnson's *The Salamander*, Dell's novel allows his heroine her sexual experience, while she—like Doré Baxter—doesn't experience any ill effects. Thus, Dell validates the importance of sexual expression as a *prelude* to conventional marital relations. Janet March has her affair, then an abortion, and finally asks her liberal father's permission to go "wild" in New York. After sowing these oats, she meets and marries Roger Leland, a bookstore owner fifteen years her senior, who comes with his own sexual history. Roger translates his reading of sexology into practical knowledge: "He did not understand what she meant until she went on to utter a string of phrases, some of which he remembered having heard, and which he realized were the professional appellations of strange and ugly practices that he had read about under quaint Latin names in the pages of Krafft-Ebing" (283). This reference to Krafft-Ebing is significant: by 1923, such sexology was so popular that its practices were accepted as part of Dell's middle-class revolution. Roger goes on to have a great affair that ends in his lover's suicide. Much altered, he waits for Janet to turn twenty-one for them to marry.

For Johnson and Dell, female sexuality leads to *eventual* heterosexual relations and healthy marriage; women's sexual experimentation serves as the means to the end of privatized marital relations. These sexual-experimentation novels end in the heroine's transition from understanding her own sexuality as voluntary—a choice—to understanding it as involuntary, an impulse that cannot be denied and thus must be channeled. The authorial trick, then, is to have the heroine orchestrate her choices so that when the involuntary passion takes over, she can exchange her sexuality for the security that the right man offers, as though women could both will and unwill their desires. With exchange as the norm of heterosexual relations, capitalism "reorganizes desire," Carol Siegel explains, so that what once seemed like the promise of sex equality and democratized gender relations ends up as the supreme act of sexual control and submission (78).

Flouting the principles of this reorganized desire, Hurst revises women's sexuality along therapeutic lines. In doing so, she rejects the idea of heterosexual love as *reciprocity*, exchange, or security and celebrates instead love that seems impractical and irrational (see Siegel 55). Unlike Dell's highly rational system for working through experiment to mature modern love, Hurst's heroines follow their often inexplicable motives for passion. They assert the primacy of feeling, a romantic response to the antiromanticism of contract.

Arguably, even Judge Ben Lindsey's public advocacy of "companionate marriage" in 1927, which replaced the idea of business contract with that of intimate partnership in the marriage market, sentimentalized what had already become the mostly business deal of the marriage. By displacing the economic with the companionate, Lindsey wanted to rescue sexuality from its debasement as a mode of exchange. Inevitably, efforts such as Lindsey's only exposed the culture's acceptance of the contract as the dominant mode of relations, however much they tried to gloss it by explaining desire and its workings as somehow exceeding contractual negotiations. Hurst invokes Lindsey's system in her autobiography, *Anatomy of Me* (1958): "The decade of experimentalists advances. Sex is a discovery. The word, which had lurked so long in the nasty silences, becomes usage. . . . Judge Lindsey of Denver pulls the rock away from sin and the nation gasps at the facts of the demoralization that crawls out from under. . . . The sane hard core of American living, for the most part intact, recedes behind phraseology of the high-kicking twenties. Petting parties. Necking. Trial Marriage. Gin. This is the order and disorder of the day" (257). Hurst objected to the publicity over "trial marriage," though she lived one out with her husband Jack Danielson. As Steven Seidman reports, Fannie Hurst's own biography provides a test case of the limits of companionate marriage. She kept her marriage secret for five years, maintaining separate residences in order to sustain her career (109). Hurst's own ambivalence about sex expression thus leads her to repudiate the idealization of erotic intimacy. In novel after novel, she melodramatizes women's growing invisibility within modern romance, while substituting her own version of love for a romantic one. Hurst imagines herself as one of the writers bound to the "nice people" by temperament and breeding and to her "Friend, The Anonymous Public," to whom she dedicates her autobiography. (These nice people bought her books in millions.) But how do "nice people" negotiate modern sexuality?

The narrative of failed desire, especially failed heterosexual coupling, became a successful paradigm for Hurst precisely because that failure forced her heroines, through a sort of sexual altruism, to create alternatives to sex power and sexual pleasure. Exactly at the time that intimacy was supposed to guarantee human happiness, Hurst shows how much pain results from this idea of modern selfhood. Within this contradiction—between the idealized promise of intimacy and the failure of desire—the true import and representativeness of Hurst's novels unfold. Utopian longing for perfect intimacy coupled with the intensity of suffering fuel her plots; the intimate self is the ideal self, but one whose love hurts.

HURST'S SEXUAL MODERNITY

My previous chapters have been centrally concerned with questions about the differences among sex power, sex pleasure, and sex rhetoric, as well as the differences between sex as an act and sex as an identity. I have discussed how women characters assumed sexuality as power and then figured sexuality as a form of pleasure or self-expression. The modern self was supposed to find gratification in sexuality that would inevitably lead to commitment, companionship, and possibly intimacy. Such rationalization of sexuality, what might even be called the bureaucracy of passion, made sexual pleasure not an end in itself but a means to companionate equality. Thus, sexuality became instrumental, no less or more so than in Harriet Beecher Stowe or Edith Wharton or ultimately in Anita Loos, whose heroines used sex power for their own aggrandizement.[4] This modernization of sexual attitudes—geared to instructing individuals in how to accept pleasure and renounce repression —served as a way to imagine self-expression in a whole new register.[5] As Steven Seidman observes, "This companionate ideal has triumphed in the twentieth century" (73).

Yet at what cost did the companionate ideal become the desideratum of American sex expression once that type of marriage was imagined to carry so much social, personal, and now sexual baggage? Reformers such as Dell reconceived intimacy as mental health but without changing the gender hierarchies that shaped the sexual division of labor. Companionate marriage might have seemed like the first step toward equalizing gender roles given its emphasis on mutual recognition, but it did not advance women's social rights. By the 1930s, modern liberalism cast legitimate sexual relations in terms of contract and property, which were screened by the promises of the companionate ideal. This era of women's writing registered a conflicted sense of allegiance to romance as an ideology and a genre, arguing for women's greater needs elsewhere, for instance, in social equality and personal satisfaction.[6] Hurst's novels situate intimacy outside of market relations in order to avoid the normative and the contractual. Love, in her view, could only be love if it were unalloyed by economic contract, beyond the gift-economy or any sort of rational exchange. Perhaps the largest part of Hurst's popularity resides in her novels' conviction that social contract could not, and should not, regulate passion.

Consider Hurst's highly ironic take on the legitimate claim to sex equality in her novel *Mannequin*.[7] As great a potboiler as Hurst ever published, *Mannequin* focuses on the daughter (Joan) of a woman obsessed with bargain hunting. In order to have more time for shopping, the mother hires a nurse (Nana), who is also a bargain since the woman comes without references except from a reform school. Driven by "greed" for maternity, the nurse steals the baby and raises her in the tenements as her own daughter, whom the nurse renames Orchid Sargossa. The heroine survives thirteen years in the tenement, while Nana becomes a drug addict, prostitute, and drunk; one day, she abandons Orchid. The novel ends with the reunion of the parents with their daughter in a courtroom scene during which Joan/Orchid is acquitted for the murder of a would-be rapist. When Nana sees Orchid's picture in a newspaper, she returns to Orchid in the courtroom, at which point the biological mother recognizes the scarf that Nana carries into the courtroom and identifies her long-lost daughter—but not before the mother is punished for her compulsive shopping by losing her daughter for two decades. And not before the father becomes the judge in his own daughter's murder case. Hurst works out the social anxieties of New Women through shopping and sexuality, even as the novel seems to indict the new consumer culture for forcing women to choose one over the other.

Mannequin struggles with the consequences of "sex equality," in Hurst's own term, showing how 1920s culture wanted women to be responsible—after the vote—for their sexual and consumer choices. Hurst complicates this question of equality and responsibility, revealing how the context of old rules of courtship, families, and sexuality are too formulaic to be trusted. Familial identification and tradition no longer suit; instead, Hurst shows how much women need to develop self-reliance rather than submit to convention. As Hurst's novels contend, women—more than men—have been greatly affected by social reorganization, so much so that desiring mothers steal other women's children, biological mothers don't recognize their own daughters, and a father judges his daughter on trial for her life. This family dynamic suggests how the split from these past social arrangements has deeply alienated Hurst's characters.

Orchid flourishes in the settlement house where she lives, and after a brief stint as a salesclerk, she becomes one of the city's famous models for a couture house until she is accosted one night by a drunken admirer in her apartment. He falls on a decorative dagger lying around, but by turning over his body, Orchid destroys evidence and is accused of having stabbed him to death. Coincidentally, Orchid's boyfriend, a young journalist, has just published a series of articles denouncing women who kill and are then acquitted. He has stirred "up agitation about the women of the country being able to get away with murder" (285). Although his words are used against her, she is nevertheless found not guilty by a jury that won't be bullied into convicting her because of the public pressure for sex equality in matters of justice—"a wave of public hysteria that has swung too far" against women (285). The lone holdout to convict her is a proud butcher with a German-Hebraic accent.[8] The other eleven men accuse him of "condemning a human soul to destruction because [he] is hysterical with mob psychology" (286). They acquit on this basis, not because Orchid is nearly raped; instead, the journalist's plea for sex equality strikes them as "hysterical" and the trial seems a form of "baiting the woman."

Of Hurst's novels, *Mannequin* is least devoted to therapeutic sexuality and more designed to repudiate standardized American culture, which Hurst represents as bourgeois social values in one of her characteristic lists: "The apartments of thousands of the standardized young families of the American commonwealth. Backbone-of-the-nation families. Statistic-builders. Willing products of the biscuit-tin system of standardization. Standardization of morals, furniture, derby hats, salad-dressing, velour upholstery, churches, colleges, amusements, silk stockings, morning cereal, and morning headlines" (6). For Hurst, the greatest form of middle-class standardization of all is the transformation of sexuality into the kind of intimacy that destroys women's quest for autonomy. In the framework of this standardized sex expression, women seemingly had to negotiate the same set of choices—standardized as taste for furniture as much as for morality or pleasure—and to make those choices seem individually tailored to their class and habitus.

How were women to negotiate standardization and create individual style? In Orchid's career, Hurst illustrates exactly how choice became no longer compensatory (as a substitute for real social power) but compulsory. Hurst emphasizes the mother's ambivalence about standardization insofar as she embarks daily on an obsessive search for the taste-defining bargain, an object or thing that is supposed to define her style. The daughter, in turn, loses all individuality completely, first as the stolen child and later as a mannequin. While the mother once desperately sought individuality in the face of standardization, the daughter makes a career of erasing her individuality in order to represent standardized style. Twenty years after her disappearance, mother and daughter don't recognize each other, so standardized—as a mannequin—has the daughter become. During the trial, she is still a mannequin, and her counsel urges her to emote in order to save herself. Like Hurst's stereotypically masochistic heroines, Orchid cannot even articulate her own defense on the witness stand. Although the daughter urges herself "to thaw," her tongue "all swollen like a dry hot potato" (262, 267), she is saved by the male jury's resistance to mob psychology, not by her own self-expression or defense, a decision that Hurst sees as social and familial confusion resulting from the American standardization of taste.

Mannequin was the novel that defined the sexual problem for Hurst to solve: the problem of sex equality and the anxiety that it prompted—that women could get away with murder. Yet rather than maintain the liberating power of sexuality or desire, Hurst's novels redefine liberation as the freedom from desire and sexual power, a liberation from sexuality in order to pursue self-sufficiency. One of Hurst's most uncomfortable novels, *Lonely Parade* tells the story of three "bachelor girls" who set up a household in New York City in 1900 as "new women" whom Hurst glamorizes even as she pities (43, 76). All three desire love, marriage, and babies, but they consider themselves first "new women," with respective careers as booking agent, interior decorator, and settlement house worker. They are all reluctant virgins, and the author spends considerable time elaborating on their ambivalence about sexuality, especially the one who is deliberately fat and takes up more psychic and physical space than Hurst's characters are usually allotted. (Hurst herself was notoriously anxious about her own weight; in *Anatomy of Me*, she advocates an "ascetic" regimen of "undereating" [341–42].) In the novel, friends and acquaintances wonder "who slept with whom" and what their "queer" household means (72, 79). Hurst explores same-sex desire here, but "lesbianism" is also listed along with menopause, clubfoot, kleptomania, hallucinations, tuberculosis, unwed pregnancy, suicidal mania, theft, drug addiction, alcoholism, and persecution complexes as "case histories" of what can go wrong with female desire (213–14). Her most stereotypical character, Sierra, known as the saint among the three for her decades-long dedication to settlement house work, is the only one still single and working at the novel's close.

Hurst everywhere insists on the invisibility of women within mar-

Irene Polini, clubfoot
Gerta Diefenbach, kleptomania
Lizzie Cronin, menopause
Mary O'Connel, hallucinations
Irene Machter, tuberculosis
Eliza Gibbons, unwed pregnancy
Sofia Szold, suicidal mania
Maria Poppola, theft
Isa Kantor, persecution complex
Clara Brown, alcoholic
Bebe Ibbetson, Lesbian
Berta Crooks, Lesbian
Lucy Smith, theft
Celia Castriani, drug addict

List of women's "case histories" from Fannie Hurst's Lonely Parade *(1942).*

riage and modern romance, a divide that means the erasure of work for sexual security. The author depicts single women's self-expression as a less desirable trade-off for sex expression, even though all of her married women become invisible or banal, and single women are frustratingly miserable. Self-expression no longer leads seamlessly to sex expression, but by 1942 self-expression and sex expression are at odds. If sex and power were once conjoined, sex here is the opposite of the power that Hurst's three heroines wield. (The only love interest in the novel is the lethargic stepson who runs off to Europe with his stepmother in order to consummate their mutual passion.) Instead, sex represents the end of business life since it separates women from the world in which they work. The last lines of the novel, in Sierra's consciousness, are perfect expressions of this sublimation: "Work. Work. Work. Thank God. Work. Work. Work" (343).

The novel itself is a case history in what Hurst variously calls the oversexed, undersexed, sexless, sex-starved dilemmas of the unmarried woman. Hurst pits self-fulfillment and female success against the "waves of compulsion"—or sex expressions—that drive "normal" women (252). This sexual compulsion corresponds to the "repression and compulsion" model that Jennifer Fleissner has analyzed in naturalist texts (25), and like Fleissner's heroines, Hurst's are "stuck" in a dated model of sexuality—and bankrupt sex expressions—from which she must rescue them.

WHEN NICE GIRLS GET THE "ITCH"

What do "nice" women do besides sublimate? In her 1950 novel *Anywoman*, Hurst tells the story of Rose Cologne, a quiet or "still" (the Hurst code for "frigid") country girl who falls hard for a swim and dance instructor at a Catskill resort. Rather than the Jewish Catskills, as Hurst makes clear in this post–World War II melodrama, this is the leisure world in which 100 percent Americans try to preserve their distance from the sexual and ethnic difference that Jews represent. Rose doesn't want to marry her safe fiancé Mark Filiatrault, a country doctor whose ambition is to stave off the onslaught of Jewish visitors and parvenus in their country valley by having as many eugenic children as possible. So her foster sister, an "It" girl whose sweaters reveal her stereotypically pointed breasts, marries him and reproduces quickly. Rose gets the sexual "itch" for Frank Caesar, for whom she'll do anything, although he continually warns her away (101). The opposite of the frigidity that the author everywhere ascribes to women, the "itch" represents the uncontrollable urge to chuck all propriety and have sex. As Frank Caesar remarks to Rose, "So you *have* got an itch that needs scratching!" (101; Hurst's emphasis). *Anywoman* ends with Rose's marriage to Frank Caesar, but not until a series of unfortunate events—his marriage to a wealthy widow whose inheritance is withheld due to legal restraints, the death of a woman seeking an abortion he had arranged with his doctor associate, the amputation of both of his legs after a plane crash that killed his rich wife—have made him acquiesce to their union. In what may be the bluntest of Hurst's novels, Rose Cologne represents a woman whose sexual inhibitions fall away once she meets a man for whom no rational desire can be explained. Frank Caesar is a gigolo, a gambler, an abortionist's procurer, and Hurst does not try to redeem him. Rather, the novel is predicated on the itch that is beyond conscious understanding—love beyond reason or rational explanation. At the end of the novel, Rose is a traveling vacuum saleswoman, happily supporting the wheelchair-bound Frank and his gambling habits.

Again and again, Hurst's novels replicate the standard tale of women's dismissal of contractual sex power and sexuality as a means to liberation, moving them through sexual ambivalence, sexual conservatism, even sexual exhaustion to something beyond what had become conventional sex expression. Many of Hurst's female heroines would qualify as sexually inarticulate; they are women who feel passion but who are far from being able to voice or explain their desires. They refuse to profit by their sexuality, operating by an ultimately private code of sexuality, one that bars any connection to liberal contract relations.

As Lauren Berlant has argued about Hurst's most famous novel, *Imitation of Life*, the white woman's most important relationship is not a product of the heterosexual revolution of the 1920s but a relationship with a black woman, and the two live as "a quasi-companionate couple" struggling to make it within "the structures of commodity capitalism and American mass culture" ("National Brands/National Body" 178). Once they do create a mass-produced commodity known as "B. Pullman" pancake restaurants, however, "the white daughter falls in love with her mother's love object; the light-skinned African-American daughter wants to pass for white, and so disowns her dark-skinned mother, whose death from heartbreak effectively and melodramatically signals the end of this experiment in a female refunctioning of the national public sphere" (178–79). Berlant's essay shows the tension between the desire of Hurst's white heroine, Bea Pullman, for female identification and her association with men in the national public sphere, which she is forced to enter when widowhood threatens the security of her father and her fatherless daughter. Bea's relation to women positions her in a kind of nostalgic intimacy, while her dealings with men put her in a necessary competition with them for public success. The outcome of both is a kind of sexual exhaustion, so tired is Bea of both domestic and capitalist arenas.[9] The novel focuses for the last twelve chapters on the very question of Bea's sexual exhaustion—her inability or unwillingness to follow in the heterosexualization of American culture. As Berlant notes, "Fame and money eroticize her in the public eye" (185), and the new beauty culture conspires with the public to advance the commodification of female sexuality. Falling in love with Frank Flake, her assistant, Bea fantasizes about a sexual life with him but gives up her fantasy quickly when she realizes that he loves her daughter.

Imitation of Life might fit better in the array of middle-age sexuality novels I explore in chapter 3—Bea is forty and "greedy" (285)—except that this novel is less about sexuality than about her long-standing ambivalence about erotic pleasure: "Was it her sensitive middle-age role to turn aside from these belated stirrings?" (263). When her daughter Jessie tells her of Frank Flake's love, Bea realizes that their youth makes the relationship "so right" (292). The eight years' difference between Bea and Flake makes her the kind of middle-aged grotesque that Atherton figured in the gerontic virgin Agnes in *Black Oxen* (see chapter 3). Both daughters—Peola and Jessie—opt for immersion in heterosexual unions, but both relationships entail the kind of hetero-invisibility that Hurst rejects. Jessie wants to marry Flake and become what her mother could not—his wife; Peola wants her mother's permission to pass as white in South America with her shell-shocked fiancé "A.M.," whom Peola refuses to name. Hurst's emphasis is less on the racial passing of the light-skinned Peola than on the difference between the generations of mothers and daughters: the mothers are highly visible symbols of success, while the daughters choose marital invisibility.

As Berlant has suggested, perhaps the daughters resist the mothers' immersion in capitalism. But what do we do with a heroine who has no powers of resistance, no self-conscious revolt from her mother? In *Lummox* (1923), Hurst's heroine is Bertha, an orphan of mostly Eastern European heritage who is of the servant class, big-boned and big-hearted. Her influence is equally big because every life she touches turns out better for her presence. At one of her first jobs, the poet-son of a millionaire rapes her, and she gives birth to a son whom she ultimately gives up for adoption. But the poet writes a famous book, *The Cathedral Under the Sea*, based on his physical understanding of her Baltic female sexual strength. Bertha moves from job to job, sometimes starving because she is too old to be hired as a charwoman but always making something emotionally right in each household she enters. The novel ends when Bertha, laid off from another cleaning job, stumbles into a bakery and, dizzy with hunger, is hired to take care of the baker's four motherless children. At long last, Bertha finds her place among the Meyerbogens, whom Hurst depicts in a series of actual drawings of stick figures, Bertha's the biggest

PAPA ESSIE ME OSCAR JIMMIE BERTHA

The Meyerbogens

Visuals from the end of Fannie Hurst's Lummox *(1923).*

of them all. Thus, Bertha reconnects with her peasant heritage among these stocky children whom she mothers. As part of the ubiquitous "servant problem," Bertha moves between and among promiscuous spaces, yet she is a woman beyond the sex stereotypes of the 1920s, neither fallen woman nor flapper.

At one of Bertha's jobs, a sensitive daughter recognizes the servant's "gift": " 'Why even Bertha—that great, white peasant girl out there in your kitchen—why there—there is something about her comes nearer to understanding the frail, delicate, tremendous little trifles about life' " (213). Bertha—the Lummox, the inarticulate and clumsy—is a creature of the unconscious, someone whose life remains inarticulate but whose passion for "frail, delicate" elements runs in impulses and drives. For Hurst, there is no inborn or inherited urge for sexual pleasure. In fact, for Bertha, sexuality of the middle-class American woman is perverse, mired in acquisitiveness and avidity. At each job she undertakes, Bertha's life is set against the failure of various sexual contracts: the Italian girl who sells herself to a sailor for a dime; the gentile wife's indifference to her Jewish husband and his mother; the woman who hides from her husband's sexual advances; the mother who drives off her daughters' suitors. Bertha eventually settles in with an immigrant family whose values more closely resemble hers; they are earthy, clean, orderly as opposed to the aridity of bourgeois life.

As late as 1960, *Family!* (one of Hurst's last novels) repeats this structure in the story of three brothers and their children, two of whom are self-made men and another a salaried worker barely making ends meet. The wife of the wealthiest brother, Charley, dies after a long mental illness (she's a self-mutilator [17]), and he takes comfort in Virgie, a woman who nurses all sorts of stray men back to temporary sobriety. Virgie is still technically married, her husband having abandoned her years earlier, so she and Charley consecrate their own marriage in her dingy apartment. Charley offers her a Cadillac, which she peremptorily refuses: "'I don't do for nobody—for anybody that I don't get real pleasure out of doing'" (70). She also refuses his offers of money and says she loves him for "real pleasure," which is Hurst's term for the authentic sexuality she promotes. While living with Charley in his St. Louis mansion, she brings the various members of his family back together in harmony, including Charley's mentally ill son, who is plagued by alcoholism and obsessive fears. (This is one of Hurst's recurrent themes: the drunken son whose battle with alcohol destroys families, as in her otherwise anomalous *A President Is Born* [1927].) Virgie banishes the son's anxieties by holding him all night in her arms, using her sexuality as a therapeutic balm for his fears. Providing therapy for others, mainly men, is "pleasure." Hurst focuses here on the notion of women's real pleasure, divorced from sexual gain and invested in authentic feeling and therapeutic health. When Charley returns home early and sees his son in bed with Virgie, he imagines the worst and sends Virgie packing; she goes to her old apartment, which is miraculously still available, and begins nursing one of her old drunken "ruins" (284). The novel ends with the family intact but with Virgie gaining nothing except her old apartment and the consolation of providing therapy for the fallen man.

Earlier, in *The Hands of Veronica* (1947), a heroine forgoes sexuality—that is, giving in to "impulses which threatened to sweep you off your feet" (182)—in order to practice her miraculous therapeutic laying on of hands to cure people's disfigurements and disabilities. However formulaic these narrative conclusions are, they give credence to the "individualized" sexual choices of the heroines. Thus, Rose and Veronica reject "safe" marriage in order to preserve their own psychologically complex ways of loving. This is Hurst's pattern: heroines seek to practice therapeutic sexuality—as Lily Browne does in *Hallelujah* when she ministers to her alcoholic husband and the paralyzed daughter of her high school crush—and they forswear traditional reproductive sexuality. Similarly, both Bertha and Virgie feel neither rage nor sadness over their rape or rejection, returning to fulfilling absorption in other people's pain.

Even in the dominant mode of melodrama, Hurst went against the grain of her contemporaries, such as Kathleen Norris, whose 1911 novel *Mother* celebrates domestic harmony. Instead, Hurst depicts women who are without passion for things or even for men but are invested in "pure" desire; that is, either for children (*Lummox*), for drunken or aging men (*Family!*), or for Christ (*Appassionata*). In *Appassionata* (1926), the heroine, Laura, does not sexually desire her fiancé, Dudley, thinking of herself as the Pieta to his wounded Christ. Dudley, however, keeps insisting on a quick wedding in order to consummate their marriage, if only to fulfill his overwhelming desire, while Laura prefers a religious ritual of submission. Her long-suffering mother and domestically abused sister look at her with fear, knowing what they do about destructive male passion and its brutalizing effects, for both are marked by their "terrible meekness" (170). In one of the strangest of Hurst's early novels, Laura struggles with her lack of desire; though she hears the "sex voice," she has no answer for it (255). At the end of the novel, she has a brief passionate fantasy about an old acquaintance, yet her ambivalence paralyzes her with fear of this stranger's passion, and in the last act of the novel she prays for guidance. Her legs are paralyzed by sexual panic until she decides to join the House of Mercy and become a nun devoted to prostitutes.

For Hurst, marriage is no longer the companionate, affectionate, or liberal modern relation it once was or seemed to be, nor does marriage guarantee heterosexual love or intimacy. In *Appassionata*, Laura finds the prospect of sex expression numbing. Marriage becomes a social necessity, organizing sexual object choice (heterosexuality) and sexual division (gender and labor) and leading Hurst to reimagine intimacy as voluntary association. For the novelist, "modern love" erases all individuality from sexual desire (even ethnic sexuality) and replaces it with a conventional, contractual relation. Female sexuality is no longer responsive to the deep drive for self-expression but instead is so standardized that it becomes the major form of social recognition. Thus, there's a reason why all of Hurst's female characters are socially indistinct: Bertha is a houseservant, charwoman, and day worker; Virgie is a morning clerk at the grocery above which she lives; the rich Jenny Avery Ratick is at financial odds with her gigolo in *Five and Ten*; Ray Schmidt is a former button-and-cloth saleswoman and kept woman in *Back Street*. Hurst's heroines test their ability to survive as individualists, financially and sexually free, involved in no sexual-adventure or mistress plots. But because they cannot find pure love, they end up choosing passivity, even the convent or death, instead of muddying their motives. Hurst's novels have been read as sentimental melodramas, but there's something else going on in them: not only does Hurst test the limits of companionate marriage versus heterosexual contract, but she also separates companionship from contract, giving the lie to Judge Lindsey's conviction that marriage could be the liberal solution to female desire. Hurst's characters cannot be accused of some profiteering or sexual adventurism because they want nothing and, of course, get nothing.

Why not just dismiss Hurst's heroines as gullible or irrational or, as some critics do, as female masochists? I argue here that Hurst's melodramas work because their visions of sexual dysfunction are coupled with her emphasis on women's self-reliance. Her plots are not indictments of male power or privilege; such condemnation is a given in Hurst's fiction. And it's not that sexual liberation triumphs over sexual repression, for these are outmoded terms for Hurst, who attempts to move beyond them as a rhetoric of sexual motives. To achieve a moral victory, Hurst's heroines relinquish the sexual power that previous novels such as *Bad Girl* or *Scarlet Sister Mary* celebrated.

"KEPT WOMEN" NOVELS

I suggest that Hurst creates a new style combining the emotional energies of postsentimental nostalgia and the newly voiced urgency of twentieth-century sex expression. The search for "authentic" rather than contractual desire becomes her *cri de coeur*. As Hurst would ask, is there an intimate, sexual self possible in opposition to economic exchanges? Frequently, she looks to answer this question in the mistress novel, a lively genre for men and women authors alike. Women writers especially portray their "kept" heroines as women who want a more authentic desire than what they can get in marriage, whether in Edith Wharton's *The Reef* (1912), Anita Loos's *Gentlemen Prefer Blondes* (1925), Jessie Fauset's *Chinaberry Tree* (1931), or perhaps most notoriously Hurst's *Back Street* (1931), certainly one of the most fantastic and heartbreaking of these mistress novels. Kept heroines are looking for a male who can deliver a passion disengaged from familial cares, unencumbered by the demands of status. (Later, as I will show, Hurst essayed the gigolo novel, too.) An authentic male sexuality may be at stake since—for Hurst—men can't give a "pure" sexual response in marriage. Beginning with Theodore Dreiser's *Sister Carrie* (1900), "kept women" novels also contribute to the antimodernist sensibility from the turn of the century: being "kept" is a relation of stasis, of preserving the status quo, since the relation can't move forward, can't progress.[10] Kept women are not creating a home (they have even less power than their married counterparts) but instead maintain a place where sexual freedom is more authentic, though circumscribed by its opposition to conventional marriage.

In fictions as various as Ellen Glasgow's earnest Depression-era *Vein of Iron* (1932) and as ironically comic as Mary McCarthy's *The Company She Keeps* (1942), women writers characterized the new sexuality through metaphors of exchange, the exchange of one kind of physicality (sex) for another (work). By the 1930s, this language is also a language of loss or mourning for the sexual expansiveness of the 1920s. This is certainly the tone of Dorothy Parker's "Big Blonde" (1929): as the heroine is kept by more and more men, she loses her sense of sexuality's carnivalesque power, preferring to drink herself out of her melancholy and ultimately taking pills in a failed suicide attempt. As in *Back Street*, Parker's story shows the price exacted from kept women. Parker's heroine must keep up appearances, keep her expression cheerful, keep her demons at bay. The men threaten to leave when she can no longer sustain her sexual vivacity. Parker's men don't want sexually depleted women but want their kept women filled with the illusion of security but the pleasures of spontaneity. The Big Blonde's loss of spontaneity occasions her depression, which for Parker is the most authentic sign of women's sex expression. Parker tries to stabilize sexuality through a new language of certainty, in this case material and domestic comforts that trump sexual intensity.

"Kept women" fiction did, however, bring mystery back to the sexuality that was ever more public and, hence, ever more part of Jackson Lears's "hegemony of the normal." The more public marriage and its issues became, the less private an expression of intimacy it appeared (remember *Bad Girl* as an example of how mystified marital relations could be). While marriage came to seem routine, even contractual, the allure of the mistress promised to restore the private nature of the sexual relation. Yet however privatized, sexual desire was no less part of the public than ever.

Zona Gale offers another version of the kept woman in *Miss Lulu Bett* (1921). In this novel, Lulu is kept in her sister's household, along with their mother and her sister's daughters, where shame compels her to do the housework. She feels guilty for taking up space at all, even as she sustains her brother-in-law's fantasy that he is "keeping" his wife's relations. In fact, Lulu contributes to his illusion of domestic control by cooking, cleaning, and even rescuing his daughter from a failed elopement. When her brother-in-law's brother comes to town, she marries him on their first excursion out of town. When he confesses that his first wife may not be dead (she left him after two years of marriage, so he may be a bigamist), Lulu decides to return to her sister's home after two weeks of marriage and resume her place. By the end of the novel, she gets married again, this time to a piano salesman who also sells sheet music and studies law in his spare time. Gale's novel explores Lulu's loneliness, but the author insists that it must end in compulsory heterosexuality. Lulu will keep house for her new husband rather than for her brother-in-law. This fantasy works by the logic of substitution, wherein the culture imagines a woman as being "kept" while she actually does all the (house)keeping. As Gale does, so does her friend Hurst: both speculate on the way that domesticity curtails desire, insofar as housekeeping is a lot like sex for these heroines—one has to keep doing it every week for it to pay off. Sex, like housework, depends on women's invisible labor to maintain proper order.

In response to these anxieties concerning ever more public sexuality, Joel Pfister argues in "Glamorizing the Psychological" that conservatives of the 1920s and 1930s pathologized female sex expression, analyzing it as a "subtextual" or "hidden 'inner' force that required domestication" (181). Moving from the sentimentalization to the "(hetero)sexualization of female emotions" (181), female sexuality became a source of interiority, an inner self that was different from whatever sexual style or codes one adopted. Either one had "It" or one didn't, "It" being a sexual sign of one's psychological complexity (182). The more sexual, even sexually neurotic, the more complex the female. Sexual ambivalence, then, was a value to be celebrated insofar as it signaled not a public expression of sexuality but a sexual interiority.

In this context, *Back Street* (1931) is one of the major expressions of sexual interiority insofar as it traces the life of Ray Schmidt, the mistress of a Jewish banker, Walter Saxel. As Hurst's novels go, this one is a rich melodrama, devoted to the complex life of feelings that make up the heroine's sexual psychology. *Back Street* shows three versions of female sexuality: married women, whose desires seem to match their husbands'; stereotypical kept women, who are in it for capital gain; and Ray Schmidt, whose sexuality is a complex mixture of submission and opposition. While the wife's story is one of ambition, an exchange of sexuality for a share of her husband's wealth, Walter keeps Ray housebound and, in a manner of speaking, "pure" because she is financially uninvested in her lover's business life.

The paradox of Hurst's kept woman is that she is passive, invisible; her sexuality is more privatized than ever. Walter wants "a woman not easy to offend, who could lie in his arms, her eyes drugged with his nearness, and yet, the next instant, turn around and prepare a dish of pig-knuckles and sauerkraut to what Walter described as the queen's taste" (122). Hurst quickly demystifies the sexual allure of the mistress by juxtaposing it with her culinary skills. This juxtaposition suggests how much sexuality is on a par with the domestic, that sexuality had to be brought back into the home and out of the public (in movies, vaudeville, magazines). Since the 1860s, women had been trying to isolate sexuality from the sentimental care with which their desires had once been associated; here, Hurst's move is to bring them back together again in a new kind of therapeutic sex expression.

Perhaps more important, Hurst glimpses the usual variety of kept women (married or single) and their motives. Most women, such logic has it, are in it for the money, for an economic parity denied them in the business world. Corinne Saxel, "in whom sex-impulses were languid," had her own marital rights (122): "The mother of his children, the banner-bearer of his respectability, his success, his stability. The handsome moleskin wrap was a banner to his success. Every aspect of his polite life was bound up in Corinne. She had rights—property rights, legal rights, moral rights, ethical rights. The woman in the flat, content with the leavings, walking surreptitiously behind the moleskin wrap, was not a menace to this security. Not even to the well-being" (127). Corinne has earned the rights of the household. Unlike Ray, who remains "simple—plain" (291), the wife has earned her status by producing children and living as a symbol of Walter's success. Corinne's "lust for the position and power and wealth of her husband and children was the animating force of her life. That was right. That was what it should be" (173). Reproductive sexuality undergirds their marriage, while Ray's sexuality is of a different sort altogether.

In fact, the beginning of the novel spends considerable time deciding what sort of sexuality Ray feels. Every male who meets her on the street imagines that she is "fly." Through the consciousness of the men who meet her, Hurst ventriloquizes the questions generally: "Where the dickens though, did a man get off with her? Say, she was swell. If a girl like Ray would go the limit—say, would she? Had she? Of course she had, and would. But had she? Darned if a fellow could tell. . . . Just how far" (13). When one man asks her directly, 'Would you sleep with a fellow?,'" Ray slaps him: "The hand that had struck out, had been the hand of some violated inner being. Something private and away from the self that was being lived here in the unsacred everydayness of existence . . . had leaped up hurt and banged in the crude form of fingertips against a human cheek, leaving imprints. One felt sick with living" (15).

Ray is divided into external and internal selves, the external marked by sexual style: "It was that external self made the men with whom she now came in contact in growing numbers delight in her free-and-easy companionship, up to that inevitable time when the demand was sure to be for more than that, and then each and every one of them, feeling somehow cheated and led on, resented her" (113). However, Ray's private self yearns for something beyond even "the decency of honest barter in giving yourself to a man for home and keep" (113). The question for Hurst is whether there is sexuality outside of the marketplace bartering, beyond capitalist desire: Where does sexual performance or style begin and "real" desire or authentic sexuality take over? On the streets, Ray is subject to any sexual interpretation men care to venture. As she fears, "This . . . is the folly of unreal people in plays and books" (162). Recognizing that she is playing an unreal role, however, does not mean that she doesn't have to play it out.

The back street apartment Walter gives her differs from the streets where Ray once met men: in the back street, she plays out a fantasy of sexual intimacy with Walter. That fantasy—of a sexuality divorced from the marketplace—she can only maintain tenuously since she still needs to eat. Her pleasure emerges only when she is secluded from the world and its speculation about her sexuality. She and Walter share fantasies predicated on opposite desires: hers for a perfectly shared and equal intimacy, his for a woman who has no desires of her own except for him. So mystifying has the relation between the sexes become that the exercise of male sexual domination has to take place on the back streets of New York City. For instance, he wants her to talk to him about his business, so their liaison begins to seem like a series of counseling sessions; for Walter, Ray represents " 'the knowledge that there is one person capable of something utterly selfless and unselfish where I am concerned. No children to come between, no social considerations, no worldly ambitions, no money-grabbing, no family politics, no consideration but me' " (176). Walter wants nothing to come between them, but this is a bitter parody of what Ray means by intimacy. Yet their fantasies oppose each other, and Ray's trauma results from Walter's misunderstanding of her psychosexual needs.

Another measure of this tension—between the public street and the private back street—is evinced in Hurst's free indirect discourse, as Hurst places in parentheses her heroine's doubts about her lover's self-obsession. This internal dialogue is the only response Ray allows herself to Walter's self-absorption (131). At one point, under the rising pressure of "slow anger," she repeats to herself an echo of what she hears Walter say to her: "a tom-tom beating itself softly into her brain. . . . I. I . . . " (168). And later she hears Walter's incessant refrain within her head, just as she hears echoes of Walter's references to her as "same old Ray . . . Old Ray. Old Ray" or her own echo: "(Me-Me-Me-Me-Me-Me-Me-Me-Me-Me)" (236, 176). Her internal voice—enclosed in parentheses throughout the novel—becomes the most authentic one, especially in contrast to the submissive voice of her responses to Walter. In a mass culture that defines women's self-expression as sex expression, Hurst shows how different the two are; the internal voice of rage is not the same as the compelled voice of submission.

Ray's rage is bracketed off from her sexual performance; the two are antithetical. Thus, Hurst dramatizes the rupture between Ray's sexual performance and her internally authentic dialogue. In this painful novel, a truly great tearjerker about the heroine's decades-long submission to her lover, Hurst explains the psychology of submission as an opposition to the too direct and, thus, demystified and rationalized sexuality of the masses. No *Story of O*, *Back Street* delivers the suppressed rage of this submission. Ray is always on the verge of lashing out at her lover, causing him pain in order to see him suffer. What keeps her from doing so is her sense of getting nothing for herself, nothing by which she could seem to have profited materially from the relationship. She even abandons Walter once, but only until he returns, begging her to take him back.

As consistent as Ray's reasons are with conventionally masochistic ones, Hurst's heroine is actually creating a different style of sex expression: "The passion of the springtime of their love, perhaps, had quieted, but the passion of her surrender to his every conviction, wish, desire, spoken and unspoken, continued to lash and dominate her unabated through the years—a slavery that was precious to her, a subservience

206

that exalted while it abased" (183). Beyond desire herself, Ray prefers to give pleasure rather than claim it (like Virgie in *Family!*). This exaltation is linked to abasement, to the condition of self-loss, through which Ray lives out her profound ambivalence about women's sexuality. Her abasement is not masochistic insofar as Walter does not submit to her fantasies—he doesn't know them—but only enacts his own. In this respect, Hurst exploits stereotypical ideas about female masochism, like Ray's abjection to the "lash" and to sexual "slavery," in order to arrive at her own fresh conclusions about female sexuality.

Masochism implies contract, and although Ray chooses the passivity of being kept (even in the passive verb form), she eschews the idea of contract—keeping him, paradoxically, by being kept. In a conventional/contractual masochistic relation, Walter would need to acknowledge Ray's unspoken desires; here he doesn't. He prefers the passive, infantile attention that is the hallmark of neither sadism nor masochism but of narcissism and, as always, a narcissism incommensurate with the recognition of the other that intimacy demands. Walter has real power, although his power is also muted by the culture's anti-Semitism, as we shall see.

Ray supports Walter's narcissism through her elaborate dinners, housekeeping, and self-suppression. The problem of the modern woman, as Hurst claims, is this failure of desire—or at least a desire based on the culture's capitalist or companionate terms. Ray muses, "It was borne in upon her, crumbling her bread into pellets, that among those sitting there, filled with intent and purpose over the pattern of their lives, only she, alone of them, found herself in the predicament of not even desiring to desire" (94). Instead, she finds a remote pleasure in anticipating her lover's desire, what Hurst calls "the perfection of complete giving" (184). Ray feels numb (her arm is asleep) while she is in bed with Walter, contemplating the "quality of her folly," an example of Hurst's deflating the idealization of erotic intimacy. Ray Schmidt's tragedy, we find, is less about sexual masochism than about suffering through the ideal of authentic or therapeutic intimacy: "The first night with him was like feeling her body become the lifestream upon the secure bosom of which he could lie blessedly safe and secure. They were elements bound tightly in the wonder of blending so perfectly. With his head at her bare breast there could never be anything so extraneous and unintimate as modesty or shyness or doubt or unfulfillment again. There were no words now needed to be spoken" (124).

Ray's illusion of romance beyond words is tricky, especially if we concede that language creates sexuality as much as it contains it. There are always words "needed to be spoken" in order to attain intimacy. In desiring something beyond language, a perfect companionship, the heroine denies the necessity of language to inform sex expression. Her silence is a sanctuary from verbal subjection and her lover's power. Walter, unconsciously or not, depends on her fantasy of wordless intimacy; that is, he depends on her silence and invisibility: "Over a period of three years, she had not ventured out of her flat for more than two or three consecutive hours, and then only at long intervals" (128). He keeps her "small" in order to be the one thing in his life beyond ambition. By contrast, she is perfectly "selfless." Walter tells Ray that she " 'can satisfy a man completely. You're tolerant of a man because you understand him. When you love a person you love him more than you love yourself' " (132). Of course, this is his fantasy of her supreme willingness to be all-giving and all-nurturing of his vulnerable narcissism, a fantasy that her own illusion supports with sad consequences, even though her parenthetical remarks spell out her resistance ("You don't!").

As one of Ray's friends remarks, Walter Saxel wants to keep Ray "little," with no flashy diamonds or expensive perfume that might draw male competition (136). Unlike other kept women whom Ray knows, she gets little financial support, which distinguishes her from the "calculating" women "with whom Ray realized she was now classed" (137). In other words, the less a man can give, the more he profits in the exchange of capitalist relations. For Ray to become calculating would mean an acceptance of the common denominator of heterosexual relations that she refuses in the first place: a capitalist reciprocity, an exchange of goods that defines this kind of sexual barter.[11]

Stephanie Bower reads *Back Street* as an instance of capitalist exchange economies deflected onto the racial melodrama of this novel. As Bower suggests, Hurst's plot is complicated by the fact that Walter is

Jewish, and Ray's sexual transgression is ostensibly greater because it crosses social and racial lines. In part, Ray is able to give herself so completely because she imagines that her tryst with the "Jew boy" already is an act of transgression: "People born Jews turned Gentile, but whoever heard of a Gentile turning Jew?" (80). And her lover Walter stays with her precisely because she isn't Jewish and thus, for him, is not part of "that solidarity of a race in which, vagaries of social ambition to the contrary notwithstanding, the clan impulse would not die" (262). He loves Ray because she has no ambitions, which he codes as "tribal" desires for advancement. As Bower concludes, "Hurst's representation of Jewishness deflects her critique of bourgeois ideology by rendering the sexual economy that transforms Ray into a living corpse a product of Walter's pathological miserliness rather than the natural consequence of an economy that positions middle-class women as domestic consumers. In other words, Walter's Jewishness works to cleanse or recuperate the sexual economy of the middle class by marking the translation of women into commodities as a product of Jewish difference" (261).

As sympathetic as I am to this reading, I think Hurst is less concerned about Walter's Jewish "pathology" than about his bourgeois compartmentalization of impulses—a compartmentalization perhaps heightened by assimilationist anxieties. For Walter, ambition is external, passion is internal. For Ray, only the internal counts, and she readily relinquishes the external sexual style she developed in order to nurture her sense of "natural" sex expression. Yet Ray's self-doubt keeps her in the domestic, privatized world, where her connection to a Jewish man justifies her self-image. Consider Ray's self-assessment: "I have all the qualities of the bad women you read about in books. I act kept. . . . I'm not fit for anything but loving. I'm not fit even to be loved" (221). In her mind, she only exists insofar as his racial otherness validates her self-negation. In contrast, he claims his relation with Ray as his right; when his son discovers their apartment and confronts them, Walter declares: " 'You have no right here. This is my right—the only right I have ever placed before the million-and-one rights of my family. You have no rights here—none of you—this corner of my life belongs to me—safe, free from every one of you—the only privacy, sanctum, home, I have ever dared claim of my own'" (275). Walter's declaration of his privacy as his sanctum sanctorum is also a regressive claim for an intimate domesticity free from demands, especially those of the sexual contract.

In Ray Schmidt, *Back Street* registers a powerful nostalgia for a time when, Hurst imagines, the main currency between men and women was sexuality, not the modern interests in ambition or money or social power or even the new companionate marriage. Ray wants to think beyond Walter's Jewishness to a pure relationship based on sexual equality, not social value. Hurst's heroine imagines a time when sexuality seemed "purer," perhaps even more sentimental than the exchange of heterosexual favors enacted in marriage. Somewhere between the permanence of marriage and the fleetingness of the affair, Hurst offers the realm of stasis as the guarantor of sexual authenticity. Romanticizing the kept woman as the only possibility for "free" sex expression, Hurst paradoxically suggests that women's sexual freedom can only be found in being kept so that their internal passion is free from external economic concerns. The "kept woman" novel returns to a nostalgic mode of relation in which women abjure all ambition for the return of the male's "pure" passion. Unencumbered by marital relations and exchanges, he is presumably free to respond with unalloyed desire. This splitting of the self into outer style and inner self—passion divorced from the sex expression or style used to signify it—marks her rejection of the new sexual freedom that failed, for Hurst, to account for women's inner needs.

Walter Saxel dies at the end of the novel without having left Ray anything, "Not a bauble. Not an object of value" (214). (That he hasn't financially emancipated her through his will is an ironic recapitulation of slavery novels.) Finally, Ray must fend for herself and is reduced to gambling for money. Later, when she can sell no more of the trifles she had received from Walter, not even his shoes, she withers away and dies after eighteen years as his mistress. Shriveled from hunger and want, with head tremors that signify her deprivation, she is found dead, clutching some money that Walter's youngest son had thrown casually to a crowd of women—either crones or cocottes—in the casino, not knowing that one of them was his father's former mistress (335). Ray's disappearance must inevitably follow Walter's since she has no self-possession to sustain her.

What sort of sexual fantasy, then, has Hurst written? It's a dream of sexual authenticity, of pure desire untainted by the commercialization of heterosexual exchanges. It is also a new sexual topography: whereas 1920s women writers had their heroines pursue sex in public, Hurst's back street scenes show her heroine's discomfort at being coded as fly, even when she prides herself on her "style." Ultimately, Ray retreats further and further from public life, where she cannot be assailed; the kept woman has the least amount of sexual freedom and sexual space— only a bedroom in some inconspicuous back street.

Yet this novel, I would argue, is more than reactionary since here the heroine's sexuality is anticipatory and creative, not just submissive and participatory. By anticipatory sexuality, I mean the heroine's willingness to wait in anticipation of her lover's arrival, potentially making every moment of her life a preparation for sexuality—that is, domesticity as extended foreplay. And for Ray Schmidt, it's as if the preparation for sexual intimacy far surpasses the experience of it. Insofar as her enjoyment comes from this extended waiting, however alone she may be, the sexuality she shares with Walter Saxel is really not about him at all. She is always in a state of sexual readiness, and thus, unlike the marital sex Hurst depicts—routinized and normalized—her life is infinitely more exciting. It's not about her response to him but about her anticipation of her own pleasure. (Whatever the pleasure is, it's certainly not conventional, although its consequences are still tragic.) Since Ray gets little else in exchange, there must be something pleasurable that sustains her passion. The novel challenges the reader to figure out what sort of sexuality may exist beyond practical exchange or rationalized contract. In other words, Ray is exceptional since she refuses to her death to settle for the deadening effects of traditional relations.

That Ray chooses this passive relation to her lover and the marketplace (to be kept is, after all, not to keep) may overturn any liberating aspects of sex power. This mistress novel shows how Ray chooses sexual expression outside of marriage, even as she assumes the economic and psychological traps of conventional heterosexuality.[12] The "kept woman" novel presupposes a world outside of the back street apartment in which women are free and active agents since the mistress can only be a mistress as opposed to other women more respectably employed or married.

The difference between keeping and being kept is the crux of *Back Street*, for this tension shows the workings of a desire that cannot be sustained except in the opposition between activity and passivity. The barriers between these active and passive forms of desire are constantly blurred, creating the urgency and intensity of the kept relationship. For women, the overwhelming fantasy of being kept stays the same: the home as a space of pure reciprocity. For all of its sentimental sexuality, Hurst's novel does try to imagine a life beyond the regulatory reproductive marriage that came to represent bourgeois sexuality.

Being kept—as a theme or trope—signifies the need to confine sexuality to a place that is free from other contaminating conditions. The kept home is a place of pure sexual availability, while the sex that occurs in marriage is paradoxically too loaded with other meanings to be controlled. While being kept harks back to the sexual parasitism that Charlotte Perkins Gilman denounced in her 1898 *Women and Economics*, the 1930s emphasis on kept women is also nostalgia for a more sexually conservative time, which the current economic conditions recall. When sexual "promises" are broken, the contract between two lovers is also a key rhetorical signifier of desire. Part of that contract involves the literal compartmentalization of sex in a culture where sexuality was starting to be seen everywhere. In this light, sex is located in an apartment, a space apart, ostensibly beyond violation. "Kept women" novels thus use sex to discipline the wider eroticization of the culture. The "kept woman" genre is related to women "keeping" house; the more women leave behind traditional housekeeping for greater sexual and social freedom, the more call for mistress novels to return sexuality and labor to the home.

Ray Schmidt has a complex desire for Walter Saxel, based on her identification with him and her inchoate desire to be him. Her desire takes the shape of submission, but the internal voice in which Hurst communicates her desire to the reader inflects her resistance to this submission. Internally divided by her simultaneous desire to be Walter

Saxel and to be his mistress, Ray Schmidt is Hurst's warning to women who want to be both the object and the subject of desire at the same time. This novel also serves as a warning that the new resexualization of women can easily become the old sex conservatism. By sex conservatism, I don't mean to suggest that everything that came before was sex radicalism; rather, in *Back Street*, the language of sex expression took a new turn into conserving rather than extending whatever sense of private sexuality could exist outside of the contract.

Once Walter dies, of indigestion no less, Ray dies of starvation. Hurst links sex and food as sustaining properties, as well as the two sites of moral indignation. Too much food, like too much sex, for Hurst, indicates a failure of control. In the end, perhaps, the most hope that *Back Street* offers exists in the figure of Emma, Ray's niece, whom she has supported through college. Ray advises Emma in a letter to "keep [herself] neat and study hard." Ray writes, "Remember, no one can ever take away your education, once you get it. Knowledge is power" (243). (The last sentence is one she uses in *Imitation of Life*.) Emma plans to be a teacher in the Midwest; she will support herself and, Ray hopes, be beyond keeping house or being kept by anyone. A female teacher in the Midwest is Hurst's new vision of female success: a fitting heroine to my mind, who also constitutes Hurst's most searching imagination at work.

KEPT MEN

Few novels, except perhaps for Gilman's 1915 *Herland*, focus on women keeping men, and there are even fewer fantasies in American women's writing of women desiring to keep men. But Fannie Hurst wrote one in her *Five and Ten* (1929), in which the wife of the thirteenth richest man in America, who made his money through a chain of dime stores, maintains her gigolo with expensive presents of cash and pearls that she snips off her own dresses as well as diamonds that she extracts from her outrageously expensive baubles. Married for twenty-six years, she finds her daughter floundering in bad affairs of her own and her teenage son suicidal. While the daughter struggles with what Hurst calls "sex antagonism," like the earlier sex equality that fueled *Mannequin*

(263, 319), Jenny Avery embodies the psychology of the guilty wife, her "temperamental frigidity" plaguing her marriage and her sexuality (64). The middle-aged Jenny falls for a Spanish dance teacher and keeps him from all the other women he has been "teaching" by slipping him $1,000 bills (136). He eventually leaves her for a "grandmother," a woman near seventy who offers the gigolo a higher rate of pay than Jenny gives. "'I cannot struggle. One must live,'" he tells her (281).

After this abandonment, her great fear is that she will reveal her sexual unconscious. As she prepares for an operation, she worries that, under ether, she will confess her affair to her husband and daughter: "Suppose . . . she should unconsciously reveal to him the tortuous secret windings of those underground rivers of her mind that carried so much along them that was traitorous to [him]" (309). There is perhaps no better definition of the contemporaneous ideas about female sexuality than Hurst's explanation of the tension between the conscious sex expression and the unconscious impulse that her heroine feels. Such a surface/depth model of sex expression dominated the works of writers such as Hurst and Atherton, which explored "the subterranean dimensions" of their sexual desires (see Pfister 180). Jenny's husband thinks about his wife's secrets in other terms: "No more than she, did he desire the revelation of those fetid places that had gathered scum in the years of swampy silence between them. Ugh" (310). Underneath bourgeois femininity's "repression" or frigidity lies layer upon layer of sexual feeling. Jenny's character reveals the sexualization of women's emotional depths, her "true" sexual identity masked by bourgeois respectability, and a new postsentimental attitude toward desire and sexuality, the "underground rivers of her mind," as the core of true identity. As Hurst shows, the sexual antagonism between husband and wife conjures up her vision of "rivers" against his view of the "scummy" swamp of her sexual psychology. She dies, as all gigolo-keeping wives must, and the novel ends with father and daughter alone, the father having divested himself of his millions and allowing his daughter only $8,000 a year after his death so she will be forced to make her own way in the world. No marriage for her, not even to the intellectual playwright whom her father had once offered to buy for her.

Hurst offhandedly refers to a book in the novel as one of "the psycho-logical novels they're writing nowadays" (115), an example of the inte-riority of female sexual desire within bourgeois families. Conscious, too, that women were reading the "sex novel" (61), she provides alternatives to the sex addiction that dominated the plots of potboilers of her day such as Olive Higgins Prouty's *Stella Dallas* (1923) and Edna Ferber's *So Big* (1924). That women read Hurst to fathom her heroines' psychologi-cal depth seems clear. Hurst has no sentimental vocabulary for sexual contact, but she invests female desire with an urgency borne out of psychological need. In her own terms, it's not "the memory of the flesh" that drives the female desire animating this gigolo novel but "memory" itself: the emotional loss triggers Jenny's "wave of self-pity, not unmixed with anger," over "life . . . passing her by" (68). Lost in reverie about her marriage, Jenny thinks to herself: "What a starveling she must be, if just the ordinary homage and admiration from a boy such as Ramon could bring about all this turmoil within her" (68). Thus, Hurst shifts the debate about female sex expression from physiology to psychology, a transition that she demonstrates in the dramas of her various heroines' therapeutic desires.

READING HURST'S EIGHTEEN NOVELS together offers a tapestry of psychological possibilities for sex expression. Hurst did not accept the idea of "sex power" at face value. Instead, she asked what sex power made psychologically possible, what it liberated, and what it suppressed in terms of "Mental Health," to borrow Floyd Dell's phrase. Was this health worth having?, Wharton and Cather both asked. Hurst goes fur-ther in parsing out what the rejection of sex expression made possible for women: it allowed a therapeutic reorientation to the demands of sexualization and standardized intimacy. Women's writing in the 1930s and 1940s was marked by the end of discussion of sexual possibilities of liberation; a novel such as Lillian Smith's *Strange Fruit* (1944) starkly responds to the optimism of Jessie Fauset's *The Chinaberry Tree* (1931). Depression-era novels brought an aversion to debates about women's sexuality, producing in women a hoarding mentality that resulted in conventional marriage and conservative lives. What they hoard is a sense of sexual passion that amounts to a zero-sum game—each woman is allotted so much passion and then she's bankrupt. While once women's sexual metaphors for expression were open to all sorts of variation, they were now firmly grounded in economic systems of value. A new sexual conservatism overwhelmed popular fiction, so much so that it seemed to shut down the kinds of debates about pleasuring that had been so daring in the 1920s.[13]

So, sex isn't everything. Yet it is quite possibly the greatest preoccupation of twentieth-century American women's writing. At least all of Hurst's novels and carefully crafted heroines lead to her dismissal of narcissistic fantasies of love's fulfillment and altruistic therapies of sexual healing. Her novels certainly oppose the notion that sex was a woman's identity, but Hurst never seems able to reconcile work and love, career and passion. They are mutually exclusive, at least in her terms of narcissism and abjection.

As we have seen, a number of American women writers doubted the efficacy of sex power—then as now—as a way to equality. Given the advent of feminism, or even just a greater frankness about sexuality, why would women choose willed passivity? How did conservative women attempt to steal the thunder of the new sex expressionists and reverse this modern-love debate? My conclusion turns to American women's writing about sexual conservatism and exhaustion.

CONCLUSION SEXUAL EXHAUSTION

James Thurber and E. B. White parodied the famous sex expression of their times: "I have known parents to go through whole books by authors like Havelock Ellis or Mary Ware Dennett without understanding a single paragraph, because they thought Man's 'eroticism' referred to his desire to be in some foreign place like Spain" (120). Despite the urbanity of such notables as Dorothy Parker or the irony of Thurber and White in their 1929 parody of sexology, *Is Sex Necessary?*, many women writers looked much more skeptically at the sexualization of American culture, some hoping to find alternatives to sex power and expression. The earlier process of self-realization, augured so forcefully by Margaret Fuller, involved rejecting the sexual component of female selfhood. In charting the literary history of sex expression as a domain of female emotional and therapeutic expertise, I have reclaimed the idea that certain women writers reasserted the sexual and revivified it as a female expertise. The advent of the sexualized culture brought these women new ways to advocate for their own power, as well as new anxieties about the reversion to women's equation with sexuality. By the end of the period of my study, female heroines were allowed to explore and experience pleasure but not to settle down. In this sense, writers like Fannie Hurst protected their heroines from pervasive romantic falsehoods that promised happiness in the contractual "ever after"; but they also taught that happiness often lies in secret, private, and necessarily temporary moments. This is sex expression under capitalism.

THE FICTIONS I HAVE EXAMINED in this book disclose how women writers understood the sexualization of culture, even as they separated it from the increasing commodification of sexuality. I have also traced three kinds of hope for sexuality, focused on transcendent, transformative, and therapeutic desires. By coining words and developing symbols such as "worse," "still," and "freezing," these writers attempted to master the new code of sex relations, thereby wresting meaning from the new sexual vernacular circulating in the late nineteenth and early twentieth centuries. The categories I have chosen to study—ugliness, middle age, sex power, inarticulate sexuality, and therapeutic intimacy—are the ones I found most crucial in the transformation of women's writing about sexuality from late Victorian to modern times. Although I might have also added deviance or pathology (including the invert and the homosexual) or exoticism (since these are better known and already identified as sexual categories and types), I wrote about codes once accessible to contemporaneous readers but now out of fashion. I wanted to recalculate their currency and thus to envision a new literary history that explored these women's writings about sexuality and their demand for a new frankness.

Like Thurber and White's misguided "parents" who confuse eroticism and exoticism, we have misread American women writers as too repressed, too polite, or too prudish without grasping their various intentions. While Mary Ware Dennett and Havelock Ellis may have made sexology part of public discourse, women writers like Mary Austin and Gertrude Atherton stylized their own versions of female sexuality. Thurber and White are ironic; at times, I am too, but my concerns are mostly engaged and encouraged by these women's serious assessments of sexuality as communication. In 1914, Austin writes as forthrightly and anti-ironically as any of her peers in defense of women's sex expression: "In this mutual crowding of the sexes into utterly untenable attitudes, women have suffered most. It is natural that from women as a class should come the most spirited rebellion. It is purely incidental that the struggle has shaped about the contest for political equality. Under all forms, the right that women are fighting for is the right to be themselves" (*Soul Maker* 251). I find this vision earnest and exciting, if also almost too utopian and optimistic about the ways that sex expression might change untenable attitudes and inequality. Yet I am utterly attracted to Austin's hope.

The story of women writers' sex expression might have a less hopeful take were I to include a different sample of books, starting with Elizabeth Stuart Phelps's *Hedged In* instead of *The Silent Partner*; Dorothy

Parker's "A Telephone Call" instead of "Big Blonde"; Djuna Barnes's or Edna Ferber's tales instead of Atherton's more vibrant fictions; Gale Wilhelm's lesbian novel *We Too Are Drifting* instead of Julia Peterkin's *Scarlet Sister Mary*; and ending with Zora Neale Hurston's several fictions instead of Fannie Hurst's eighteen novels. Yet by including Hurst rather than her friend and paid companion Hurston, I have described the less familiar and perhaps more dramatic but no less encompassing story of women's belief in the therapeutic value of sexuality (Hurst) instead of a story of a woman's subjugation by three husbands (Hurston). In contrast, Hurston's vision (like Barnes's and Wilhelm's) yields the by-now familiar tale of the general culture's debility—or even inarticulateness—over matters sexual. Or I could have asked why a host of novelists were interested in "the virgin question" in books such as Dorothy Day's 1924 *The Eleventh Virgin*, Frances Newman's best-selling 1926 *The Hard-Boiled Virgin*, and Kathleen Norris's 1928 *The Foolish Virgin*. Why this sudden preoccupation with virginity?

It may have been easier to deal with the imagined essentialized character of sexuality than with a heroine's formless or inarticulate desires, as many authors crafted stories about "other women's" sex expression. The difference between "other women" and "good women" depends on experience and language, but this opposition between good and bad women soon breaks down.

For example, Phelps's *Hedged In* (1870) tells the story of Eunice "Nixy" Trent, who as an unwed mother at age fifteen has been turned out of her job as a dining saloon waitress. She cannot find a job to support her baby and still stay "honest"; the concert hall is the only place that will employ her, but staying honest there is an impossibility (42). Shunned by all of the would-be reformers who talked out of both sides of their mouths about that "erring class" (148), Nixy wanders and suffers, abandoning her baby at someone's door, before she is saved by a true reformer, a girl roughly Nixy's age who convinces her mother that they need to practice their untested Christian principles. Mrs. Purcell and her "pure" daughter Christina take Nixy in, and Nixy soon reforms herself. She becomes a grammar school teacher, even as she is haunted by rumors of her illegitimate baby and is troubled once she reclaims her son Kent from the nursery where he was being raised. Phelps struggles with the question of inherited tendencies for sex, the "taints of blood and brain" that "were lodged in the poor girl's growing life" (114). When Christina falls in love and marries the local doctor, Nixy dies the night of her friend's wedding. Although *Hedged In* condones only respectable, marital sex and urges her readers to help wayward girls recover their self-esteem, by the time she writes *The Silent Partner* a year later, she acknowledges the pleasure of sexuality for working girls and suggests that middle-class reformers offer very little to compete with sexual pleasure.

Phelps is careful to observe that Nixy "sinned once" but is "not a wicked girl" (110–11), a distinction that points to the difference between *Hedged In* and *The Silent Partner*, in which working girls have sex all the time but no sexual "sin" is ever mentioned. The distinction between sexual experience and "wicked," "immoral," or "bad" choices is central to my study insofar as it signals that women writers were distancing themselves from the religious and moral evaluations of sexuality and insisting instead on their own interpretations.

The difference between sexuality as respectability and sexuality as self-help or redemption is decisive: in telling this particular story about the struggle over women's sexual expression, I find the greatest possibility for rescuing sexuality from its characterization as either liberated or repressed, democratized or coercive. Moreover, these binaries are not useful or even particularly relevant for the debates in which women writers created a language that would encompass more variable ways of symbolizing desire.

Of course, Phelps's reform story is not the only one I could tell about American women writers' invention of sexual discourse and their recovery of a passion once prohibited or repressed or one they had to invent in the first place. Sometimes they created a new truth about sexuality; sometimes they expressed their ambivalence; often, they retreated to the old model of repression because the new truth denied too many of the problems of reproductive intimacy or patriarchal protection. But that protection and intimacy were in short supply, thereby eliciting even more narratives about women's potential use of sexual power and sexual passion.

I could end by telling the tale of women's rejection of sex as therapy and the ever-greater commodification of sexuality and intimacy, whereby sex came to seem another consumer choice. Or I could end with Thurber and White's *Is Sex Necessary?*, a hilarious parody of sex manuals and treatises like V. F. Calverton and Samuel Schmalhausen's exploration of modern sexuality *Sex in Civilization*. Hurst echoes Thurber and White's question in her *Lonely Parade*, in which she says, "Sex isn't everything," in response to the culture's obsession with sexuality. This was a serious enough question for Hurst. While she concludes that sex is necessary (but not "everything"), Thurber and White argue that it's not everything and, indeed, overrated. They offer a list of "Sex Substitutes" that will do just as nicely: bowling, craps, baseball, six-day bicycle racing, and fudge-making (for women). As they say, "Writing is a form of sexual expression . . . , and it takes just as much out of a person" (45). They diagnose women interested in their erotic lives as having "*Schmalhausen* trouble," whereby they might see "three sides to sex" (87–88; Thurber and White's emphasis). They conclude: "Sex is by no means everything. It varies, as a matter of fact, from only as high as 78 per cent of everything to as low as 3.10 per cent" (133–34). I can't offer as definite a quantification of how much sex expression occupied women writers except to say that this concern with assessing sexual freedom is one of the most pervasive of the many untold stories of American women's sex expression.

After 1930, female sexuality ended up looking like some form of trouble, Schmalhausen or otherwise; comedic send-up, such as in screwball comedies or gold-digger scenarios, as David Shumway argues persuasively in *Modern Love*; or consumer choice. Sex expression rarely appeared any longer as hope or liberation. A common narrative was open to heterosexual and lesbian couples alike: a narrative of suffering and misery. Cutting across these narratives of sex expression—from Viña Delmar's *Bad Girl* to Gale Wilhelm's *We Too Are Drifting*—is the same assumption: that intimacy meant sharing a sexual trajectory. Wilhelm's title—about the drifting of lovers on the current of familial and cultural convention—speaks to the general state of intimacy by the mid-1930s. Sexual intimacy had to be both private and public, a merging

Fig. 1.
Sex Substitutes (Übertragung Period): Baseball.

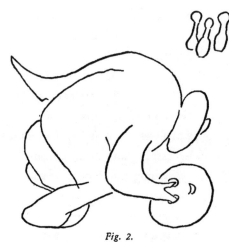

Fig. 2.
Sex Substitutes (Übertragung Period): Bowling.

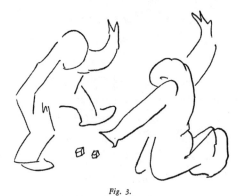

Fig. 3.
Sex Substitutes (Übertragung Period): Craps.

FUDGE-MAKING.

"The female, equipped with a Defense far superior in polymorphous ingenuities to the rather simple Attack of the male, developed, and perfected, the Diversion Subterfuge. The first manifestation of this remarkable phenomenon was fudge-making."

A series of "Sex Substitutes": baseball, bowling, craps, and fudge-making.
From James Thurber and E. B. White, Is Sex Necessary? (1929).

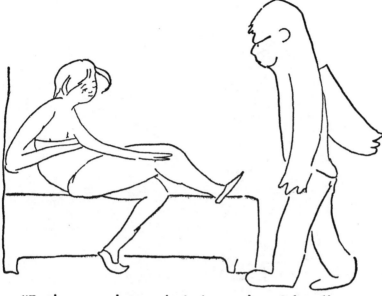

"Furthermore, she was beginning to have Schmaulhausen trouble."

"Schmaulhausen trouble." From James Thurber and E. B. White,
Is Sex Necessary? (1929).

of the realms of authenticity and social equality, and the public realm
was denied to Wilhelm's couple. Failed intimacy was a specific form of
suffering, and it provided the culture with a new shared language of
psychic negotiation. This social suffering was to be shared across classes,
races, sexualities, so much so that suffering became, according to Illouz,
its own emotional habitus (see *Cold Intimacies* 66–68). This emotional
habitus—with its own forms of intimacy—was an effect of social class
and class training in levels of intimacy.

As we have seen, the invention of the New Woman threatened to
provide a new kind of sexual power; the "bad girl," too, had to be
domesticated, as Delmar had done in her popular novel. The endangered couple must be defended against the anxiety that this unmoored
female sexuality aroused, along with the fear that women would leave
home and family. Companionate marriage became the solution to this
threat by yoking sexuality to contract, a bond through which men and

I am told that one type has actually been known to get the man of her choice down and sit, as it were, side-saddle of him.

Women's "side-saddling." From James Thurber and E. B. White,
Is Sex Necessary? (1929).

women could ostensibly exchange goods neutrally, equally. The new modern contract was now laden with emotions and made ostensibly more gender-neutral or gender-equal. But the story of sex expression became one of drifting away from something new and exciting to a conventionalized suffering, loss, and weightlessness.

Emotionality was then channeled into companionship, which was ostensibly fueled by intimacy—that sense of deep commitment to the other that must be publicly performed. Sexuality was identified no longer as an impulse or primitive awareness but as a discourse, a language that could approximate the sense of interiority that intimacy was supposed to name. New concepts about the self's inner life (such as "anxiety") marked out the territory in the self that could be created, managed, and analyzed. Women were enjoined to develop their emotional skills in order to succeed at communication, by which they might achieve sexual compatibility and intimacy. Intimacy came to be at the crossroads of emotional and sexual life. To achieve emotional and sexual liberation meant to achieve intimacy, for intimacy was to be the new signification of equality. Intimacy as sexual egalitarianism meant that contract was equal, for intimacy could only be achieved in the face of each partner's equal rights and a fair exchange of rights and pleasures.

Without a new lexicon to explain these pleasures, women could claim neither liberation nor equality. This is both a feminist and a rationalized movement, for it speaks to women's desires even as it seeks to codify and use sexuality to fulfill the social need to quantify intimacy. Eventually, American women writers came to terms with this new misery about sexual intimacy. How were women to express their desires, achieve equality, and earn social recognition? Such narratives of intimacy required new stories and new styles that could channel these desires into tales of inner lives discovered and fulfilled. The suffering self, on the contrary, was neurotic, in need of adjustment and therapy, transformation and recovery, or stories of sexual and intimate failures because of an incommunicative partner, inarticulate lover, or conventional sex relations.

Thus, sex expression did not leave out lesbianism, but writers thought that a generally expressed sexuality would include everything by virtue of its democratized language.[1] The move to make sexualities distinct—to emphasize difference rather than sameness—came later in the 1940s and 1950s. That may be due to a failure of imagination, but it may be just as well that authors like Gail Wilhelm and Mary McCarthy did not differentiate sex expression based on object choice.

Gale Wilhelm's *We Too Are Drifting* (1935) tells the story of woodcut artist Jan Morale, who calls off an affair with her married lover Madeline after falling in love with a young admirer, Victoria. Madeline is angry, and the two lovers fight each other violently. Victoria is engaged to a law student whose mother is best friends with Victoria's mother. Victoria's family does not know of her affair with Jan, and the mothers of the engaged couple arrange for their families to spend a two-week vacation together. At the end of the novel, Victoria leaves Jan, despite her desire for her, to fulfill her family's arrangement. The novel's subplot shows the cooperative relationship between Jan and the sculptor Kletkin, for whom Jan sat as a model for his celebrated work *Hermaphroditus*. She has no family but Kletkin, since her twin brother was hanged for some unnamed crime.

After Jan dismisses Madeline and ends their affair, Madeline cuts Jan with a spitzsticker—a sharp-pointed graver used in woodcutting—and "somehow there was a long bleeding gash on the upper side of Jan's thumb and blood running toward her wrist" (78–79). Later, Jan tries to choke Madeline for interfering with her relationship with Victoria: "She saw Madeline's face close to hers and she woke out of a long terrible loneliness of sleep and she hated Madeline and this hatred was awake again and she rose swiftly striking Madeline's knees with hers, her body striking Madeline's like a tree falling in a storm. She caught Madeline's throat with her hands and she thought of nothing but the long humiliated hatred and her hands fitting Madeline's neck like a tight necklace. . . . She knew she was stronger and resistance was beautiful; it was a thing to prolong and subdue and finally kill and hold wilted in your hands" (111–12). Jan takes out her sexual frustration on her old lover, while she confesses her lack of agency to Victoria. She is capable of a kind of frustrated violence, even as she recognizes its futility.

When it is not recounting violence, the novel details the sexual excitement and tension between Jan and her new lover Victoria. This excitement is the key emotion on which the narrative turns: "Jan had no clear image of her face, she had looked at her face only twice, once indifferently and then once again almost blindly. Then how had the excitement got into her throat? What in the voice, in the body walking had shown her that radiance?" (35). Wilhelm repeats Jan's interior sensation, "it was exciting," over and over again, as if to mark the difference between drifting and the fixation on physical pleasure (39).[2] Wilhelm represents the two ends of the sexual spectrum—from excitement to drifting—and shows that this tension causes Jan's social suffering.

Victoria tries to muster the courage to call off the vacation. But Jan cautions her: "You see, my dear, you'll never be able to say to your family I'd rather go to the mountains with my friend than go to Chicago with you. You see that's simply a way of saying, My dear family, to hell with you, and you couldn't possibly be expected to say that" (109). Jan imagines sex expression as distinct from what one can say to one's family. Jan knows that her lover cannot discuss her desire or turn away from her family's plans. Victoria may not want to leave Jan, but she won't disengage from her family for her either. She can't tell her family "to hell with you," and this linguistic inhibition marks the failure of her relationship with Jan. Victoria is ashamed because she will do "a weak thing" by going off with Dan and their mothers (116). One might argue that her tribal alliance to family overcomes her romantic attachment to Jan (see Blum 344).

But what exactly disposes Jan and Victoria to "drift"? It is not so much the unspeakability of lesbianism but rather the distance from emotional authenticity—being able to say "to hell with you"—that creates the disruptive current. This sense of being unmoored in emotional life leads Jan and Madeline to try violence as a way to anchor these emotions since "resistance is beautiful" and has a much longer history than does intimacy. If sociologists such as Eva Illouz call emotional life under late capitalism chaotic, American literary history bears out the chaotic effects of intimacy's demands.

So why the shift from pleasuring and intimacy to satire and shopping or just plain drifting? What did it mean for women writers to give up the comforts of sentimentality or the directness of sex expression that Mary McCarthy calls the "freedom of speech," a freedom missing in *We Too Are Drifting* as much as it is in *Bad Girl*? You can see such a power in Meridel Le Sueur's Depression-era novel, *The Girl* (1939). Le Sueur writes as explicitly as anyone about female sexuality, of the unnamed girl's desire to be entered: "Something had entered me, broken me open, in some kind of terrible hunger" (51). Le Sueur describes the experience of penetration for the girl. This representation of heterosexual penetration and pleasure makes Le Sueur's fiction a breakthrough in sexual explicitness. These are traditional sexual relations, sometimes even abusive ones, but they are nonetheless expressed in an untraditional freedom to speak. After her first sexual experience, the girl imagines about herself: "You would never be a wall, a closed door, an empty bowl" (51). Searching for the right figures for the end of her virginity, Le

Sueur's girl thinks of herself as open but not empty, tropes distinctly related to the depths of the Depression. She anticipates the next entry, the filling up of her body as an end to sexual hunger and alienation (the wall, the door). While Paula Rabinowitz persuasively reads heterosexual desire in *The Girl* as linked to historical processes and class consciousness (123), I see Le Sueur's emphasis on the opening up of language as a way to express the sexual experience of interiority: no wall, no door, no empty bowl, the female experience of sexuality is instead one of fullness and openness. Instead of sentimental ties as the glue of social relations, sexual ties hold the social and political body together.

Sex was sometimes a painful adventure, as we see in Mary McCarthy's *The Company She Keeps* (1942). With the sexual bruises her heroine in one story gets as a result of her three-day affair onboard a cross-country train, McCarthy brings us full circle to the idea of sex as a physical mark. Her work heralded a sexual explicitness that was matched by mourning over the lost possibilities of sexual freedom. By the time McCarthy publishes *The Group* in 1963, her trademark is a great ironizing of sexual explicitness, treated with dry realism: "[Dottie] and Mother had talked it over and agreed that if you were in love and engaged to a nice young man you perhaps ought to have relations once to make sure of a happy adjustment. . . . Dottie thought it very important to arrange that side of marriage properly; defloration, which the girls were always joking about in the smoking room, frightened her. Kay had had an awful time with Harald; five times, she insisted, before she was penetrated, and this in spite of basketball and a great deal of riding out West" (28). This sex expression occurs between mother and daughter; Harald's wife's virginity is a problem even for her girlfriends.

Her most explicit story in *The Company She Keeps*, "The Man in the Brooks Brothers Shirt," calls attention to male style as material and physical, with power an effect of the man's shopping choice. The heroine's style is more indirect, a question of how far she will go, a question of boundaries, not personal brands—nothing so detectable as Brooks Brothers but, instead, a more muted style. Women can only announce themselves obliquely in McCarthy's sense of bourgeois decorum. In the first story of this collection, "Cruel and Barbarous Treatment," the heroine is traveling to Reno for her first divorce, but she will only announce "West" as her destination on the train. "It would probably be best, she decided, to say 'West' at first, with an air of vagueness and hesitation. Then, when pressed, she might go as far as to say 'Nevada.' But no farther" (22). Not admitting to the destination means not revealing her personal life or committing to the divorce. To go "West" or to "Nevada" or to "Reno" involves a much greater level of specificity about the heroine's determination, when, in fact, her sexual vagueness does not invalidate her need to engage other people. For McCarthy, geographical discourse is a measure of how far her heroine will go sexually. She will, of course, go all the way, but she cannot announce it. McCarthy's prose depends on her reader's part as eavesdropper to her heroine's inner dialogue; she casts her readers as private interlocutors who are party to the internal desires that need not be spoken but can be read in the heroine's demeanor, her manner, even her evasions. The style is meant to avoid vulgarity and cheapness, though McCarthy concedes that it's very hard to avoid vulgarity when, as the girl thinks, she embodies the look of "the-girl-who-sits-in-the-club-car-and-picks-up-men" (65). For McCarthy, true desire is necessarily vulgar, too direct.

This geographical code is even more pronounced in the encounter with the "Brooks Brothers" man. She meets him on a train going west, goes to his compartment, and ends up naked. But the trick is in the telling: McCarthy seems to give her heroine only two sexual choices— timidity or malleability—neither of which seems to equal agency. Nothing happens to McCarthy's heroine that is ostensibly of her own choosing. Instead, her sexuality is determined by the negative or the passive voice:

> She had felt tired and kind, and thought, *Why not?* Then there had been something peculiar about the love-making itself—but she could not recall what it was. She had tried to keep aloof from it, to be present in body but not in spirit. Somehow that had not worked out and she had been dragged in and humiliated. There was some comfort in this vagueness, but recollection quickly stabbed her again. There were (oh, holy Virgin!) four-letter words that she had

been forced to repeat, and, at the climax, a rain of blows on her but-
tocks that must surely (dear God) have left bruises. (82; McCarthy's
emphasis)

Once again, the sexually active heroine is worried about the marks upon
her body, along with the change in expression, that this sexual encounter leaves.

Sex expression erupts in the four-letter words and in the "freedom of
speech of hers [that] was a kind of masquerade of sexuality, like the
rubber breasts that homosexuals put on for drags" (80). Sex expression
is a masquerade, a trying on of different sexual styles, but it seems to be a
requirement for American women writers inventing a new way of explaining social relations. While once the American woman writer would
have asked "why" sexuality had to dominate human relations, McCarthy's question is a glib, even resigned, "why not?"

OF COURSE, THIS GROWING SEXUALIZATION of the culture was tied
to the formation of the middle class. Sexualizing relations became a way
of marking the middle class off from what once were the "decadence"
and delinquence of the working class and the absolute sanctuary of the
leisure class and its unspoken, sometimes unexplained, sexual practices.
It was also a way—as Eric Haralson argues about Henry James—of
condensing all experiences into passion and passion into sexuality or at
least the "sexual imperative" to devote one's life to sex expression ("Excellent Adventure" 179, 183). While James could afford to resist this
Americanizing impulse to treat all expression as sex expression, most
American women writers could not or did not want to do so. While, for
James, the French novel was superior in this respect, American women
writers found too much to gain in writing sex expression for themselves.

I date the emergence of sex expression from the late nineteenth
century, but one could trace further back the idea that love and passion,
appetite and desire could be disassociated from kinship and familial
relations. Sex expression emerges perhaps first in Walt Whitman and
certainly in the onanism and Mormon polygamy debates of the 1840s
and later. Sex expression itself took on its mass-mediated and popular

form in the post-Freudian period when sex was distinct from appetite, considered a choice rather than a drive. What other expressions besides self-expression and sex expression could be developed? Sex expression goes through various stages of advancement and restraint, though I have never equated sex expression with progress or freedom (as Calverton did in the book from which I borrow my title). Indeed, the literature of sex expression provides the matrix through which debates about women's freedom took place, supplying the language that allowed women's sexual subjectivity to be drafted. The sexualization of American culture is no narrative of progress or decline but a newly imagined sexual rhetoric— including marks of passion, middle-age crisis, kept women, pleasuring —that can be traced to American women's writing during the ongoing sexual revolution, from 1860 to 1940.

NOTES

Introduction

1 Male writers, too, were fascinated with these tropes. Hawthorne's Coverdale in *The Blithedale Romance* (1852), for example, was obsessed with the question of not only whether Zenobia was a virgin but also how he might tell if she was experienced. He scans her for signs of that expression, hoping to discern the marks of sexuality by which he can classify her: "Her unconstrained and inevitable manifestation, I said often to myself, was that of a woman to whom wedlock had thrown wide the gates of mystery" (44). Hawthorne also embeds a tale told by Zenobia, "The Silvery Veil," which deploys the fear that the woman's veil masks an ugliness so profound that it would blight the male sexuality of whoever beheld her. The fear of the ugly woman's sexual powers is so great that Theodore refuses the hope of a sexual union with perhaps the fairest woman in the world: the ugliness of sexual vice and passion trumps the promise of beauty every time. "Gates of mystery" and "silvery veils" are such overwrought metaphors for female sexuality that women writers frequently rejected them and stylized their own figures for sexuality.

2 V. F. Calverton, the chosen pen name for George Goetz, was the famous editor of the *Modern Quarterly* in the 1920s and the radical who tried to Americanize Marx. As Leonard Wilcox writes, Calverton and Samuel Schmalhausen, one of his early collaborators, participated in symposia about sex and psychology, one of which was titled "Sex is Necessary! Or, Why You Don't Feel the Way You Should" (78). Calverton's career followed the social necessity of sex and politics.

3 See Peiss 56. For instance, hats bedeviled Charlotte Perkins Gilman, who saw them as a sign of sexual availability, as well as the infantilizing drive for self-expression.

4 See Eric Haralson's reading of *The Ambassadors* in "Lambert Strether's Excellent Adventure" as a tour de force of Strether's heterosexual diffidence. Marilee Lindemann's *Willa Cather: Queering America* and Haralson's *Henry James and Queer Modernity* are eloquent arguments about how American literature was "queer," populated with alienated characters, ethnic "othering," and anxieties about the foreign. For Cather and James especially, the drama of heterosexual desire waned entirely, which made their works evidence of a new sort of sex expression altogether (5).

5   As Pamela Haag argues, the Elinor Glyn–named "It girl" experienced a similar sort of inarticulateness because her sexual magnetism was completely unself-conscious, a particular sex expression that was alien and irrational because it was beyond language. Haag questions how to negotiate this conscious/unconscious divide: "How, then, could young women, perceived as naturally alienated from their sexuality, claim desire as part of a culturally legitimate identity?" (" 'Real Thing' " 566). According to Haag, the 1920s and 1930s saw "the disjunction between unconscious sexual instinct and conscious self-possession" in working-class women (566).

6   As Elizabeth Lunbeck contends in *The Psychiatric Persuasion*, once sexuality became of interest to the middle classes, it was not imagined as a conscious decision (as it was for the working classes) but was considered a set of unconscious motivations and impulses. The working classes could seemingly control their sexualities, but the middle classes first had to relinquish themselves to their unconscious desires (207). Thus, hypersexuality gave way to frigidity as a new sexual problem. On the contrary, according to Julian Carter, the "heart of whiteness" could be found in erotic self-control coded as "normal." This sexual normality consolidated the ideal of whiteness as "American civilization's legacy" (14).

7   Fannie Hurst, for instance, wrote throughout the 1950s and 1960s but often replicated plots that she had originally used in the 1920s and 1930s.

Chapter 1

1   Sociologist Eva Illouz poses the question, "Is modern romantic love a utopia, that is, a category of the imagination that articulates values alternative to the market and commodity exchange, or is it an ideological system serving and furthering the interests of capitalism? To put the question more broadly, how is the meaning of love affected by its incorporation within the culture of capitalism?" (*Consuming* 145).

2   As Pamela Haag argues, and as I will show in the realm of women's fiction, "Sexual and political modernity in America were both coincident and causally interdependent" (*Consent* 94). Liberalism itself was sexualized in this first period of modern American culture. This is also the project that Bruce Burgett identifies as the "sexualizing process," in which "sex" is historicized rather than normalized and studied as part of other politicized processes in the United States ("Mormon Question" 78).

3   Julia Stern was among the first to signal this shift to the "postsentimental" in her reading of *The Morgesons* (123).

4   As Lucy Bland argues, turn-of-the-century England witnessed the same search

for "an adequate language" for sexuality and passion—something in between sexology and the vernacular of the streets (273). Thus, I document the move from the sentimentalization of femininity to the (psycho)sexualization of femininity.

5 Countering Foucault, Anthony Giddens argues that we cannot ignore the constraints of gender, the ideology of romantic love, the policing of the family, and, above all, the Foucaultian "conception of the self in relation to modernity" (24). Scholars have emphasized the discourses of restraint (and the constraints of discourse), and sometimes of pleasure, at the expense of new and specifically gendered ways that people imagined sex expressions outside of the norms of conventional sexuality.

6 Pamela Haag explains how classical liberal ideology "defined individualism as freedom of exchange in the property of self" (*Consent* xviii). "Notions of normal heterosexual identity were not unaffected by the entrenchment of a laissez-faire culture in the late nineteenth century" (26). Haag's understatement notwithstanding, liberal culture changed women's writing from a sentimental to a postsentimental, even sexualizing, production. In general, Haag explains this move as the emergence of the "private person," whereby modern liberalism guaranteed individual free choice, especially in sexuality (xix). Mark Seltzer, in another context, sees this transition as inaugurating "statistical persons," or what he considers the increasing abstraction of persons even as their materiality and physicality are emphasized, creating a new kind of representative or typical person (14), who was a function of "the body-machine complex" (101).

7 Nancy Fraser explains social-needs discourses as those that "exceed the apparently (but not really) self-regulating domestic and official economic institutions of male-dominated, capitalist societies" (156). Women's fictions about sexuality also emerge from this social excess, but in the context of linguistic absence. Women writers created a language of their own to describe sexual needs.

8 See David Shumway's caveat about Anthony Giddens's "larger utopianism" about social change suggested by the "pure relationship" (155).

9 See Helen Horowitz's excellent discussion of sex debates in nineteenth-century culture. Sex expression became a topic of popular discussion, as Horowitz argues, as early as the 1870s, when the concept of "sexual starvation" came into play (336).

10 As Emily Leider argues in her biography of Atherton, *Hermia Suydam* "represents a serious, though aesthetically crude, attempt to grapple with . . . sexual morality and a woman's legitimate right to express passion outside of marriage" (80).

11 See Leider 81–83. In Laura Daintrey's 1892 novel *Actaeon*, for instance, the heroine Pauline Belmore carries on an affair for two years before killing herself

with "the drugged oblivion of chloral" after her enemy Bleecker Falk threatens to expose her (95). Here, Daintrey links sexuality with chloral addiction, as Edith Wharton will come to do in her novels.

12 The interracial and intraracial dimensions of sexuality complicate the belief in the sexual frankness of the 1920s. Pamela Haag brilliantly analyzes, for instance, Ida B. Wells's attack on both rape and lynching, two elements of race and gender tyranny (*Consent* 131).

13 See Peel 307.

14 As Lauren Berlant and Michael Warner describe it, their purpose is not just to imagine "a safe zone for queer sex but the changed possibilities of identity, intelligibility, publics, culture, and sex that appear when the heterosexual couple is no longer the referent or the privileged example of sexual culture" (548). Their essay works by collapsing sentimentality and heterosexuality—as though these are the same historical and national discourse. As I have been arguing, however, it is not the referent or the privileged dyad that is so crucial but, instead, it is the means of persuasion by which sex is portrayed.

Chapter 2

1 Nina Miller renames "middle-brow" as "popular modernism" in order to signify the various media by which the modern self was being negotiated in mass culture (88).

2 As Walter Benn Michaels suggests, in a market economy, "the love of freedom may come to seem as perverse as the love of tyranny," given that one may have to trade one's body and enslavement for food and shelter. Michaels insists that all contracts become claims about owning and being owned in the market economy (62).

3 Chapter 3 deals with Rebecca Harding Davis, who uses a train wreck as a metaphor for the end of a middle-aged woman's desires, thwarting her immersion in teenage dreams of sexual romance.

4 Instead of focusing on heterosexuality or homosexuality, masochism or sadism, or any other binary that resulted in part from the new sexological studies, I have been writing about the way that sex expression came to refract emotions and desire registered in American literature.

5 See Nancy Bentley on the nature of accidents in Wharton as "a violent symptom of modern conditions" ("Wharton, Travel, and Modernity" 176).

6 See Jennifer Putzi's excellent chapter on the scar and sexuality in which she argues for Stoddard's grasp of the relation between tattoos and scars as signifying marks on the body. Putzi has also edited Stoddard's *Two Men*, a novel that deals with the interracial sexuality between one of those men, Parke, and an

African American woman in town. To his mother, Parke cries, "What she is, mother, *I* have made her; and, as her cup of disgrace is full, so is mine, and I shall drink it" (165). *Two Men* is another postsentimental novel of American dynamics of sexuality.

7 As Julia Stern remarks, Cassandra hates conventional learning, except for reading Byron and especially "Don Juan" (111).

8 She is five years older than her husband, who married her when he was nineteen or twenty, and they have the baby when Cassandra is roughly fifteen years old (9, 12). As Amanda Claybaugh remarks in her astute reading of the reform subtexts of this novel (temperance, antislavery, and property reform), "The novel is full of vaguely adulterous mothers, mothers whose late-life babies cannot be entirely explained" (112).

9 Or as Joseph Boone writes in *Libidinal Currents*, "Frankness in writing about female sexuality is no guarantee that the dams of repressive tradition will be broken—or, more to the point, that the waters that flow upon their breaking will give birth to anything other than traditionally restrictive iconographies of 'Woman' " (68).

10 From the 1860s on, social reform movements such as the Female Moral Reform Societies that historians such as Carroll Smith-Rosenberg analyze attempted to purify society of the double sexual standard. When these efforts failed, social engineering came into vogue as a way to contain the proliferation of the unruly masses, considered to be reproducing at an unparalleled rate.

11 Ann Douglas's *The Feminization of American Culture* identifies only one woman as "ugly": the unsentimental Margaret Fuller, whose ugliness inhibited her sexual fulfillment even as it spurred her intellectual achievements. "Fuller's great romantic peers and predecessors abroad, Madame de Staël and George Sand, however, had special precedents, sanctions, and abilities denied their American counterpart for making their intricacies in some sense part of their allure. . . . De Staël and Sand were beautiful, well-born, wealthy; they had access to a sympathetic milieu, and dozens of devoted lovers. Fuller was not good-looking, and it galled her to be 'ugly'; she did not know a man's love until she was thirty-seven, although she often sought it" (261–62). Intentionally or not, Douglas links Fuller's failure of sex expression to her ugliness, and that failure spurs Fuller's intellectual goals of self-culture. For Douglas, the legacy of sentiment only cheapens culture, debasing a great intellect such as Fuller's rather than celebrating her conquering of desire. Ugliness, in Douglas's treatment of Fuller's career, redirects sexuality into intellectual power. Fuller's intellect notwithstanding, ugliness once provided the very rationale for sexual intimacy or pleasure, a topic that Douglas banishes from her antebellum literary history.

12 Joanne Dobson notes in her "Reclaiming Sentimental Literature" that "if sexual relation is a component of sentimental connection, it tends to be mediated through and subsumed within affectional love" (286). Although Dobson is correct about the sentimentalization of sex, the sentimental reformers had to face sexual relations outside of the affectional model being promulgated by domestic authors.

13 See Susan Power's *The Ugly-Girl Papers; or, Hints for the Toilet* (1874) to explore how ugliness was to be overcome when women mastered beauty.

14 Eric Sundquist also claims in *To Wake the Nations* that debates about blood were common in racialist thinking, and African American historiographers as well as fictionists often complicated the issue of blood and heredity by invoking Africanist consciousness or the advantages of miscegenation.

15 When Lucia True Ames Mead writes in *To Whom Much Is Given* (1899) that women's benevolence to girls might consist of "a bath, . . . clean underwear, and . . . mend[ed] clothing," we see the symbolic displacement of sexuality onto dirty underwear or, in Faulkner's *Sound and the Fury*, Caddy's muddy drawers (33).

16 "Years ago," Jean Yellin claims, "Ann Douglas charged women and clergymen with responsibility for 'the feminization of American culture' in the nineteenth century, but *Margret Howth* presents an important instance in which the leading member of the white male literary [Howells] establishment demanded that a nineteenth-century woman writer 'feminize' her text" (217) by changing the ending from a bleak critique of industrialization to a happy celebration of domestic abundance.

17 Pamela Haag suggests the logic of a working woman's fall: "A woman's work and poverty, first, corroded her modesty. This corrosion of modesty, barring interventions by reformers themselves, culminated in the woman's sexual seduction; her ruination would lead to sexual commerce. . . . The working girl, lacking the class-specific '*luxury*' of modesty and virtue, would eventually stumble into passion and sexual commerce, indeed, passion *as* sexual commerce" (*Consent* 44; Haag's emphasis).

18 Beryl Satter's *Each Mind a Kingdom* gives insightful readings of the prodesire factions of New Thought.

Chapter 3

1 See Mary Odem's chart of the legal ages of consent in 1885 and 1920 (14–15).

2 Floyd Dell's novel is a free-love manifesto that decries the possible fate of the heroine, who worries about being "an old hag of thirty-two" (*Love without Money* 75). Despite the other obsessions that Dell registers in his novel (lesbian-

ism and homosexuality, abortion, feminism, adolescent sexuality, along with what he generally calls "the American ideal of sexless companionship" among youth), he does maintain the myth that sex eludes women after thirty. The heroine, Gretchen Cedarbloom, mentally rebukes the old maid, Carol Martin: " 'I don't think she's ever gone to bed with anything except a hot-water bottle. She thinks that sex is something you read about in a novel by James Branch Cabell' " (329). While Cabell's romances emphasized sex, Dell's concerned modern realism, even though sexual intimacy is relegated to the postadolescent "Flaming Youth." The novel focuses on the hero's and heroine's search for a bed to make love in since both characters live at home and cannot afford a hotel. The novel ends with the hero saying, " 'Here we are, in spite of all the devils in hell, mothers included!' " (365).

3 As Jennifer Fleissner reminds us, this narrative of decline was also linked to the narrative of modernity, as well as the "decline in national birthrates" (204).

4 The *New York Times Book Review* heralded Atherton's novel for its treatment of "what has been but recently shown to be a scientific possibility," rejuvenation through the increased development of the sex cells. The reviewer, however, laments the inclusion of "the unnecessary and very ugly episode of Agnes Trevor," which "nauseated the Countess Zattiany, and has much the same effect upon the reader."

5 See Julie Prebel's meticulous reading of Atherton's novel.

6 As many historians of the settlement workers write, settlement reformers tended to see sexuality as "relief from the poor wages and conditions of the workplace," with no "profit" or pleasure of its own (Abrams 448). As Alexander explains, the growth of "sexualized youth cultures" kept both working- and middle-class parents busy at deterring their children's sexuality (59).

7 See, for instance, the report entitled *The Settlement Horizon* by Robert A. Woods and Albert J. Kennedy, issued by the Russell Sage Foundation in 1922. The chapter entitled "Mixed Company" explains that supervised dancing, informal entertainment, and choral singing were the only activities allowed during the intermixing of the girls' and boys' clubs. In the appendix on sex education, the author explains how settlement workers dealt with sex: "They knew that once sex instinct is aroused, to control it is difficult. Their prescription, as we have seen, was to delay its conscious awakening" (409).

8 Popular-magazine fiction used the settlement as a ground for analyzing contemporary issues of sexuality. For instance, Grace Sartwell Mason's story "The Lotus Eater" (1918) represents the Protestant male reformer as a "sediment worker" who relishes the sexual attentions of the "garment-shop girls" he would "cultivate" (101).

Chapter 4

1 For an excellent general discussion of the unprecedented focus on heterosexual intimacy, see Christine Stansell's *American Moderns*. She describes "sexual modernism" as "paradoxical, self-deluding, sometimes harmful" (267), even when some of the practitioners of the new intimacies could "will" themselves into equality.

2 The reviews of *Linda Condon* remark upon Hergesheimer's character study of the beautiful but cold Linda, a woman whose beauty gives her the only emotional connection to her husband and children.

3 Scholars have offered substantial and incisive analyses of prostitution as the urgent issue of late nineteenth- and early twentieth-century progressive reform (see Stanley; Stansell; Gilfoyle; Katie Johnson). But an alternate discourse of what was respectable sexuality was generated alongside this language of reform.

4 See Jesse Battan and Caroline Levander for excellent discussions of these linguistic battles.

5 The popular novelist Kathleen Norris denounces this power in such romances as *The Foolish Virgin* (1928), in which the heroine Pamela ruins her reputation by staying out all night with her boyfriend after they run out of gas and take refuge in an abandoned house. While they still love each other, he nevertheless abandons her for the sake of his social reputation but finds himself enthralled by her power: "It was as if Chester's eyes made Pamela conscious of her own beauty to-night, and his low voice taught her her power. She seemed to herself intoxicated with the heady wine of it, the ecstasy of knowing that this man was hers, to be controlled by the laziest lift of her heavy lashes, or the faintest intonation in her voice" (271). Such power was, in Norris's heightened awareness, "simply madness," a power that Pamela must abandon in order to marry the rightful suitor, the familial and stolid Gregory (for whom she works as a companion to his aged mother). Overwrought and clichéd, Norris's numerous heroines refuse such power for more stable relations. In Norris's *The Beloved Woman* (1921), the heroine Norma Sheridan discovers almost too late that money and power mean little compared to her stable marriage to an engineer. On the day that he is leaving to take a new job in California, Norma discovers that she cares little for her inheritance or for the discovery of the identity of her real parents, the wealthy and influential Melroses.

6 Austin revises Dreiser's *Sister Carrie* and redeems her heroine as a "good" sexual woman.

7 See Hamilton Fyfe's description of the third sex as a woman more drawn to work than to sex: "With the numbers of women and men in England there had come into existence what might almost be called a Third Sex. This was made up

of women who, foreseeing no probability of marriage to provide them with interest and occupation, either worked for a living or threw their energies into work of a social or charitable kind, and included a great many who have laboured with most commendable results in the fields of education, medicine, literature, commerce, science, and social reform" (1891). Michael North concludes that the authors in the 1920s believed "the contradiction between women and work so strong" that Fyfe invented this "Third Sex" to identify women whose energies were devoted to work and reform (185).

8 See Katie N. Johnson's *Sisters in Sin: Brothel Drama in America, 1900–1920* for a discussion of the myth of the actress as whore (27).

9 Sex power does not inevitably lead to a change in hierarchical relations between men and women, nor does it change the fantasy of sexual empowerment that women once invested in liberated, unrepressed sexuality. Perhaps we need to look not to sexuality but to fantasy as an indication of women's changing relation to power. If women's sexual fantasies (of escape or rescue, domination or subordination) remain the same in women's writing, perhaps those fixed scripts of sexuality are more important than how women use sexuality to advance or flee.

10 See my "Addiction and Intimacy," which elaborates on these texts. Wharton rejected women's sexual power because it results in personal as well as cultural alienation. Even more important, her novels, from *The House of Mirth* (1905), to *The Fruit of the Tree* (1907), to *Ethan Frome* (1911), substitute the language of drugs for that of sexual liberation or women's freedom from Victorian mores. Drugs, not sex, take the place of her heroines' tragedies of alienation. Lily Bart takes chloral to sleep, perhaps to die; Bessy Amherst dies of a morphine overdose; Zeena is addicted to patent medicines; Mattie becomes a lifelong invalid and, by extension in a culture devoted to painkillers, an addict. Drugs even literalize the metaphorical destruction of sexual intimacy.

11 For better or worse, these early novels level Wharton's critique against the democratizing effects of liberating sexuality and, in a larger vein, the commodification of American culture. At the time when the flapper was being invented as the figure of misdirected or wanton passion, Wharton's preoccupation with the life of passion led her to embellish the figure of middle-age desire. These plots include Lawyer Royall's attachment to Charity Royall in *Summer* (1917), Kate Clephane's interest in a younger man in *The Mother's Recompense* (1925), and Martin Boyne's fascination with Judith Wheater in *The Children* (1927). Unlike the new celebrants of sexual liberation focused on the young and the beautiful, Wharton was willing to see passion in the lives of characters supposedly beyond the pale of sexual experience: middle-aged men and women, mothers, and their pre- and postadolescent children.

12 R. W. B. Lewis dates the Palmato fragment at 1935, while Jennie Kassanoff puts it at 1918–19.

13 See Jean-Michel Rabaté's *1913: The Cradle of Modernism* for his reading of Undine's aggression and neurosis: "It is no coincidence that it was the alleged cynicism of this novel that cost Wharton the Nobel Prize in 1927. While 'cynicism' may not be the right term, there is deep ambivalence in Wharton regarding her heroine. Should we absolve Undine because she is only reproducing the 'custom of the country'?" (195).

14 As Nancy Bentley argues, Mrs. Spragg is "waxen" and "idol-like," a perfect specimen of the tensions of the modern woman (*Ethnography* 170–71). And with Undine, Bentley suggests, we feel a fascinated identification and repugnance, which is a mark of Wharton's "operative ambivalence" (175).

15 Jennie Kassanoff expertly analyzes Wharton's anxiety about race and the "vanishing American" in this novel, and Wharton's anxiety about sexuality is inextricable from her concerns about racial degeneration.

Chapter 5

1 Eva Illouz calls this new emergence the "therapeutic emotional style," characterized by increased attention to talking through the normality and pathology of the self in relation to others (*Cold Intimacies* 6–8).

2 *Bad Girl* sold a record 200,000 copies, *Scarlet Sister Mary* was a best seller and Pulitzer Prize–winner, but *Salome of the Tenements* was neither a critical nor a popular success.

3 As Joseph Boone writes, "Sex has come to signify the central but hidden *essence* of one's nature" (69; Boone's emphasis). Muriel Dimen makes a similar point: "Sexuality has become a relation, not a force. If, with Freud, we thought that your sex is what makes you who are, now we think that who you are shapes what sex you are and what sex you like. . . . The self, we now think, is born in relationship, not in the continuously flowing impersonal excitement—libido—located by Freud beneath psychic process and structure" (157). This emphasis on relationship posits what is crucial about sex expression: it is beyond standardized or therapeutic self and depends on reciprocity.

4 See Sharon Ullman's first chapter in *Sex Seen* for an important analysis of the culture's rejection of ugliness and middle age in turn-of-the-century films. Ullman writes about the "potency" of ugliness as a "destructive power" to female desire and sexual agency (20). But is the "old maid" asexual because of her age or because of her ugliness? Or both?

5 What is more, Sonya continually refers to Manning as her "patron saint." This Christian discourse cannot be reconciled with her Jewish faith. The mythology

of Christian sainthood attracts her to Manning, but neither can sustain the illusion of his sacrificial martyrdom for the cause. Thus, Sonya's explicit Jewishness mixes with a Christian submission to a power outside of herself.

6   In *Love in the Machine Age* (1930), Floyd Dell cites the statistic that some women had "as many as 40" abortions in the 1920s (175), though Dell's figures seem more like urban myth than fact.

7   Deborah McDowell claims that Nella Larsen wrote about women's sexuality ambivalently in *Quicksand* (1928) and *Passing* (1929), while Jessie Fauset retreated to the domestication of desire that Claudia Tate analyzed as part of the literary history of African American novels of the 1890s.

8   One reviewer claims the novel is devoid of "implied moral purpose" since he sees Peterkin's stories as "uncolored by any open desire to uplift the negro race or the American people" (Law 455–56).

9   Following Ann duCille's lead in her reading of the use of white characters in Zora Neale Hurston's *Seraph on the Suwanee* (1948), I am wondering whether it is possible for Peterkin to use black characters in *Scarlet Sister Mary* to deal with the ideas of women's heterosexual pleasure *without* assigning to black men (or all black people) characteristics of sexual license. Does Peterkin use Mary as Hurston used Arvay Henson to make a point about female sexuality (duCille 127–28)? In other words, is there a difference between Hurston's use of race and Peterkin's? Or even between Peterkin's writing that Mary slept with all sorts of men on the plantation and Fauset's writing that Judy Strange in *Chinaberry Tree* slept with "men . . . from the South, big, hard, sweaty, black fellows" (15)? What's the difference when black and white writers explore female sexual pleasure?

10 As Patricia Guthrie explains in *Catching Sense*, community women served their communities as midwives. On the South Carolina Sea Island of St. Helena, for instance, the old Penn School was the site of a vocational school until the 1950s (8). By the 1940s, southern public-health work focused on regulating midwives (see Litt 73).

11 Many of the African American women's novels of the 1920s—from Zara Wright's virtually ignored *Black and White Tangled Threads* and *Kenneth* in 1920, to Larsen's much-discussed *Passing*, to Zora Neale Hurston's first published work in *Fire!!* (the short story "Sweat")—also promulgate the necessity for black women to achieve either self-expression or sex expression.

12 What Carol Batker calls Fauset's "integrationist politics" extends to the novelist's treatment of sexuality (71). Just as Fauset's politics are subtle and complex, so too are her sexual dynamics (Batker 84, 88).

13 In fact, dressmaking became a way for ex-slaves, as Elizabeth Keckley documents in *Behind the Scenes*, to make a world of self-expression and commodity

consumption available to black women after emancipation. As Lori Merish writes, "Fashion is again the symbolic matrix within which desire—especially the desire for 'freedom'—is negotiated" (239). Fauset explores the legacy of bondage relations attached to the figure of the dressmaker at length.

14 Jane Kuenz argues that "rather than read the moments of forced resolution in Fauset's novels as signs of her personal failure as a writer or a thinker—as I believe most of her feminist readers still do—I would suggest instead that they mark the point at which the texts' internal contradictions overlap with and threaten to give voice to those contradictions general in the culture and, in this instance, in New Negro gender and racial ideology in particular. . . . Yet even in those earlier texts, including *There is Confusion*, readers can accept an overly cheery resolution only by first recognizing the problems Fauset's feminist critique makes evident: Maggie's economic and sexual dependency in relation to both white and black men, Joanna's uncomfortable relation to the kinds of sacrifices expected of her as an actually talented Talented Tenth woman" (95). As Kuenz has it, Fauset's novel is largely about the tension between sexuality and race.

15 Women's "sex charm" (275) yields a kind of benevolence once they use it as a means to empower a sexual sisterhood.

16 For influential social critic Floyd Dell, in *Love without Money* (1931), the question of sex was about not persons but places—that is, where one could have sex, a question of geography, especially when lovers had no room of their own.

Chapter 6

1 *New York Times* book critic Wilbur Watson writes that "speaking out of a comedy of the Nineteen Twenties, a Kaufman-Hart character described Cosmopolitan as something Fannie Hurst wrote everyday. The description would seem as valid today: few of our lady novelists have been more prolific—and few have labored more earnestly to hold a loyal public. Miss Hurst's new novel is devoted to the all-for-love theme. Or perhaps the girl-gets-wrong-boy pattern would be a more accurate classification for *Anywoman*" (32).

2 Sex power led to a number of rejuvenation strategies, as we saw in chapter 3 and the new focus on middle-age sexuality. Fannie Hurst's story "The Smirk, a Light Tragedy That Has an Entirely New Moral" focuses on Alicia's attempt to win back her old lover, Dr. Elmer Channing, a philosophy professor whom she had not married for fear of genteel professorial poverty; he is now a wealthy widower with a three-year-old daughter. In order to renew his sexual interest, she decides to have plastic surgery at age forty-two: "There were ravages in the face of Alicia. Ravages of disappointment in gutters under her eyes, and her cheeks

had dropped a little, like clay down a hillside. . . . At forty-two Alicia looked it. The muscles of her mouth sagged as if there were little weights hung on the inside of her lips" (79). She felt that her previous powers of sexual attraction needed bolstering with a new face.

Yet this new face leaves her marked with an unchanging smile, one that remains a mask, "planted" with a sly, slightly satiric smirk. Alicia is left with a form of sex expression that she hadn't imagined and one that gives her acquaintances " 'the creeps' " and scares his young daughter (79). More important, the face cannot reflect her emotions, thus making it a less reliable register than it had been before, even though that previous expression reflected her tired disappointment at life. She cannot change the smirk; her expression is "indelible" and impermeable. In it, Hurst explores the effects of sex power on its user. The face-lift has unintended and disastrous effects. Hurst is skeptical of the efficacy of a plastic surgery that erases personality in the name of rejuvenated sex expression.

3 I am tempted here to use Jennifer Fleissner's terms from her masterful reading of naturalism to explain how Hurst's forty-year career demonstrates the "stuckness" and obsessive-compulsiveness of her characters. But unlike the female heroines that Fleissner analyzes, Hurst's almost always work through their compulsions through some variation on the therapeutic mode.

4 What sort of intimacy would work when women's desires are inherently social, since contractual relations are by nature liberal models of association? Yet Hurst's intimacy is also inherently resistant, since the same liberal models can't account for women's transgressive desire. The model of desire that Wharton espouses is an apt one for this dilemma: her ideal is for a therapeutic model of intimacy, while her plots reveal that all such intimacies are addictive. Wharton posits sex expression as an addiction to a therapeutic "inner life" when she herself struggles to create the lexicon of sex expression in the face of such elusiveness and contradiction.

5 So vital did sexuality seem to modern American selfhood that personal happiness was lodged in sex expression, as David Shumway suggests in *Modern Love*, in which he argues that "the emergence of the discourse of intimacy should be understood as a response to the crisis in marriage" (134) starting in the 1920s and continuing with greater force through the 1940s. From this crisis, Shumway concludes, emerges the "relationship"—not quite marriage, not quite romance, but something more mixed and in needing of fixing. Following Anthony Giddens's analysis of "intimacy as democracy," Shumway charts advice about how to achieve the "pure relationship" (140). My sense is that women writers became tired out by their emotional work in creating this democratic intimacy.

6 According to Eva Illouz, Anthony Giddens's model of the "pure relationship" is

"based on a communicative rationality that assumes that two persons are equal to each other, can make claims about their needs, and base these claims on agreed-upon norms of equality and reciprocity" (*Consuming* 206). Wendy Langford's vehement argument against Giddens cites the impossibility of such democratization since women can never be equal under current social organizations. For Hurst's readership, however, the social theory was less relevant than social practice, especially in terms of how this readership was to live out its sexual life.

7 In a 1919 issue of *Catholic World*, Maurice Egan predicts Hurst's literary formula: "Miss Fannie Hurst has discovered the type of the haughty 'saleslady' or the scornful cloak model whose business it is to appear as fashionable as possible, but who in her heart longs only for domestic life, with mission furniture or Louis Quatorze or whatever is the mode, a husband who is a good provider, and a certain number of children. At the heart of these novels, which evidently contain a great amount of truth, occasionally enameled with touches of romance, there is the admission that the life of a contented family is the highest possible object to which human nature can attain" (295). Of course, this is all wrong, given Hurst's rejection—again and again—of conventional family arrangements.

8 In *Anatomy of Me* (1958), Hurst explains her parents' attitude toward the word "kike." Her mother met the word with indifference: "I doubt if the opprobrium 'kike' had retained much of its impact for Mama. It hopped about like a toad in the idiom of the German-Jewish community of our town. It connoted a race divided against itself. Similarly, light Negroes and dark Negroes. Touchables and untouchables. 'Kike' denoted the Jew originally out of Eastern Europe. Russian, Polish, Galician. The caste system held rigidly, German Jew segregated from Eastern Jew. The usage of 'nigger' was still so general that it was only as a young adult (the [Washington] University played no role in awakening this consciousness) that I began to be aware of its connotation" (90–91).

9 Stephanie Lewis Thompson's chapter on Hurst in *Influencing America's Tastes* reads the published novel against the manuscript version, entitled *Sugar House*. Thompson notes that the question of Bea's sexuality, both straight and lesbian, is much more explicit in the unpublished version (188–90).

10 Arguably the most famous of "kept women" is Carrie Meeber in Theodore Dreiser's *Sister Carrie* (1900), a novel that sets the gold standard for mistress fiction. Whether one reads Carrie as an "unattached woman" (she is neither a traditional fallen woman nor yet a New Woman) or a "scab" (as Stephanie Smith does, since Carrie does the work of a wife for less money and security than a wife would), Dreiser sparked decades-long reverberations about what being "kept" actually means in a culture increasingly devoted to compulsory

marriage. As I discussed in chapter 2, what's important for my project is Dreiser's vision of middle-age male sexuality in George Hurstwood, whose decline into a stereotyped midlife crisis is set against Carrie's rise. In turn, Carrie's transformation depends on her abandoning her invisible labor as mistress—baking biscuits and keeping house, since her duties for Hurstwood are not only sexual—for the visible labor of performance.

11 Walter Michaels's reading of *Summer* in "The Contracted Heart" is crucial to this reading of exchanging goods in sexual relations.

12 Elizabeth Janeway's 1945 *Daisy Kenyon* might be the exception that proves the rule. Although she supports herself, Daisy is still caught between two lovers and raped by one before she commits to leaving her career to be a military-base wife to the other. The rape (committed by her married lover of eight years) sends her from the city she loves (New York) to an unknown place in California at the side of her officer-husband. This formula is repeated throughout novels of the 1920s and 1930s as a variation on sexual nostalgia: from Carrie Meeber's decision in *Sister Carrie* to pretend to be Hurstwood's wife rather than work to David Graham Phillips's portrayal of the eponymous heroine in *Susan Lenox: Her Fall and Rise* in his 1917 novel.

13 As Lauren Berlant claims in a dialogue with Jane Gallop over the Clinton-Lewinsky affair, American culture has always desired "a heterosexuality that doesn't need language because it has no structural problems or excesses" ("Loose Lips" 248).

Conclusion

1 I don't reduce the specificity of lesbian culture here, but it's clear that such misery about the failures of intimacy cuts across many of the narratives about sex expression.

2 An exception is Gale Wilhelm's *Torchlight to Valhalla* (1938), which ends with the twenty-one-year-old heroine in love with a seventeen-year-old new neighbor; there is no trauma, drama, or suffering, except for the one man who falls in love with the heroine and her grief over her father's death.

BIBLIOGRAPHY

Abrams, Laura S. "Guardians of Virtue: The Social Reformers and the 'Girl Problem,' 1890–1920." *Social Service Review* 74.3 (September 2000): 436–52.

Addams, Jane. *Twenty Years at Hull House.* New York: Macmillan, 1910.

Aiken, George L., and George C. Howard. *Uncle Tom's Cabin.* 1852. *Nineteenth-Century American Musical Theatre.* Vol. 5. Ed. Thomas Riis. New York: Garland, 1994.

Alcott, Louisa May. "Behind a Mask; or, A Woman's Power." 1866. *Louisa May Alcott Unmasked: Collected Thrillers.* Ed. Madeleine Stern. Boston: Northeastern UP, 1995. 361–429.

Alexander, Ruth M. *The "Girl Problem": Female Sexual Delinquency in New York, 1900–1930.* Ithaca: Cornell UP, 1995.

Ammons, Elizabeth. "Edith Wharton and Race." *The Cambridge Companion to Edith Wharton.* Ed. Millicent Bell. Cambridge: Cambridge UP, 1995. 68–86.

Apter, Terri. *Secret Paths: Women in the New Midlife.* New York: Norton, 1995.

Atherton, Gertrude Franklin. *Black Oxen.* New York: A. L. Burt, 1923.

———. *Hermia Suydam.* New York: John W. Lovell, 1889.

———. *Patience Sparhawk and Her Times.* London: John Lane, 1897.

———. *A Question of Time.* New York: John W. Lovell, 1891.

Austin, Mary. *Everyman's Genius.* Indianapolis: Bobbs-Merrill, 1925.

———. *Love and the Soul Maker.* New York: D. Appleton, 1914.

———. *No. 26 Jayne Street.* Boston: Houghton Mifflin, 1920.

———. "Regionalism in American Literature." *English Journal* 21 (1932): 97–107.

———. "Sex in American Literature." *The Bookman* 57.4 (June 1923): 385–93.

———. *A Woman of Genius.* 1912. New York: Feminist Press, 1985.

Banner, Lois. *In Full Flower: Aging Women, Power, and Sexuality.* New York: Knopf, 1992.

Barnes, Elizabeth. *States of Sympathy.* New York: Columbia UP, 1997.

Batker, Carol. *Reforming Fictions: Native, African, and Jewish American Women's Literature and Journalism in the Progressive Era.* New York: Columbia UP, 2000.

Battan, Jesse F. " 'The Word Made Flesh': Language, Authority, and Sexual Desire in Late Nineteenth-Century America." *American Sexual Politics.* Ed. John C. Fout and Maura Shaw Tantillo. Chicago: U of Chicago P, 1990. 101–22.

Bauer, Dale M. "Wharton's 'Others': Addiction and Intimacy." *The Historical Guide to Edith Wharton.* Ed. Carol Singley. New York: Oxford UP, 2003. 115–45.

Baym, Nina. "Women's Novels and Women's Minds: An Unsentimental View of Nineteenth-Century American Women's Fiction." *Novel* 31 (Summer 1998): 1–16.

Bell, Millicent, ed. *The Cambridge Companion to Wharton.* Cambridge: Cambridge UP, 1995.

Benstock, Shari. *No Gifts from Chance.* New York: Scribner's, 1994.

Bentley, Nancy. *The Ethnography of Manners: Hawthorne, James, Wharton.* Cambridge: Cambridge UP, 1995.

———. "'Hunting for the Real': Edith Wharton and the Science of Manners." *The Cambridge Companion to Edith Wharton.* Ed. Millicent Bell. Cambridge: Cambridge UP, 1995. 47–67.

———. "Wharton, Travel, and Modernity." *A Historical Guide to Edith Wharton.* Ed. Carol J. Singley. New York: Oxford UP, 2003. 147–79.

Berlant, Lauren. "The Female Complaint." *Social Text* 19–20 (Fall 1988): 237–59.

———. *The Female Complaint: The Unfinished Business of Sentimentality in American Culture.* Durham: Duke UP, 2008.

———. "National Brands/National Body: *Imitation of Life.*" *The Phantom Public Sphere.* Ed. Bruce Robbins. Minneapolis: U of Minnesota P, 1993. 173–208.

———. "Poor Eliza." *American Literature* 70.3 (September 1998): 635–68.

———. *The Queen of America Goes to Washington City.* Durham: Duke UP, 1997.

Berlant, Lauren, with Jane Gallop. "Loose Lips." *Our Monica, Ourselves.* Ed. Lauren Berlant and Lisa Duggan. New York: New York UP, 2001. 246–67.

Berlant, Lauren, and Michael Warner. "Sex in Public." *Intimacy.* Spec. issue of *Critical Inquiry* 24.2 (Winter 1998): 547–66.

Birken, Lawrence. *Consuming Desire: Sexual Science and the Emergence of a Culture of Abundance, 1871–1914.* Ithaca: Cornell UP, 1988.

Bland, Lucy. *Banishing the Beast: Feminism, Sex, and Morality.* London: Tauris Parke Paperbacks, 1995.

Blum, Virginia. "Love Studies; or, Liberating Love." *American Literary History* 17.2 (Summer 2005): 335–48.

Boone, Joseph. *Libidinal Currents: Sexuality and the Shaping of Modernism.* Chicago: U of Chicago P, 1998.

Bower, Stephanie. "The Wages of Virtue." *Middlebrow Moderns: Popular American Women Writers of the 1920s.* Ed. Lisa Botshon and Meredith Goldsmith. Boston: Northeastern UP, 2003. 245–62.

Brennan, Teresa. "Social Physics: Inertia, Energy, and Aging." *Figuring Age: Women, Bodies, Generations.* Ed. Kathleen Woodward. Bloomington: Indiana UP, 1999. 131–48.

Brodie, Janet Farrell. *Contraception and Abortion in Nineteenth-Century America.* Ithaca: Cornell UP, 1994.

Burgett, Bruce. "On the Mormon Question: Race, Sex, and Polygamy in the 1850s and the 1990s." *American Quarterly* 57.1 (March 2005): 75–102.

——. "Sex." *Keywords of American Cultural Studies*. Ed. Bruce Burgett and Glenn Hendler. New York: New York UP, 2007. 217–21.

Burstein, Jessica. "A Few Words about Dubuque: Modernism, Sentimentalism, and the Blasé." *American Literary History* 14.2 (Summer 2002): 227–54.

Calverton, V. F. *Sex Expression in Literature*. New York: Boni & Liveright, 1926.

Calverton, V. F., and Samuel D. Schmalhausen. *Sex in Civilization*. Garden City, NY: Garden City Publishing, 1929.

Carby, Hazel. "Policing the Black Woman's Body in an Urban Context." *Critical Inquiry* 18.4 (Summer 1992): 738–55.

Carlin, Deborah. " 'What Methods Have Brought Blessing': Discourses of Reform in Philanthropic Literature." *The (Other) American Traditions*. Ed. Joyce W. Warren. New Brunswick: Rutgers UP, 1993. 203–25.

Carter, Julian. *The Heart of Whiteness: Normal Sexuality and Race in America, 1880–1940*. Durham: Duke UP, 2007.

Castronovo, Russ. "Incidents in the Life of a White Woman: Economies of Race and Gender in the Antebellum Nation." *American Literary History* 10.2 (Summer 1998): 239–65.

Cather, Willa. *A Lost Lady*. 1923. Lincoln: U of Nebraska P, 1997.

——. "Paul's Case." 1905. *Willa Cather: Early Novels and Stories*. New York: Library of America, 1992. 111–31.

Chauncey, George, Jr. "From Sexual Inversion to Homosexuality." *Salmagundi* 58/59 (Fall 1982/Winter 1983): 114–46.

Chopin, Kate. "The Storm." 1898. *The Awakening and Selected Stories*. Ed. Sandra Gilbert. New York: Penguin, 1984. 281–86.

Clarke, Edward H. *Sex in Education; or, A Fair Chance for Girls*. Boston: James R. Osgood, 1873.

Claybaugh, Amanda. *The Novel of Purpose: Literature and Social Reform in the Anglo-American World*. Ithaca: Cornell UP, 2007.

Creel, Margaret Washington. *"A Peculiar People": Slave Religion and Community-Culture among the Gullahs*. New York: New York UP, 1988.

Curtis, Susan. *A Consuming Faith: The Social Gospel and Modern American Culture*. Baltimore: Johns Hopkins UP, 1991.

Daintrey, Laura. *Actaeon*. New York: Empire City, 1892. Wright bibliography number 1371, reel D-3.

Davis, Rebecca Harding. "Anne." 1889. *A Rebecca Harding Davis Reader*. Ed. Jean Pfaelzer. Pittsburgh: U of Pittsburgh P, 1995. 329–39.

——. *Margret Howth*. 1862. New York: Feminist Press, 1990.

Dean, Carolyn J. *Sexuality and Modern Western Culture*. New York: Twayne, 1996.

Dearborn, Mary. *Pocahontas's Daughters: Gender and Ethnicity in American Culture.* New York: Oxford UP, 1986.

Degler, Carl N. *In Search of Human Nature: The Decline and Revival of Darwinism in American Social Thought.* New York: Oxford UP, 1991.

Delamotte, Eugenia C. *Gates of Freedom: Voltairine de Cleyre and the Revolution of the Mind.* Ann Arbor: U of Michigan P, 2004.

Dell, Floyd. *Janet March.* New York: Knopf, 1923.

———. *Love in the Machine Age: A Psychological Study of the Transition from Patriarchal Society.* New York: Farrar & Rinehart, 1930.

———. *Love without Money.* New York: Farrar & Rinehart, 1931.

———. "Sex in American Fiction." *American Mercury* 66 (January 1948): 84–90.

Delmar, Viña. *Bad Girl.* New York: Grosset & Dunlap, 1928.

Dickinson, Robert Latou, and Lura Beam. *The Single Woman: A Medical Study of Sex Education.* Baltimore: Williams & Wilkins, 1934.

Dimen, Muriel. *Sexuality, Intimacy, Power.* Hillsdale, NJ: Analytic Press, 2003.

Dobson, Joanne. "Reclaiming Sentimental Literature." *American Literature* 69.2 (June 1997): 263–88.

Dollimore, Jonathan. *Sex, Literature, and Censorship.* Malden, MA: Blackwell, 2001.

Douglas, Ann. *The Feminization of American Culture.* New York: Knopf, 1977.

———. *Terrible Honesty: Mongrel Manhattan in the 1920s.* New York: Farrar, Straus, Giroux, 1995.

Drake, Mrs. Emma F. Angell. *What a Woman of Forty-five Ought to Know.* Self and Sex Series. Philadelphia: Vir, 1902.

Dreiser, Theodore. *Jennie Gerhardt.* 1911. New York: Penguin, 1994.

———. *Sister Carrie.* 1900. Philadelphia: U of Pennsylvania P, 1981.

duCille, Ann. *The Coupling Convention: Sex, Text, and Tradition in Black Women's Fiction.* New York: Oxford UP, 1993.

Egan, Maurice Francis. "American Family Life in Fiction." *Catholic World* 110 (December 1919): 289–304.

Elmer, Jonathan. *Reading at the Social Limit: Affect, Mass Culture, and Edgar Allan Poe.* Stanford: Stanford UP, 1995.

Enstad, Nan. *Ladies of Labor, Girls of Adventure: Working Women, Popular Culture, and Labor Politics at the Turn of the Twentieth Century.* New York: Columbia UP, 1999.

Erlich, Gloria C. "The Female Conscience in Wharton's Shorter Fictions." *The Cambridge Companion to Edith Wharton.* Ed. Millicent Bell. Cambridge: Cambridge UP, 1995. 98–116.

Farland, Maria Magdalena. "*Ethan Frome* and the 'Springs' of Masculinity." *Modern Fiction Studies* 42.4 (Winter 1996): 707–29.

Fauset, Jessie. *The Chinaberry Tree and Selected Writings.* 1931. Boston: Northeastern UP, 1995.

——. *Comedy, American Style.* 1933. Boston: Beacon Press, 1994.

——. *Plum Bun.* 1929. Boston: Beacon Press, 1990.

——. *There Is Confusion.* 1924. Boston: Northeastern UP, 1989.

Fetterley, Judith. " 'Checkmate': Elizabeth Stuart Phelps's *The Silent Partner*." *Legacy* 3 (1986): 17–29.

Fisher, Philip. *Hard Facts: Setting and Form in the American Novel.* New York: Oxford UP, 1987.

Fleissner, Jennifer. *Women, Compulsion, Modernity: The Moment of American Naturalism.* Chicago: U of Chicago P, 2004.

Fowler, O. S. *Creative and Sexual Science.* New York: National, [1875].

Fraser, Nancy. *Unruly Practices: Power, Discourse, and Gender in Contemporary Social Theory.* Minneapolis: U of Minnesota P, 1989.

Freud, Sigmund. "Female Sexuality." *The Standard Edition of the Complete Psychological Works of Sigmund Freud.* Vol. 21. Trans. James Strachey. 1931. London: Hogarth Press, 1953. 223–43.

——. *Totem and Taboo.* 1913. Trans. James Strachey. New York: Norton, 1950.

Frost, Laura. "The Romance of Cliché: E. M. Hull, D. H. Lawrence, and Interwar Erotic Fiction." *Bad Modernisms.* Ed. Douglas Mao and Rebecca Walkowitz. Durham: Duke UP, 2006. 94–118.

Fuller, Margaret. "The Great Lawsuit: Man versus Men." 1843. *Norton Anthology of American Literature.* 6th ed. Ed. Nina Baym. New York: Norton, 2003. 1620–50.

Fyfe, Hamilton. *Peoples of All Nations: Their Life Today and the Story of Their Past (Danzig to France).* Vol. 3. London: Fleetway House, 1922.

Gale, Zona. *Miss Lulu Bett.* New York: D. Appleton, 1921.

Gandal, Keith. *The Virtues of the Vicious.* New York: Oxford UP, 1997.

Giddens, Anthony. *The Transformation of Intimacy: Sexuality, Love, and Eroticism in Modern Societies.* Stanford: Stanford UP, 1992.

Gilfoyle, Timothy J. *City of Eros: New York City, Prostitution, and the Commercialization of Sex, 1790–1920.* New York: Norton, 1992.

Gillette, Meg. "The Making of Modern Parents." *Modern Fiction Studies* 53.1 (2007): 50–69.

Gillman, Susan. *Blood Talk: American Race Melodrama and the Culture of the Occult.* Chicago: U of Chicago P, 2003.

——. "Pauline Hopkins and the Occult: African-American Revisions of Nineteenth-Century Sciences." *American Literary History* 8.1 (Spring 1996): 57–82.

Gilman, Charlotte Perkins. *Herland.* 1915. Introd. Ann J. Lane. New York: Pantheon, 1979.

——. *Woman and Economics.* 1898. Ed. Carl Degler. New York: Harper, 1966.

Glenn, Susan. *Female Spectacle: The Theatrical Roots of Modern Feminism.* Cambridge: Harvard UP, 2000.

Glyn, Elinor. *Man and Maid*. Philadelphia: J. B. Lippincott, 1922.

Goldman, Emma. "The Traffic in Women." 1910. *The Traffic in Women and Other Essays on Feminism*. Trumansburg, NY: Crossing Press, 1970. 19–32.

Goldman-Price, Irene. "The Perfect Jew and *The House of Mirth*: A Study in Point of View." *Edith Wharton Review* 16.1 (Spring 2000): 3–9.

Gordon, Linda. *Woman's Body, Woman's Right*. New York: Penguin, 1974.

Gullette, Margaret Morganroth. *Declining to Decline: Cultural Combat and the Politics of Midlife*. Charlottesville: U of Virginia P, 1997.

Guthrie, Patricia. *Catching Sense: African American Communities on a South Carolina Sea Island*. Westport: Bergin & Garvey, 1996.

Haag, Pamela. *Consent: Sexual Rights and the Transformation of American Liberalism*. Ithaca: Cornell UP, 1999.

——. "In Search of 'The Real Thing': Ideologies of Love, Modern Romance, and Women's Sexual Subjectivity in the United States, 1920–40." *Journal of the History of Sexuality* 2.4 (1992): 547–77.

Halttunen, Karen. *Confidence Men and Painted Women*. New Haven: Yale UP, 1982.

Haralson, Eric. *Henry James and Queer Modernity*. New York: Cambridge UP, 2003.

——. "Lambert Strether's Excellent Adventure." *The Cambridge Companion to Henry James*. Ed. Jonathan Freedman. Cambridge: Cambridge UP, 1998. 169–86.

Hawthorne, Nathaniel. *The Blithedale Romance*. 1852. New York: Norton, 1978.

Hegeman, Susan. "Taking *Blondes* Seriously." *American Literary History* 7.3 (Fall 1995): 525–54.

Hendler, Glenn. "The Limits of Sympathy." *American Literary History* 3.4 (Winter 1991): 685–706.

Hergesheimer, Joseph. *Linda Condon*. New York: Knopf, 1919.

Heywood, Angela. "Creative Dualism—Motherhood." *The Word* November 1888: 3.

——. "The Ethics of Touch—Sex-Unity." *The Word* June 1889: 2–3.

——. "The Grace and Use of Sex Life." *The Word* June 1890: 3.

——. "Human Sex-Power—Fleshed Realism." *The Word* December 1892: 2–3.

——. "Marriage Moloch—Free Love." *The Word*: n.p.

——. "Penis Literature—Onanism or Health?" *The Word* April 1884: 2.

——. "Seed Forces—Personal and Collective." *The Word* November 1884: n.p.

——. "Sex Nomenclature—Plain English." *The Word* April 1887: 2–3.

——. "Sex Service—Ethics of Trust." *The Word* October 1889: 2–3.

——. "The Woman's View of It—No. 4." *The Word* April 1883: 3.

Higonnet, Margaret. "Speaking Silences: Women's Suicide." *The Female Body in Western Culture*. Ed. Susan Rubin Suleiman. Cambridge: Harvard UP, 1986. 68–83.

Hopkins, Pauline. *Of One Blood*. 1903. *The Magazine Novels of Pauline Hopkins*. New York: Oxford UP, 1988.

Horowitz, Helen Lefkowitz. *Rereading Sex: Battles over Sexual Knowledge and Suppression in Nineteenth-Century America*. New York: Knopf, 2002.

Howe, Julia Ward. *The Hermaphrodite*. [1846–47?]. Ed. Gary Williams. Lincoln: U of Nebraska P, 2004.

——. *Sex and Education: A Reply to Dr. E. H. Clarke's "Sex in Education."* 1874. New York: Arno Press, 1972.

Hull, E. M. *The Sheik*. 1919. Philadelphia: Pine Street Books, 2001.

Hurst, Fannie. *Anatomy of Me*. London: Jonathan Cape, 1958.

——. *Anitra's Dance*. New York: P. F. Collier & Son, 1934.

——. *Anywoman*. New York: Harper & Brothers, 1950.

——. *Appassionata*. New York: Knopf, 1926.

——. *Back Street*. London: Jonathan Cape, 1931.

——. *Family!* New York: Doubleday, 1960.

——. *Five and Ten*. New York: Harper & Brothers, 1929.

——. *Fool—Be Still*. Garden City, NY: Doubleday, 1964.

——. *Great Laughter*. New York: Collier, 1936.

——. *Hallelujah*. New York: Harper & Brothers, 1944.

——. *The Hands of Veronica*. New York: Harper & Brothers, 1947.

——. *Imitation of Life*. Ed. Daniel Itzkovitz. 1933. Durham: Duke UP, 2004.

——. *Lonely Parade*. New York: Harper & Brothers, 1942.

——. *Lummox*. New York: Harper & Brothers, 1923.

——. *Mannequin*. New York: Knopf, 1926.

——. "The Smirk, a Light Tragedy That Has an Entirely New Moral." *Harper's Bazaar* 61 (January 1926): 78–79, 122.

——. *Star-Dust: The Story of an American Girl*. New York: Harper & Brothers, 1921.

Hurston, Zora Neale. *Their Eyes Were Watching God*. 1937. Urbana: U of Illinois P, 1978.

Illouz, Eva. *Cold Intimacies: The Making of Emotional Capitalism*. Malden, MA: Polity Press, 2007.

——. *Consuming the Romantic Utopia: Love and the Cultural Contradiction of Capitalism*. Berkeley: U of California P, 1997.

——. *Oprah Winfrey and the Glamour of Misery: An Essay on Popular Culture*. New York: Columbia UP, 2003.

Israel, Betsy. *Bachelor Girl: The Secret History of Single Women in the Twentieth Century*. New York: William Morrow, 2002.

Janeway, Elizabeth. *Daisy Kenyon*. Garden City, NY: Doubleday, 1945.

Johnson, Barbara. *The Feminist Difference: Literature, Psychoanalysis, Race, and Gender*. Cambridge: Harvard UP, 1998.

Johnson, Katie N. *Sisters in Sin: Brothel Drama in America, 1900–1920*. New York: Cambridge UP, 2006.

Johnson, Owen. *The Salamander*. Indianapolis: Bobbs-Merrill, 1913.

Kaplan, Amy. *The Social Construction of American Realism*. Chicago: U of Chicago P, 1988.

Kaplan, Carla. *The Erotics of Talk: Women's Writing and Feminist Paradigms*. New York: Oxford UP, 1996.

Kassanoff, Jennie. "Corporate Thinking: Edith Wharton's *Fruit of the Tree*." *Arizona Quarterly* 53.1 (Spring 1997): 25–59.

——. *Edith Wharton and the Politics of Race*. New York: Cambridge UP, 2004.

Katz, Jonathan Ned. *The Invention of Heterosexuality*. New York: Dutton, 1995.

Keckley, Elizabeth. *Behind the Scenes: Or, Thirty Years a Slave, and Four Years in the White House*. 1868. New York: Oxford UP, 1988.

Kelley, Edith Summers. *Weeds*. 1923. Old Westbury, NY: Feminist Press, 1982.

Kevles, Daniel J. *In the Name of Eugenics*. Cambridge: Harvard UP, 1995.

King, Andrew J. "Constructing Gender: Sexual Slander in Nineteenth-Century America." *Law and History Review* 13.1 (Spring 1995): 63–110.

Klimasmith, Betsy. "A Taste for Center Stage: Consumption and Feminism in *A Woman of Genius*." *Exploring Lost Borders: Critical Essays on Mary Austin*. Ed. Melody Graulich and Betsy Klimasmith. Reno: U of Nevada P, 1999. 129–49.

Koshy, Susan. *Sexual Naturalization: Asian Americans and Miscegenation*. Stanford: Stanford UP, 2004.

Kowaleski-Wallace, Elizabeth. "The Reader as Misogynist in *The Custom of the Country*." *Modern Language Studies* 21.1 (1991): 45–53.

Kraut, Alan M. *Silent Travelers: Germs, Genes, and the "Immigrant Menace."* New York: Basic Books, 1994.

Kroeger, Brooke. *Fannie: The Talent for Success of Writer Fannie Hurst*. New York: Random House, 1999.

Kuenz, Jane. "The Face of America Performing Race and Nation in *There Is Confusion*." *Yale Journal of Criticism* 12.1 (1999): 89–111.

Lang, Amy Schrager. "The Syntax of Class in Elizabeth Stuart Phelps's *The Silent Partner*." *Rethinking Class: Literary Studies and Social Formations*. Ed. Wai Chee Dimock and Michael T. Gilmore. New York: Columbia UP, 1994. 267–85.

Langford, Wendy. *Revolutions of the Heart*. New York: Routledge, 1999.

Law, Robert Adger. "Mrs. Peterkin's Negroes." *Southwest Review* 14 (1928–29): 455–61.

Leach, William. *Land of Desire: Merchants, Power, and the Rise of a New American Culture*. New York: Pantheon, 1993.

Lears, Jackson. *Fables of Abundance: A Cultural History of Advertising in America*. New York: Basic Books, 1994.

——. "Sherwood Anderson: Looking for the White Spot." *The Power of Culture: Critical Essays in American History*. Ed. Richard Wightman Fox and T. J. Jackson Lears. Chicago: U of Chicago P, 1993. 13–37.

———. *Something for Nothing: Luck in America*. New York: Viking, 2003.

Leider, Emily Wortis. *California's Daughter: Gertrude Atherton*. Stanford: Stanford UP, 1991.

Le Sueur, Meridel. *The Girl*. 1939. Cambridge, MA: West End Press, 1978.

Levander, Caroline Field. *Voices of the Nation: Women and Public Speech in Nineteenth-Century Literature and Culture*. New York: Cambridge UP, 1998.

Lewis, R. W. B. *Edith Wharton: A Biography*. New York: Harper & Row, 1975.

Lindemann, Marilee. *Willa Cather: Queering America*. New York: Columbia UP, 1999.

Lindsey, Judge Ben B., and Wainwright Evans. *The Companionate Marriage*. New York: Boni & Liveright, 1927.

Litt, Jacquelyn S. *Medicalized Motherhood: Perspectives from the Lives of African American and Jewish Women*. New Brunswick: Rutgers UP, 2000.

London, Jack. *Martin Eden*. 1908. New York: Amsco School Publications, n.d.

Loos, Anita. *Gentlemen Prefer Blondes*. 1925. New York: Penguin, 1989.

Lott, Eric. "The Whiteness of Film Noir." *American Literary History* 9.3 (Fall 1997): 542–66.

Lunbeck, Elizabeth. *The Psychiatric Persuasion: Knowledge, Gender, and Power in Modern America*. Princeton: Princeton UP, 1994.

Mason, Grace Sartwell. "The Lotus Eater." 1918. *Breaking the Ties That Bind: Popular Stories of the New Woman, 1915–1930*. Ed. Maureen Honey. Norman: U of Oklahoma P, 1992. 94–112.

McCarthy, Mary. *The Company She Keeps*. New York: Simon and Schuster, 1942.

———. *The Group*. New York: Signet, 1963.

McDowell, Deborah. *"The Changing Same": Black Women's Literature, Criticism, and Theory*. Bloomington: Indiana UP, 1995.

Mead, Lucia True Ames. *To Whom Much Is Given*. New York: T. Y. Crowell, 1899.

Mellencamp, Patricia. *High Anxiety: Catastrophe, Scandal, Age, and Comedy*. Bloomington: Indiana UP, 1992.

Merish, Lori. *Sentimental Materialism*. Durham: Duke UP, 2000.

Michaels, Walter Benn. "The Contracted Heart." *New Historicisms, New Histories, and Others*. Spec. issue of *New Literary History* 21.3 (Spring 1990): 495–531.

———. "The Phenomenology of Contract." *Raritan* 4.2 (1984): 47–66.

Miller, Nina. *Making Love Modern: The Intimate Public Worlds of New York's Literary Women*. New York: Oxford UP, 1998.

New York Times Book Review 21 January 1923: 14.

Norris, Charles G. *Seed*. Garden City, NY: Doubleday, 1930.

Norris, Kathleen. *The Beloved Woman*. Garden City, NY: Doubleday, 1921.

———. *The Foolish Virgin*. Garden City, NY: Doubleday, 1928.

———. *Mother*. New York: Grossett & Dunlap, 1911.

North, Michael. *Reading 1922: A Return to the Scene of the Modern*. New York: Oxford UP, 1999.

Odem, Mary. *Delinquent Daughters: Protecting and Policing Adolescent Female Sexuality in the United States, 1885–1920*. Chapel Hill: U of North Carolina P, 1995.

Parker, Dorothy. "Big Blonde." 1929. *Dorothy Parker: Complete Stories*. New York: Penguin, 1995. 105–24.

———. "General Review of the Sex Situation." 1926. *Norton Anthology of American Literature*. 6th ed. Ed. Nina Baym. New York: Norton, 2003. 1615.

Peel, Robin. *Apart from Modernism: Edith Wharton, Politics, and Fiction before World War I*. Madison: Fairleigh Dickinson UP, 2005.

Peiss, Kathy. *Cheap Amusements*. Philadelphia: Temple UP, 1986.

Peterkin, Julia. *Scarlet Sister Mary*. 1928. Athens: U of Georgia P, 1998.

———. "What I Believe." *Forum and Century* 83.1 (July 1930): 48–52.

Pfister, Joel. "Glamorizing the Psychological." *Inventing the Psychological: Toward a Cultural History of Emotional Life in America*. Ed. Joel Pfister and Nancy Schnog. New Haven: Yale UP, 1997. 17–59.

Phelps, Elizabeth Stuart. *Hedged In*. Boston: Fields, Osgood, 1870.

———. Reply to Dr. E. H. Clarke's *Sex in Education*. *Sex and Education*. Ed. Julia Ward Howe. 1874. New York: Arno Press, 1972.

———. *The Silent Partner*. 1871. New York: Feminist Press, 1983.

Power, Susan. *The Ugly-Girl Papers; or, Hints for the Toilet*. New York: Harper, 1874.

Prebel, Julie. "Engineering Womanhood: The Politics of Rejuvenation in Gertrude Atherton's *Black Oxen*." *American Literature* 76.2 (June 2004): 307–37.

Putzi, Jennifer. *Identifying Marks: Race, Gender, and the Marked Body in Nineteenth-Century America*. Athens: U of Georgia P, 2006.

Rabaté, Jean-Michel. *1913: The Cradle of Modernism*. Malden, MA: Blackwell, 2007.

Rabinowitz, Paula. *Labor and Desire: Women's Revolutionary Fiction in Depression America*. Chapel Hill: U of North Carolina P, 1991.

Rafter, Nicole Hahn. *Creating Born Criminals*. Urbana: U of Illinois P, 1997.

———, ed. *White Trash: The Eugenic Family Studies, 1877–1919*. Boston: Northeastern UP, 1988.

Raub, Patricia. *Yesterday's Stories: Popular Women's Novels of the Twenties and Thirties*. Westport: Greenwood, 1994.

Review of *Bad Girl*, by Viña Delmar. *New York Herald Tribune* 8 April 1928: 7.

Review of *Bad Girl*, by Viña Delmar. *New York Times Book Review* 22 April 1928: 8.

Review of *Bad Girl*, by Viña Delmar. *Saturday Review of Literature* 3 March 1928: 4.

Review of *Bad Girl* (play), by Brian Marlow and Viña Delmar. *Outlook and Independent* 156 (22 October 1930): 156.

Review of *Black Oxen*, by Gertrude Atherton. *New York Times Book Review* 21 January 1923: 14.

Review of *Linda Condon*, by Joseph Hergesheimer. *New York Times Book Review* 19 November 1919: 24.

Review of *Linda Condon*, by Joseph Hergesheimer. *The Nation* 29 November 1919: 693.

Review of *Linda Condon*, by Joseph Hergesheimer. *New Republic* 21 (3 December 1919): 29–30.

Review of *Linda Condon*, by Joseph Hergesheimer. *New Statesman* 17 July 1920: 422–23.

Review of *Plum Bun*, by Jessie Fauset. *Literature Review* 12 April 1924: 661.

Review of *Plum Bun*, by Jessie Fauset. *International Book Review* June 1924: 555.

Review of *Plum Bun*, by Jessie Fauset. *Booklist* 35 (May 1929): 321.

Review of *Plum Bun*, by Jessie Fauset. *New York Evening Post* 23 February 1929: 10.

Review of *Salome of the Tenements*, by Anzia Yezierska. *Boston Evening Transcript* 24 February 1923: 5.

Review of *Salome of the Tenements*, by Anzia Yezierska. *New York Tribune* 17 December 1922: 26.

Review of *Salome of the Tenements*, by Anzia Yezierska. *New York Times Book Review* 24 December 1922: 22.

Review of *Scarlet Sister Mary*, by Julia Peterkin. *New Republic* 26 December 1928: 172–73.

Review of *Scarlet Sister Mary*, by Julia Peterkin. *New York Herald Tribune* 28 October 1928: 6.

Review of *Scarlet Sister Mary*, by Julia Peterkin. *Saturday Review of Literature* 3 November 1928: 5.

Review of *Scarlet Sister Mary*, by Julia Peterkin. *Outlook and Independent* 180 (21 November 1928): 1212, 1215, 1222.

Roberts, W. Adolphe. "My Ambitions at 21 and What Became of Them." Interview with Anzia Yezierska. *American Hebrew* 15 (25 August 1922): 342, 358.

Ross, Edward Alsworth. *The Old World in the New: The Significance of Past and Present Immigration to the American People*. New York: Century, 1914.

——. "Positions and Attitudes." 28 August 1935. Madison: Wisconsin State Historical Society. Microfilm reel 32, frames 0816–34.

——. "Society of Western South America." [1914]. Madison: Wisconsin State Historical Society. Microfilm reel 33, frames 150–66.

Rubin, Herman H., M.D. *Eugenics and Sex Harmony: The Sexes, Their Relations and Problems*. New York: Pioneer, 1943.

Russett, Cynthia Eagle. *Sexual Science: The Victorian Construction of Womanhood*. Cambridge: Harvard UP, 1989.

Sánchez-Eppler, Karen. "Bodily Bonds." *Touching Liberty: Abolition, Feminism, and the Politics of the Body*. Berkeley: U of California P, 1997. 14–49.

Satter, Beryl. *Each Mind a Kingdom: American Women, Sexual Purity, and the New Thought Movement, 1875–1920*. Berkeley: U of California P, 1999.

Seabury, David. "The Bogy of Sex: Life Is a Conclusive Denial That Sex Is a Central Concern." *Century* 114.5 (September 1927): 528–36.

Seidman, Steven. *Romantic Longings: Love in America, 1830–1980*. New York: Routledge, 1991.

Seltzer, Mark. *Bodies and Machines*. New York: Routledge, 1992.

Sheldon, Charles. *In His Steps*. New York: Odyssey, 1895.

Shumway, David. *Modern Love: Romance, Intimacy, and the Marriage Crisis*. New York: New York UP, 2003.

Siegel, Carol. *New Millennial Sexstyles*. Bloomington: Indiana UP, 2000.

Smith, Stephanie. *Household Words: Bloomers, Sucker, Bombshell, Scab, Nigger, Cyber*. Minneapolis: U of Minnesota P, 2006.

Smith, Theophus H. *Conjuring Culture: Biblical Formations of Black America*. New York: Oxford UP, 1994.

Somerville, Siobhan B. *Queering the Color Line: Race and the Invention of Homosexuality in American Culture*. Durham: Duke UP, 2000.

Squier, Susan. "Incubabies and Rejuvenates: The Traffic between Technologies of Reproduction and Age-Extension." *Figuring Age: Women, Bodies, Generations*. Ed. Kathleen Woodward. Bloomington: Indiana UP, 1999. 88–111.

Stanley, Amy Dru. *From Bondage to Contract*. Cambridge: Cambridge UP, 1998.

Stansell, Christine. *American Moderns: Bohemian New York and the Creation of a New Century*. New York: Metropolitan Books, 2000.

Stern, Julia. " 'I Am Cruel Hungry': Dramas of Twisted Appetite and Rejected Identification in *The Morgesons*." *American Culture, Canons, and the Case of Elizabeth Stoddard*. Ed. Robert McClure Smith and Ellen Weinauer. Tuscaloosa: U of Alabama P, 2003. 107–27.

Stockham, Alice B. *Karezza: Ethics of Marriage*. 1896. *Sex, Marriage, and Society: Sexual Indulgence and Denial*. New York: Arno Press, 1974.

Stoddard, Elizabeth. *The Morgesons*. New York: Carleton, 1862.

———. *Two Men*. Ed. Jennifer Putzi. Lincoln: U of Nebraska P, 2008.

Stowe, Harriet Beecher. *Pink and White Tyranny: A Society Novel*. 1871. New York: New American Library, 1988.

Sundquist, Eric. *To Wake the Nations*. Cambridge: Harvard UP, 1993.

Tate, Claudia. *Domestic Allegories of Political Desire: The Black Heroine's Text at the Turn of the Century*. New York: Oxford UP, 1992.

Thomas, Brook. *American Literary Realism and the Failed Promise of Contract*. Berkeley: U of California P, 1998.

Thompson, Stephanie Lewis. *Influencing America's Tastes: Realism in the Works of Wharton, Cather, and Hurst*. Gainesville: UP of Florida, 2002.

Thomson, Rosemarie Garland. "Benevolent Maternalism and Physically Disabled Figures: Dilemmas of Female Embodiment in Stowe, Davis, and Phelps." *American Literature* 68.3 (September 1996): 555–86.

——. "Crippled Girls and Lame Old Women: Sentimental Spectacles of Sympathy in Nineteenth-Century American Women's Writing." *Nineteenth-Century American Women Writers: A Critical Reader*. Ed. Karen L. Kilcup. Malden, MA: Blackwell, 1998. 128–45.

Thurber, James, and E. B. White. *Is Sex Necessary?* Garden City, NY: Blue Ribbon Books, 1929.

Thurman, Suzanne. "Shaker Women and Sexual Power: Heresy and Orthodoxy in the Shaker Village of Harvard, Massachusetts." *Journal of Woman's History* 10.1 (Spring 1998): 70–87.

Trask, Michael. *Cruising Modernism: Class and Sexuality in American Literature and Social Thought*. Ithaca: Cornell UP, 2003.

Travis, Jennifer. "Pain and Recompense in *Ethan Frome*." *Arizona Quarterly* 53.3 (Autumn 1997): 37–64.

Tremper, Ellen. *I'm No Angel: The Blond in Fiction and Film.* Charlottesville: U of Virginia P, 2006.

Tuttleton, James. "*The Fruit of the Tree*: Justine and the Perils of Abstract Idealism." *The Cambridge Companion to Edith Wharton*. Ed. Millicent Bell. Cambridge: Cambridge UP, 1995. 157–68.

Twain, Mark. *Letters from the Earth*. Ed. Bernard DeVoto. New York: Harper, 1962.

Ullman, Sharon R. *Sex Seen: The Emergence of Modern Sexuality in America*. Berkeley: U of California P, 1997.

Urch, Kakie. "The [Em] Space of Modernism and the Possibility of *Flaneuserie*: The Case of Viña Delmar and Her 'Bad Girls.' " *Modernism, Gender, and Culture: A Cultural Studies Approach*. Ed. Lisa Rado. New York: Garland, 1997. 17–46.

Waid, Candace. *Edith Wharton's Letters from the Underworld*. Chapel Hill: U of North Carolina P, 1991.

Wald, Gayle. *Crossing the Line: Racial Passing in Twentieth-Century U.S. Literature and Culture*. Durham: Duke UP, 2000.

Warner, Michael. *The Trouble with Normal: Sex, Politics, and the Ethics of Queer Life*. New York: Free Press, 1999.

Warren, Kenneth W. *Black and White Strangers: Race and American Literary Realism*. Chicago: U of Chicago P, 1993.

Watson, Wilbur. "Mr. Wrong." *New York Times* 30 April 1950: 32.

Wharton, Edith. *The Children*. 1928. New York: Macmillan, 1992.

——. *The Custom of the Country*. New York: Scribner's, 1913.

——. *Ethan Frome*. 1911. New York: Bantam Books, 1987.

——. *French Ways and Their Meaning*. New York: D. Appleton, 1919.

——. *The Fruit of the Tree.* 1907. New York: Scribner's, 1907.

——. *The House of Mirth.* 1905. New York: Berkley Books, 1981.

——. *The Mother's Recompense.* 1925. New York: Scribner's, 1986.

——. *Summer.* 1917. New York: Perennial, 1980.

Wilcox, Leonard. *V. F. Calverton: Radical in the American Grain.* Philadelphia: Temple UP, 1992.

Wilhelm, Gale. *Torchlight to Valhalla.* 1938. Tallahassee: Naiad P, 1985.

——. *We Too Are Drifting.* 1935. Tallahassee: Naiad Press, 1985.

Williams, Susan. *Reclaiming Authorship.* Philadelphia: U of Pennsylvania P, 2006.

Wilson, Harriet. *Our Nig.* 1859. Nottingham: Trent Editions, 1998.

Wolff, Cynthia Griffin. *A Feast of Words: The Triumph of Edith Wharton.* New York: Oxford UP, 1977.

Woods, Robert A., and Albert J. Kennedy. *The Settlement Horizon.* New York: Russell Sage Foundation, 1922.

Woodward, Kathleen. *Aging and Its Discontents: Freud and Other Fictions.* Bloomington: Indiana UP, 1991.

——, ed. *Figuring Age: Women, Bodies, Generations.* Bloomington: Indiana UP, 1999.

Wright, Zara. *Black and White Tangled Threads and Kenneth.* 1920. New York: G. K. Hall, 1995.

Yellin, Jean Fagin. "The 'Feminization' of Rebecca Harding Davis." *American Literary History* 2.2 (1990): 203–19.

Yezierska, Anzia. *Salome of the Tenements.* 1923. Urbana: U of Illinois P, 1995.

Zagarell, Sandra A. " 'Strenuous Artistry': Elizabeth Stoddard's *The Morgesons*." *The Cambridge Companion to Nineteenth-Century American Women's Writing.* Ed. Dale M. Bauer and Philip Gould. Cambridge: Cambridge UP, 2001. 284–307.

INDEX